Political philosophy and social welfare

Essays on the normative
basis of welfare provision

Raymond Plant BA, PhD, AKC
Professor of Politics, Southampton University

Harry Lesser BA, BPhil
Lecturer in Philosophy, Manchester University

Peter Taylor-Gooby BA
Lecturer in Social Administration, University of Kent

Routledge & Kegan Paul
London, Boston and Henley

First published in 1980
by Routledge & Kegan Paul Ltd
39 Store Street,
London WC1E 7DD,
9 Park Street,
Boston, Mass. 02108, USA and
Broadway House,
Newtown Road,
Henley-on-Thames,
Oxon RG9 1EN
Printed in Great Britain by
Redwood Burn Limited, Trowbridge and Esher

British Library Cataloguing in Publication Data

Plant, Raymond
    Political philosophy and social welfare. – (The
    international library of welfare and philosophy).
    1. Public welfare   2. Social policy
    I. Title   II. Lesser, Harry
    III. Taylor-Gooby, Peter   IV. Series
    361   HV31   80 41279

ISBN 0 7100 0611 X
ISBN 0 7100 0631 4 Pbk

Contents

Preface

This book was written while its three authors were lecturers at the University of Manchester. Raymond Plant and Harry Lesser were members of the Philosophy Department and Peter Taylor-Gooby a member of the Department of Social Administration. There has been a long tradition of co-operation between the Department of Philosophy and the Faculty of Economic and Social Studies in the University and the authors hope that this book makes a reasonable contribution to that tradition. Recently, co-operative work of this sort in Manchester has been fostered in a series of seminars held in the convivial surroundings of Hillel Steiner's home, and the authors are grateful to Hillel and Miriam for providing an atmosphere so conducive to both work and enjoyment. Most of the chapters of the book were originally tried out as papers at this seminar and subjected to very searching criticisms. Of course, the authors are responsible for their failure to respond more adequately to the points that were argued against them.

Raymond Plant also owes a special debt to David Braybrooke of Dalhousie University, a man with considerable experience of working in these fields, with whom he discussed the notion of need at some length on two of Professor Braybrooke's visits to Manchester.

The book falls into three parts, although there is a central theme running through the whole volume. The first part, after an introductory chapter on the role of political philosophy in debates about social policy, is devoted to an extensive discussion of the concept of need and its relation to wants and desires. The second part deals with the way needs are (or are not) expressed through political and social processes. The final part deals with the role of community in thinking about welfare.

Acknowledgments

Although the book was written as a co-operative enterprise, individual chapters are the responsibility of particular authors. Raymond Plant wrote chapters 2, 4, 5, 9 and 10; Peter Taylor-Gooby wrote chapters 1, 6 and 8, Harry Lesser chapters 3 and 7.

Raymond Plant would like to thank Geraint Parry and W.E. Connolly for their comments on chapter 9. Chapter 10 was first given as a paper to a conference of libertarian scholars held in Oxford at Easter 1979. He would particularly like to thank F. von Hayek, Max Hartwell, Stanislav Andreski and John Gray for their vigorous response to a paper which was perhaps not altogether welcome.

1   Political philosophy and social welfare

> Narrowly defined, social administration is the study of
> the development, structure and practices of the social
> services. Broadly defined, it is an attempt to apply
> social science - including philosophy - to the analysis
> and solution of a changing range of social problems.
> It must be taught in both of these senses if it is to
> be of any value.
>
> [Donnison, 1961]

This book attempts to apply some of the insights derived
from political philosophy to the study of social welfare.
Political philosophy has traditionally been concerned with
questions of citizenship, rights, duties, forms of government, political obligation and the nature of civil society
rather than issues of need, of social service provision
and of state responsibility for the welfare of the community. Yet perhaps the most striking feature of present-
day society is the massive political and economic weight
of the state, and its growth has been one of the most
significant trends in recent history. The most important
single aspect, whether measured by expenditure, by number
of personnel or by volume of legislation, and the most
impressive continuing growth area of the state, is its
social welfare activities. The study of these activities
may legitimately claim a place on the agenda of political
philosophy.

THE EXPANSION OF THE WELFARE STATE

The findings of various writers who have charted the growth
of state expenditure in the UK and elsewhere are conveniently summarized by Gough (1975, pp. 59-60). In the UK
the proportion of the GNP consumed or allocated by the

state has increased from 12.7 per cent in 1910 to 50.5 per cent in 1970. Moreover, the proportion of state expenditure devoted to social welfare has increased from 31 per cent to 49 per cent over the period. OECD statistics suggest that this trend is mirrored in the experience of the developed industrial world. Bacon and Eltis (1976, pp. 13-14) show that a steadily increasing proportion of the labour force has been absorbed into state welfare activities:

> Between 1961 and 1974 employment by local authorities rose 54% and by central by 9%. By contrast in the remaining services ... employment expanded only 13% on average, so the shift from industry has been most rapid into public employment.... Within the public sector employment in education at all levels has risen and employment in the provision of health and welfare services.... All would agree that these are vital to any civilised community, and it is a realisation of this by all political parties that has done so much to bring about these very great shifts in the labour force.

Perhaps the very obtrusiveness of the welfare state has led to a trend over recent years for political theorists to become more conscious of the need to tackle the issues that arise from state provision of services to meet need. There is evidence of attempts to recapture the heritage of a relationship that once existed between political philosophy and the government's welfare activities. The influence of utilitarianism on the development of Victorian poor law policies has been discussed by many writers, and the contribution of neo-Hegelianism to the liberal welfare settlement that preceded the First World War is now being recognized. It is perhaps an indication of the lack of philosophical concern with social welfare issues in the more recent past that no comparable influence on debate at the time of the Second World War settlement can be traced. Instead, we turn to positivist social sciences as exemplified in the work of Keynes and Rowntree to discover the conceptual basis of Beveridge's liberalism.

THE RESPONSE OF POLITICAL PHILOSOPHY

The growth of state-organized welfare is now impossible to ignore. Views on the political significance of this development differ. One influential work claimed at the close of the 1950s that ideology, which was once a road to action, has come to a dead end (Bell, 1960, p. 393). The thesis that ideological conflict between essentially opposed viewpoints was exhausted, in view of the growth in advanced industrial countries of practical consensus on

the direction of social advance, has been subsequently
belied by both intellectual and political developments.
Neo-liberal and neo-marxist schools of thought have en-
joyed a vigorous and contentious revival on both sides of
the Atlantic. Thus Nozick's 'Anarchy, State and Utopia'
(1974), which contains a critique of the moral basis of
state intervention in social life, has been described as
'the best piece of sustained analytical argument to have
appeared in political philosophy for a very long time'
(Steiner, 1975, p. 120). The definitive statement of
Hayek's position is now available (Hayek, 1973; 1976).
At the same time there is a revival of interest in marxist perspectives, ranging from the urban sociology of
Castells to the political theory of Miliband (1969), from
the metaphysics of Althusser (1970) to the interpretive
sociology of Habermas (1975).

Such invigoration of intellectual debate reflects a
polarization. The comfortable certainties of two-party
government in this country are seriously upset. On the
continent of Europe, communist mass parties are formu-
lating challenging ideological positions. The issue of
the desirability of state welfare is hotly contested.
This debate is pointed by economic recession, and by
political decisions to reduce welfare spending. Just how
significant these decisions are remains to be seen. However, their implications for the study of welfare may be
readily illustrated. As recently as 1970, Donnison could
summarize a popular viewpoint, describing (p. 203):

> the process by which policies for the equalization of
> income, wealth and living standards extend freedom
> and promote innovation and developments which ensure
> the continuing economic growth that makes further
> progress towards equality possible. [cf. Crosland,
> 1974, pp. 57-8]

Equality, growth and welfare are all desirable things.
A more recent government expenditure White Paper (Cmnd
6721, 1977, para. 56) points out: 'a modern civilised
society needs an adequate level of public services. These
are prerequisites of efficiency, as well as welfare and
personal freedom.' However, the argument concludes: 'at
this juncture, further social improvements must depend
on the prior achievement of our industrial and economic
objectives.' Thus there are good political reasons why
the struggle between different viewpoints on the relative
merits and on the various ways of attaining different
social goods has become less avoidable and more determined. This conflict has its implications for debate in
political philosophy.

POLITICAL PHILOSOPHY AND THE STUDY OF SOCIAL POLICY

Social policy is now a matter of central political concern.
How should political philosophers approach this phenomenon?
Let us consider the problems that have been generated in
the study of social policy through the discipline that has
traditionally concerned itself with that area: social administration. Social administration contains an important,
if somewhat uncritical, tradition of inquiry concerned
with the delineation of the precise characteristics of
social problems, understood as aspects of a positive social
world, and the construction of remedies to these problems
within a consensual analytic framework. Repeated criticisms of this tradition are ably summarized by George and
Wilding (1972). However, it is possible to claim that it
is not without its merits in contributing to the ameliora-
tion of social conditions - practical rather than academic
though these merits may be.
     The 'social engineering' school is only one among
several. Mishra (1977) identifies four other traditions,
concerned with charting the expression of an ideal of
citizenship through social policies, with producing a
functionalist account of welfare within a problematic
originally set by Durkheim, with the convergence theories
of Kerr and Rostow, and with the various strands of
marxist interpretation of the welfare state. To these
we may add the Fabian tradition exemplified in Crosland,
Tawney and some of Titmuss's work, and the phenomenology
of Carrier and Kendall.
     What is the common concern of these various traditions?
Carrier and Kendall conveniently summarize definitions
of the subject area given by its major exponents (Heisler,
1977, p. 27): social administration is the study of the
activities of states whose 'manifest purpose is to influence differential "command over resources" according
to some criteria of need'. This definition is echoed by
Mishra (1977, p. 7). The problem is that it links together two areas of interest - social institutions and
the normative notion of need. It is not immediately clear
how we are to yoke together two such awkward beasts.
     Pinker points out: 'in social policy and administra-
tion, we begin with fact-finding and end in moral rhetoric'
(1971, p. 12). Heisler claims 'there is a large chink in
the armoury of social administration ... interposed between social philosophy and the assumed understanding of
actual conditions' (1977, p. xi). Need, in the sense that
the concept is used to provide criteria for the performance of social institutions, lives in the house of moral
philosophy. Here, if anywhere, can we expect to find

satisfactory accounts of the values that underlie any
delineation of need. The task of describing social institutions, the activities of states, falls to social
science. Values are certainly involved in the theories
that provide the foundations for the characterization of
social elements. However, the role of values in this area
is less obvious and direct than it is in the study of
needs. The problem is, can moral philosophy and social
science be done in the same breath? What is the relation
between our conceptualization of social institutions and
the project of evaluating the performance of those institutions?
     Two areas of concern in political philosophy seem rele-
vant. First, there is the endeavour to justify particular
interpretations of relevant values, such as social justice,
freedom and equality. Such substantive theory tackles the
problem of characterizing need head-on. Second, there is
the attempt to understand the relation between particular
forms of society and the concepts that are current within
them, particularly those reflexive concepts that are used
to analyse social orders. We shall consider the production
of substantive values and the reflexive use of ideology, in
order to explore the resources available in political philosophy for the study of social welfare policy.

SUBSTANTIVE THEORY

In this area there had been little positive development in
recent times until the path-breaking work of Rawls (1972).
Daniels (1975) claims that Rawls's work represents 'a welcome return to an older tradition of substantive rather
than semantic political and moral philosophy' (p. xi).
Thus it pumps new life into what had seemed to be the bankrupt tradition of liberal political thought. Such theory
offers students of social policy the tempting prospect of
a sure foundation for their normative analysis. 'Rawls' ...
theory contains a fairly specific conception of social
justice which could be used ... to evaluate government's
social policies, and to many people this has seemed a
cardinal virtue of the theory' (Miller, 1976, p. 342). The
alacrity with which the theory has been taken up by academic philosophers and by more practical men of affairs is
hardly 'surprising.
     Similarly, Nozick is engaged in (among other things)
     substantive theory (Steiner, 1975, p. 120): Professor
     Nozick's aim is to demonstrate (and incidentally to
     commend) the kind of political order implied by a moral
     position assigning priority to the requirements of

Kant's second formulation of the categorical imperative, that we treat persons as ends and not merely
as means.

However, substantive moral theory, appropriate though
it is to the justification or rejection of a normative
notion of need, has been perpetually haunted by the awkward empirical fact that competent philosophers often disagree on the unique meaning to be given to moral terms.
Without entering into such debate here (a good summary of
counter-arguments to Rawls's approach is given in Barry,
1973, and Daniels, 1975), it does seem at first sight that
procedures for choosing between the evaluative uses of
moral language are subject to question. One of the ways
in which we differentiate values from facts is that the
former are in principle empirically untestable.

However, moral beliefs are strongly held, and obsti-
nately contested, and so far as the relation of political
philosophy and social welfare is concerned, this struggle
is by no means trivial. Thus when Crosland writes to commend the view that socialism is basically concerned with
a particular conception of equality (1974, p. 15), he
immediately derives practical consequences from it embracing a wholesale redirection of state policies in the
fields of housing, social security, town planning, industrial organization and control and so on. For this reason
we move on to consider reflexive political philosophy,
which endeavours to understand the social location of
political concepts, and to account for the complexities
of their use in social terms. How useful is this approach
in coming to terms with the discussion of social welfare?

REFLEXIVE THEORY

In this area political philosophy has moved away from
theoretical fortress-building. The task is no longer the
definitive construction on one universally applicable and
eternally defensible interpretation of the concept in hand.
We will examine Gallie's attempt rigorously to characterize
the nature of controversy over some social concepts, and
then discuss Miller's project of locating the various ways
of understanding a concept in different sociological perspectives.

Gallie's contention is that 'there are concepts which
are essentially contested, concepts the proper use of which
inevitably involves endless disputes about their proper
uses on the part of their users' (1955-6, p. 169). He
illustrates the implications of this suggestion through a
highly artificial example: that of a game in which various

teams compete for a title which is claimed by their sup-
porters on the grounds that the chosen team has 'played
the game best'. No scores, no common objective; a pure
form of struggle. 'There is therefore continuous competition between the contesting teams not only for acknowledge-
ment as champions, but for acceptance of ... the proper
criteria of championship' (p. 171).

   Such a procedure does seem analogous to some of the
everlasting debates in social and political philosophy,
between, for example, the exponents of negative and positive interpretations of freedom, or the various characterizations of social justice. As we have seen, it is such
debate that has in practice vitiated the various attempts
to establish particular theses in substantive political
philosophy, and to solve the normative problems of the
study of social welfare.

ESSENTIALLY CONTESTED CONCEPTS

Gallie sets out four formal conditions for a concept's
being necessarily subject to such debate; being, as he
terms it, 'essentially contested'. It must be appraisive;
the achievement it evaluates must be of an internally
complex character; the achievement must be initially
capable of being described in various ways; and it must
be such as to admit of considerable modification in the
light of changing circumstances. In other words, the
accredited achievement must be sufficiently complex and,
at first sight, ambiguous to allow for the formation of
various schools of thought, and it must be persistently
vague enough to tolerate their continuance.

   One point should be made: Gallie is not simply
rigging out the oft-noted relativist position in more
formal dress. This rests on the problem that it is hard
to see how disputes over value-judgments can be rationally
resolved. The position is plausible because values are
untestable beliefs. Such a view has the disadvantage
that it puts an end to any sensible political debate. In
the absence of criteria for rational argument it is
claimed we must simply sulk or agree to differ. Gallie,
however, is pointing to a particular group of value-
concepts whose proper and justifiable use in sensible
political argument involves value-debate. This is not the
futility of relativism. There is a point to such a debate,
which emerges when we consider the use of such concepts.

   Gallie adds a further condition, specifying the role of
essentially contested concepts. To use such a concept
'means to use it against other uses and to recognize that

one's own use of it has to be maintained against these
other uses' (p. 172). In other words, essentially contested concepts are used aggressively and defensively.
Two additional conditions are finally included, to guard
against the argument that what has been described as a
contested concept might simply be the confused and overlapping use of several rather similar concepts, and that
the debate is therefore pointless. These turn on the
suggestion that all the various competing users must
recognize the authority of an exemplar, and 'the plausibility of the claim that the continuous competition ...
between the contestant users of the concept, enables the
exemplar's achievement to be sustained and/or developed
in optimum fashion' (p. 179). The acknowledged exemplar
serves to knit together and organize the various positions.
The idea of traditions linking these positions to a respected common ancestor lends point to the continued use
of contested concepts. The plausibility of the suggestion
that the contest is in a real sense creative means that it
makes sense to persist in the struggle that constitutes
the correct use of an essentially contested concept despite the perennial and irresoluble nature of value-
conflict.

The idea that the use of some concepts necessarily
involves conflict is a powerful explication of one of the
central problems of political and social philosophy:
that people differ and that in philosophy, unlike that
natural sciences, there seems to be no universally ack-
knowledged way of settling the disputes, so that the subject cannot be seen as progressive. However, a number of
puzzling questions are raised by the idea. Let us consider
four: the scope of the thesis, the way debate in essentially contested areas is to be conducted, the likely
impact of the thesis itself on debate, and its implications for the understanding of the use of such concepts.

THE LIMITS TO ESSENTIAL CONTESTABILITY

First, how are we to mark off the sphere of essential
contestability from other areas of value-debate? It seems
necessary to prevent the idea from infecting the central
concepts of ethics 'whose everyday use appears to be
uniquely describable and universally acknowledged' (p. 187).
However, as Gallie hints in the passage where he touches on
this question (pp. 194-5), it is difficult to see how it
is possible to accomplish the restriction. Thus the notion
of duty, if it is to have moral force, must be taken as
describing what different people ought to do 'in a similar

situation'. However, adherence to contested concepts,
such as social justice, informs our conception of duty.
Is 'duty' then to be subject to relativistic reinterpretation? It seems hard to draw limits to the capacity of
essential contestability to infect moral concepts. The
thesis seems to open the door to the reduction of all
moral, social and political theory to an endless and
fruitless debate, and thus to triviality.

THE LOGIC OF CONVERSION

The second point springs out of this. Debates appear endless. It is an empirical fact however that people's views
alter in the course of argument in essentially contested
areas. Is there any logic of conversion that could be
used to drag dispute in this area out of the morass of
relativism? A certain piece of evidence or argument put
forward by one side in an apparently endless dispute can
be recognized to have a definite logical force, even by
those it fails to win over; the conversion of a hitherto
wavering opponent can be seen to be justifiable given the
waverer's previous state of information and the grounds
on which he previously supported one side.
    Such justifiable but nevertheless value-based conver-
sions are probably most common in political discussions.
Thus it is easy to understand the detachment of right-
wing members of the Labour Party, who strongly emphasize
pluralist values in their political ideology, from that
party, if we bear in mind their belief that the Labour
Party is becoming increasingly dominated by what they see
as illiberal left-wing views, and by an emphasis on class
and on particular class interests. The notion of a logic
of conversion has practical application to our understanding of the development of the positions taken by particular people in debate. However, it is hard to see how the
idea enables us to devise a cogent resolution of the problem of basic values. It remains impossible to devise objective proofs of particular positions.

CONVERSION AND THE LEVEL OF ARGUMENT

The third issue provides an interesting sidelight on
Gallie's views on the relation between the essential contestability thesis and the problem of relativism in debate.
He asks: 'in what ways should be expect recognition of the
essentially contestable character of a given concept to
affect its future use by different contestant parties?'

(p. 192). He stresses that what we are looking for is the
practical effect of such recognition, for there do not
seem to be any necessary entailments between the character
of a concept and the way philosophers employ it. Prac-
tically, there are two likely results: either 'a recognition of rival uses as ... of permanent potential critical
value to one's own', and therefore 'a raising of the level
of the quality of argument' (p. 193), or the exact opposite, on the grounds that there's no truth, so cut the
cackle. The only effective form of political debate is to
punch the opposition on the nose!
     The interesting feature here is the use of a notion of
'quality of level of argument' in conjunction with the previous recognition that there is no universally cogent
logic of conversion. This seems to be an extension of the
idea that in some areas contests may plausibly be claimed
to develop a traditional interpretation of an exemplar.
But what is the relation between quality of argument and
the development of a tradition? Is any work within a tradition to be seen as a raising of quality? Exactly how
political arguments are to be well conducted by rational
men in the face of a nagging essential contestability is a
problem that Gallie does not explore.

THE SOCIAL HISTORY OF CONTESTED CONCEPTS

However, the final issue does open out a hopeful prospect
for political philosophy in this perplexity: Gallie concludes his article by offering a defence against the argument that to stress the various traditions through which an
exemplar is developed is to retreat from philosophy to an
inconclusive historicism. He counters with the view that
there are two ways in which we can be said to understand a
concept: the 'logical', which means '(a) conforming to
and (b) being able to state the rules governing its use',
and the 'historical', which means knowing 'the whole gamut
of conditions that have led to and now sustain the way we
use it' (pp. 196-7). We can immediately see that the
notion of historical explanation is here used in the widest
possible sense, for the study of a whole gamut of conditions
must include the history of ideas, the sociology of knowledge and the whole range of features of social organization that have plausibly been claimed by competing theorists
to affect the production of and enthusiasm for political
ideas within it. Gallie continues (p. 198):
     if we want to see *just what* we are doing when we apply
     a given appraisive concept, then one way of learning
     is by asking from what vaguer and more confused version

... our currently accepted version of the concept ...
has been derived.

It seems that this conclusion is rendered virtually inescapable once we have accepted the idea that schools of
thought differ on how certain concepts are to be used, and
that the resulting conflict is logically irresoluble. If
we are to attempt the job of understanding the conflict
between various uses - if that rather than the resolution
of the conflict is to be our focus of attention - we will
have to attempt to understand how it is that various uses
have in practice been espoused and promulgated at various
times. This consideration certainly opens up a large
arena into which Gallie does not venture, an arena that
centres on the sociology of knowledge but includes other
disciplines. Crucially, it involves relating concepts to
characterizations of the social orders within which they
are deployed (with more or less success) and in the description of which they are employed. Political concepts as
reflected in human ideology influence courses of action
through justification or encouragement. Thus creative debate between essentially contested concepts in one sense at
any rate both attempts to describe and is political conflict. For this reason the development of contested traditions has a point, and a very important point.

Two unresolved issues remain: the exact scope of the
thesis, and its implications for the way in which political
argument is to be carried out. There are powerful reasons
for suggesting that the scope of the thesis is large indeed.
This consideration makes the question of what counts as
argument in this area all the more important. Gallie summarizes the grounds on which it makes sense to continue to
use an essentially contested concept as 'the probability
or plausibility of the claim that the continuous competition ... enables the original exemplar's achievement to be
sustained and/or developed in optimum fashion' (p. 180).
Later he mentions the possibility that widespread recognition of the force of the thesis will tend to raise the
'quality of the level of argument'. It seems difficult
to interpret these statements without some idea of what
is meant by plausibility or quality. How can we set up
objective criteria for the use of such concepts? In the
case of plausibility, such criteria would involve us in
assertions about the present state of the exemplar's art
and how it can best be developed. But this is to engage
in the contest. 'Quality of argument' cannot refer to
cogency, because cogency is inapplicable in these matters.
What non-trivial and desirable feature of arguments does
it delineate?

It seems clear that the essential contestability
thesis succeeds in hanging an ominous question mark over
all efforts to carry out substantive debate in this
area. In particular, problems arise in any attempt to
situate a group of concepts for which we may be content
to accept the force of the essential contestability thesis,
in relation to a second group of value-concepts where that
thesis does not apply. We have seen the capacity of essential contestability to infect a whole range of related
concepts; we have also seen that it is impossible to
specify any point to the use of essentially contested
concepts without appealing to uncontested concepts. Certainly to engage in political debate is to do something
that seems very similar to what is more rigorously defined
in the conditions of use of an essentially contested concept. However, for there to be any point to debate about
who's 'playing the game best' we need to have some independent way of keeping the score. We turn to the idea of
understanding through the historical explanation of the
various uses of the concepts of political philosophy.

POLITICAL PHILOSOPHY AND THE SOCIOLOGY OF KNOWLEDGE

An important writer who has suggested and illustrated a
methodology for proceeding in this area is Miller. In
the introduction to 'Social Justice' (1976) he criticizes
the use of linguisti c analysis in relation to political
concepts on two grounds: first, it is an empirical fact
that the interpretations of the concepts change over time.
Second, there is 'often acute disagreement over the use of
some of these ideas which arises *within* societies....'
(p. 4). Gallie's historical approach to the explanation
of traditions of thought was founded in the recognition of
a substantially similar problem. Miller (p. 5) develops
the insight into a tool for the analysis of the role of
political concepts in the contemporary social order:
> to uncover the full range of uses which a concept such
> as fairness has, it is therefore not enough to examine
> verbal transactions between individuals; it is neces-
> sary in addition to look at the concept's place within
> the whole set of beliefs which compose an ideology;
> and at the functions which that ideology serves.
Thus we must first analyse the range of different uses
of the concept in which we are interested (Miller illustrates
such analysis by pointing to Berlin's distinction (Berlin,
1969) between two concepts of liberty) and then consider
why the concept should display such a diversity of meaning.
'The answer is that each version of a particular concept

finds its natural home in a different way of looking at
society' (Miller, 1976, p. 7). The variety of social perspectives explains the variety of uses of our social concepts. The best way of analysing these perspectives is
through sociology. Thus can political philosophy place
both the interpretation of the concept 'and the view of
society in a social context, asking about the type of
society which fostered these ideas, about the classes
which adopted them, and so on' (p. 9). The problems that
afflicted Gallie's essential contestability thesis are not
resolved. However, the sociological perspective has the
effect of circumventing them. If understanding involves
the relation of concepts to social situations, the questions of the scope of contestable concepts, the nature
of the conflict and the evaluation of the level of argument
become social facts, to be analysed in the same way as the
concepts themselves.

Miller carries out his project in relation to 'social
justice'. The concept is defined by the root meaning *suum
cuique* - to each his own. In the first section of the book,
a conceptual map of interpretations of this notion is drawn
in terms of desert, right and need. In the second, each
of these contested substantive characterizations of the term
is related to its expression in the work of a political
philosopher. Miller refers his interpretations of justice
to Hume, Sidgwick and Kropotkin, respectively. The third
section attempts 'to place the idea of social justice in
sociological perspective by comparing the conceptions of
justice found in several different social contexts' (p. 13).

The first and second sections conform closely to
Gallie's programme for the explication of an essentially
contested concept, although the debate is situated in the
context of the social use of different interpretations of
the concept by the various traditions. Miller remarks
(p. 245):

> the theme which underlies the foregoing studies is that
> in adopting one or other of the rival conceptions of
> social justice, one is neither deciding on the correct
> use of a shared concept, nor making an isolated moral
> choice, but rather committing oneself to a much wider
> view of what societies are and ought to be ... If ...
> we were to object to Hume that there are perfectly
> legitimate uses of the concept of justice for which he
> does not allow, this would be to miss the real point:
> namely that Hume is trying to persuade us to restrict
> the concept's view in the way he recommends, because
> of the role which justice plays in society as he sees
> it.

Thus Miller, like Gallie, sees the concept as evaluative,

complex, vague, and above all, used aggressively and defensively.

What is the outcome of Miller's attempt to locate
various approaches to social justice in society? After
a close analysis of three forms of society - primitive,
hierarchical and market - he concludes that the essentially legalistic concept has no place in primitive
orders. 'A traditional network of close personal relationships produces a commitment to values such as generosity' (p. 388). The hierarchical order that stresses
social ranking leads to 'a primary emphasis on justice as
the protection of established rights and a secondary emphasis on ... the relief of the needy'. Market societies
are more complex; the impersonal exchange relationships
of a (more or less) free market generate a view of justice
as the requital of desert 'though the transformation of
these societies brought about chiefly by the rise of cor-
porate groups has changed the basis of desert and reintro-
duced the principle of need' (p. 389).

In this way the project of socially locating various
notions of social justice is completed. Miller concludes
by contrasting his approach with Rawls's attempt to sub-
stantiate a particular principle, and claims that 'the
whole enterprise of constructing a theory of justice on
the basis of the choices hypothetically made by individuals abstracted from society is mistaken', for 'men hold
conceptions of social justice as part of more general
views of society, and they acquire these views through
their experience of living in actual societies with a
definite structure' (pp. 341-2). The object of political
philosophy should be 'to explicate the ideas and principles
found in [a] culture and to find out whether there are any
decisive arguments for taking up particular prescriptive
standpoints, using the criteria that are available' (p. 343).

PROBLEMS IN MILLER'S APPROACH

The first part of such a programme seems eminently practicable. Problems arise with the second. The question is
whether we can use decisive arguments for a particular
perspective, given that people differ on the interpretation of concepts and that their differences relate to
their differing implicit or explicit political or sociological standpoints. As Gallie points out, no cogent way
of choosing between these has yet been found.

Miller's answer to this objection rests on the notion
of 'agreed criteria'. Thus he maintains that it is impossible for the political theorist to argue conclusively

view may be somewhat mortifying to the 'glory, jest and
riddle of the world'. It also makes it hard to understand
how it is that man produces the social fabric. For certainly no one else does. The idea that there is an intelligible connection between a man's relationships with
other men and his idea of social justice is only one side
of the coin. Winch (1958) traces the other: 'a man's
social relations with his fellows are permeated with his
ideas about reality. Indeed "permeated" is hardly a strong
enough word: social relations are expressions of ideas
about reality' (p. 23).

If Miller's approach is designed to give us a way of
understanding the relation between social institutions
and ideas, Winch is pointing to a reciprocal relation between ideas and human society. Berger and Luckman, in
their phenomenological sociology of ideas (1971, pp. 78-9),
attempt to integrate both perspectives:

  man and his social world interact with each other. The
  product acts back upon the producer.... Society is a
  human product. Society is an objective reality. Man
  is a social product ... an analysis of the social world
  which leaves out any one of these three moments will be
  distortive.

If the perspective of the sociology of knowledge is to
provide a useful approach to the study of the political
philosophy of social welfare, it seems that the project is
in its infancy. Substantive moral theory has failed so
far to produce satisfactory characterizations of moral
concepts. Reflexive theory comes to terms with the diversity of ideology. Yet it fails to provide an adequate
account of the relation between ideology and society.
What can political philosophy contribute to the task that
is set by the study of social policy?

ESSENTIAL CONTESTABILITY AND THE STUDY OF SOCIAL POLICY

Two problem areas were distinguished earlier in the study
of the welfare activities of modern society: the difficulties involved in the characterization of a normative
concept of need, and the questions raised in the analysis
of the success of social institutions in meeting needs.
In this volume, an emphasis on the essential contestability
of the concepts used in the discussion of welfare serves to
link these two areas of interest. Substantive moral
theory, such as that of Nozick and Rawls, is considered
only in so far as it is relevant to contemporary debate in
this area. The emphasis, in analysis of concepts such as
need, right, stigma. want and community, is on the dis-

tinction between the various uses of these notions that
are current within our culture and on the relation of these
notions to the views on society contained in various political ideologies. Essentially contested concepts underlie
the use of the notion of 'need'. If we accept Winch's
contention that 'social relations really exist only in and
through the ideas which are current in society' (1958,
p. 133), it follows that these contested notions underlie
the institutions that serve to meet need. It is hoped
that a clarification of these issues will be one step in
the direction of the 'very desirable consequence of ... a
marked raising of the level of quality of arguments in the
disputes of the contestant parties' (Gallie, 1955-6, p.
193). However, if contested concepts inform political
institutions, political debate about such concepts is in
a very real sense politics. In this sense the quotation
from Weber that stands as epigraph to Runciman's 'Relative
Deprivation and Social Justice' (1972) seems peculiarly
apposite: 'any meaningful assessment of someone else's
aspirations can only be a criticism of them in the light
of one's personal view of the world, a struggle against
alien ideals from the standpoint of one's own' (p. xii).

Part One

Needs, welfare and social policy

'The word "need" ought to be banished from discussion
of public policy, partly because of its ambiguity but
also because ... the word is frequently used in
"arbitrary" senses.'

[Alan Williams on 'needology']

'Needs create obligations.'

[Simone Weil]

Needs, rights and welfare

NEEDS AND THE GOALS OF WELFARE

The concept of need is absolutely fundamental to the understanding of contemporary social policy and the welfare state. In the view of some commentators, the recognition and satisfaction of need marks the welfare function of the modern state from its other functions, and at the same time the relationship between needs and rights is at the heart of the much discussed problem of stigma on the part of the recipients of welfare benefits.

Some theorists have argued that it is the concept of need that differentiates the social services from other types of institutions in the modern state. Forder, for example, in 'Concepts in Social Administration', argues that: 'The definition of need presents a central problem for the social services, since this defines the objectives of the services' (1974, p. 39), and much the same view is to be found in Jonathan Bradshaw's 'New Society' article, The Concept of Social Need (1972, p. 640):

The concept of social need is inherent in the idea of social service. The history of the social services is the history of the recognition of social needs and the organisation of society to meet them. The Seebohm Report was deeply concerned with the concept of need, though it never succeeded in defining it. It saw that the personal social services are large scale experiments in ways of helping those in need.

Similarly Walton, in Need: A Central Concept (1969), argued that the notion of need might well be a way of characterizing and fixing the scope of the social services. Dorothy Thompson argued in 1958 that: 'The range of benefits are provided purely on the basis of need and not of cash payment or any abstract conception of social value. This conception is a profoundly anticapitalist one' (p. 56).

Much the same idea has been expressed by George and
Wilding in their characterization of radical social
policy (1976):

> The fundamental principle of radical social policy
> is that resources, whether in the field of health,
> education, housing or income, should be distributed
> according to need. Contemporary welfare capitalism in
> the form of the welfare state cannot meet this basic
> objective, for it is guided by the social values and
> economic interests of the dominant class in society.

On such a view not only will the concept of need allow
us to delineate the appropriate role for the social services, but it will also enable us to point up fundamental
discrepancies between this ideal and the performance of
the social services within capitalist society. We might
try to formalize this approach by saying that the satisfaction of need is the only proper criterion for the distribution of social service resources - merit, moral worth,
potential, ability, are not proper grounds for the distribution of such resources. The satisfaction of need is the
internal goal (Nozick, 1974, p. 234) of the social services, and it is by means of this distributive principle
that the social services are to be delineated from market
transactions. It would seem on such a basis that, if
needs do specify the objectives of the social services,
then all that has to be done is for needs to be empirically
discovered for the objectives of the social services to be
made completely determinate and specified - in much the
same way as some educational theorists have argued that to
be able empirically to specify the needs of children would
be to be able to determine the content of the school curriculum. If needs can be fixed in some straightforward,
neutral, objective way, then the goals of the social services could equally be fixed objectively, thus bypassing
contestable appeals to social and political values. Questions about the social services would no longer be questions about moral or political values but of matching
means to needs, which might be thought to be a technical
rather than an ideological problem. In addition, such a
conception of the social services and their relation to
need fulfilment would also yield a neutral way of assessing the performance of the social services. Presented
with a set of clearly defined and objectively determined
needs, it could then be argued that the social services are
more or less efficient according to the extent to which
they do manage to meet these needs. Indeed, the whole
social indicators movement may well be based upon just
this view (see p.101 below).

A very great deal depends upon the characterization of
the concept of need before it can really be decided
whether or not needs can fulfil this function of specifying in a neutral manner the objectives of the social
services. The conception of need that is presupposed on
this sort of view is that need is a non-normative concept -
that needs can be discovered in some kind of objective
manner by sociologists, social workers, psychologists,
educationalists and others - and it is just such a conception of need that evaporates on analysis.
 At the same time, in the discussion of the internal relationships between the social services and needs, the
concept of need is being used in such a way as to make it
different from wants, preferences and desires. It would
be absurd to argue that the social services exist to satisfy people's wants and desires, and in arguing that they
exist to satisfy needs there is a presumed contrast
operating between wants and needs. The economic market is
usually to be the institution within which wants as preference are satisfied, and it is just because people have
needs that are not being satisfied via the market that the
services have developed. Needs and their satisfaction
characterize the social services on the general welfare
aspect of society: the market exists to satisfy preferences and wants.
 Again, the coherence of these assumptions depends considerably upon the characterization of needs. If the
concept of needs is clear and incontestable and is marked
off by a determinate boundary from wants, then the division of labour between the social services and the market
will be justified; on the other hand, if there is no
clear distinction between needs and wants, and if there
is a rather murky area in which needs shade off into
wants, then other values and principles are going to have
to be introduced to try to fix the boundary between the
market and the welfare sphere.

NEEDS AND STIGMA

The concept of need is also crucial to the social services
in that the relationship between needs and rights lies at
the heart of the problem of stigma and social service
provision. Titmuss (1974) points out that 'stigma'
'originally meant a mark physically branded on a slave or
a criminal. What it is generally taken to refer to today
is an imputation attaching to a person's reputation or
standing' (p. 43). In the context of the recipients of
social service provision, the term is used to indicate

be distributed on a private, personal basis and that it
might be distributed rather haphazardly. A right to welfare entails a strict obligation to provide it; on the
other hand, generosity, charity, benevolence and humanity,
while highly commendable virtues, are not strict obligations. For even if we think that there is a duty to be
benevolent in general terms, we need not think that there
is a duty of benevolence in any particular case. E Telfer
has summarized the position here quite well (1976, p. 107):

> I shall take it that the *laissez-faire* system is agreed
> to be inadequate; indeed, under such a system the state
> would in my view be abrogating its responsibilities
> towards the needy. It is true that the needy might be
> very well provided for if there were a strong enough
> tradition of charity of this kind. But it seems too
> haphazard a basis for such an important service. In
> any case, it might be said that the opportunity for
> health care allied to welfare is a basic human right;
> if this is so, receiving it should not have to depend
> upon people's goodwill, however forthcoming that good-
> will is.

Again, a clear understanding of the concept of need and
its relationship to that of right is quite fundamental to
clear thinking about the provision of welfare and the whole
structure of the welfare state. Stigma and dependence
may be misplaced attitudes on the part of recipients of
welfare transfers if these transfers are based upon some
kind of general right. Naturally stigma does not arise
in market transactions because men think that they have a
right to what they buy and to what they produce and sell:
stigma would be equally inappropriate if welfare were seen
to be a basic right which men may claim off society. At
the same time, to see welfare provision in terms of rights
and obligations instead of humanity and benevolence will
sanction a commitment to government responsibility to
welfare and a corresponding institutional welfare structure
which will not necessarily be required if welfare is seen
in terms of humanity and charity.

NEEDS AND WANTS

If the satisfaction of need is said to be the basic or
internal goal of the social services, the concept of need
is being used in such a way as to assume a distinction
between needs and wants. It would certainly be odd to say
that the welfare services exist to satisfy wants - I may
desire or want a colour television set or a new car, but
these are not goods that are available from the social

services. On the contrary, in fact, those who use the
concept of need to demarcate the sphere of the social
services are willing to concede that, at least within
Western societies, it is the economic market that provides
the institutional framework within which wants are articulated and satisfied, to the extent that they are. So it
is crucial for drawing the distinction between the market
and welfare institutions in terms of need that there
should be some fairly precise difference between needs
and wants. However, it is important not to beg this question at the outset. Some have held that there is no real
distinction and have tried to utilize this point to argue
in favour of an extension of the market into what may be
seen as the welfare section of society on the view outlined above (Seldon, 1968) and others have taken a quicker
line and suggested that needs are wants that people have
but are not prepared to pay for, and certainly in the use
of economic analyses in cost-benefit studies this is the
only way in which needs enter. Needs are taken to be
desires or wants that a person would be willing to pay
a hypothetical price to have satisfied. Indeed, unless
needs are seen as wants, and therefore as having some kind
of economic value, it is difficult to see how they could
enter into economic calculation at all. So it must not
be assumed that there is a clear-cut distinction between
needs and wants.

One major feature that needs and wants have in common
is that they are complex concepts. The full specification of a want or a need expression will require that its
structure be spelt out, and from this expansion of both
want and need expressions certain important consequences
follow.

The structure of want and need expressions can be set
out as follows:

X wants Y for Z
A needs B for C

That is to say, in all cases in which the verb 'to want'
or the verb 'to need' are used there has to be a subject,
not necessarily animate in the case of need, who wants or
needs or who has the wants or needs ascribed to him; there
must be an object which is wanted or needed; and finally,
there must be some end goal, purpose or function which the
object is wanted or needed for. In modern philosophy this
characterization in regard to wants has been put forward
most forcefully by Professor G.E.M. Anscombe in her
'Intention' (1957), para. 37:

But is not anything wantable, or at least any perhaps

attainable thing? It will be instructive to anyone who
thinks this to approach someone and say: 'I want a saucer
of mud' or 'I want a twig of mountain ash'. He is
likely to be asked what for; to which let his reply be
that he does not want it *for* anything, he just wants
it....
      It is not at all clear what it meant to say: this
man simply wanted a pin. Of course, if he is careful
always to carry the pin in his hand thereafter, or at
least for a time, we may say that he really wanted that
pin. Then perhaps the answer to 'what do you want it for?'
may be 'to carry it about with me', as a man may want a
stick. But here again there is a further characterisa-
tion ... to say 'I merely want this' without any charac-
terisation is to deprive the word of sense; if he insists on 'having' a thing we want to know what 'having'
it amounts to.

The same is true of needs. A claim by B that X is needed
is fully intelligible only when the purpose for which it
is needed is exhibited; and from this it follows that for
any claim to want or need to be intelligible, the end or
purpose in question has to be specified. These goals or
purposes for which things are wanted or needed are called
'desirability characteristics' by Professor Anscombe, and
in order for a need or a want expression to be fully understood, the desirability characteristics of the goal or
purpose have to be cited, and not only cited but drawn from
a common stock of desirability characterizations. In most
cases these desirability characterizations remain tacit or
latent in the use of need or want expressions, not because
these expressions do not require these characteristics,
but because they are conventional and obvious:

> I need a holiday
> I need a new pen
> I want a new pair of trousers
> I want to see the new film

In these cases it would, in normal circumstances, be pointless to cite the ends in question just because they are
tacitly understood. On the other hand, the use of uncon-
ventional examples shows that, when the claim to have a
want or a need is not fully understood, it is the end in
question that renders the claim intelligible. For example:

> I want a saucer of mud
> I want a twig of mountain ash
> I need poison

are all made intelligible once the ends, purposes or goals
in question are spelled out; viz.,'for my child to make a
model'; 'to use in a floral decoration'; 'to clear my greenhouse of mice'. As Taylor (1969) p. 254, argues, 'The
only criterion for understanding a want is understanding
what state of affairs will satisfy it, which is equivalent
to understanding what use the person whose want is in
question expects from the object of his want' (p. 254).
This does seem to follow from what it would mean to satisfy
a want, and the same would hold true a fortiori for the case
of needs.

However, reference to ends and uses is not just relevant
to making the want or need intelligible; it is also central when questions of justification arise. Usually questions of this sort arise only in the case of need, and we
can see clearly that at least part of the justification
to claim to need something would have to involve reference
to the purposes involved and the uses to which the things
needed would be put. Only if such purposes and uses are
themselves regarded as legitimate will the needs generated
by such uses and purposes be regarded as legitimate. In
order for my need for poison to be justified, the use that
I expect to derive from it must also be justified. Clearly,
to rid my greenhouse of mice would usually be considered
a legitimate use; to rid my greenhouse of my sleeping
mother-in-law, an illegitimate use. In the first case the
claim to need would be vindicated; in the second case it
would not. Although this may appear to be platitudinous,
a very important point emerges, namely, that reference to
need is not itself enough to act as a claim to resources.
As Brian Barry has pointed out in 'Political Argument'
(1965, pp. 48-9), only when the ends or purposes for which
things are needed are both articulated and found to be
justified does the appeal to need have any moral force.
To recognize this is already to move away from the view
that needs can be established in some morally neutral way
by sociological research; rather, the classification of
needs is going to depend crucially upon ends, goals and
purposes, the justification of which is an ineradicably
moral enterprise and one that may be morally contestable.

However, this still leaves unresolved the question of
the status of these ends which play such a crucial legitimating role in need contests. These ends, purposes, uses,
etc., play this legitimating role, but how are they themselves to be legitimized? It seems clear, in the first
instance at least, that these ends are themselves objects
of human wants, desires and needs. The end, goal, purpose
or use that renders a want or need intelligible and on
occasion justifiable is itself wanted, desired or needed.

This again seems to be clear enough in ordinary usage:

> I need poison (initial need statement)
> Why?
> To clear my greenhouse of mice (initial justifying goal)
> Why do you want to clear your greenhouse of mice? (Initial justifying goal itself revealed as a want)
> Because the mice will eat the produce which I intend to sell (the broader goal which justifies the initial goal)
> ...
> and so on

Here the end or use that justified the need for poison is (itself) an object of desire. It is clear therefore that, if we want to give a full account of a particular want or need expression, we have to put it into a framework of broader generality of other goals and purposes which give direction and meaning to specific more episodic ends that a person may pursue. The question that we shall have to answer when we ask whether there are basic or human needs is whether there are certain goals and purposes that all persons desire and that are wanted as ends in themselves, so that they can act as basic justifying principles for the needs and wants that they generate, and whether all persons can be said to have the same basic ends and therefore the same basic needs and wants as the necessary means to attain such ends.

NEEDS, WANTS AND PSYCHOLOGY

However, before taking up this very large question we shall consider another proposal for drawing a fairly sharp distinction between needs and wants. Some theorists have suggested that the difference between needs and wants should be looked for in terms of wanting being a psychological state, whereas needing something is a kind of objective, publicly discernible fact about a person. This position is developed by David Miller in 'Social Justice' (1976, p. 129):

> wanting is a psychological state, which is ascribed on the basis of a person's avowals and his behaviour....
> Needing, on the other hand, is *not* a psychological state, but rather a condition which is ascribed 'objectively' to the person who is its subject.

Similarly, Benn and Peters, in 'Social Principles and the Democratic State' (1959), argue that wants are states of mind whereas needs imply a failure to measure up to an

understood standard. This kind of difference between
needs and desires or wants has been insisted upon by
David Braybrooke in his important essay, Let Needs
Diminish that Preferences may Flourish (1968a, p. 90):

> in a case where there is evidence that N does desire
> something and equally weighty evidence that he doesn't,
> his testimony will decide the issue, provided at least
> that we have general grounds for thinking him habitually
> sincere. But in a case where there is evidence both
> ways about N needing something, his saying so only
> begs the question. It carries no more weight than the
> opinion of anyone else equally observant.

Certainly the kinds of considerations that have led
philosophers to hold this view are important and uncontro-
versial; what is controversial is whether these considerations sanction the drawing of the distinction in terms of
wants being psychological states and needs being objective
external states of affairs. The kinds of considerations
in question are cases where a person may need or 'really'
need something that he may not want and cases where he may
want something that he does not need. Examples of the
first sort would be:

(a) 'He needs insulin' (He may be a diabetic although he
    does not know it and therefore does not want or
    desire insulin).

(b) (To a young child) 'You need to eat more cabbage"
    (Cabbage is a healthy food: the child may know this
    but he still doesn't want to eat it).

(c) 'You need a break from work' (in a situation in
    which I have a project which I wish to finish and
    I do not want to take a break from work).

None of these cases is in any way artificial and they do
give some plausibility to the idea that needs can be
ascribed independently of wants or desires and indeed in
known opposition to an individual's psychological avowals.
In this sense the ascription of needs may be objective and
the ascription of need does not necessarily entail the
presence of a corresponding psychological state. Examples
of the second case, where one may want something that one
does not need, are in fact similar and in a sense merely
reversals of the previous examples:

(a) 'He wants another ice cream' (When he has had one
    already - he doesn't need it).

(b) 'He wants some more of the orange-flavoured vitamin
    pills' (He has had his quota for the day - in the
    sense that the body does not require more - he
    doesn't need any more).

(c) 'He wants a holiday' (But he hasn't been working very
    hard recently - he doesn't really need one).

Again, these kinds of examples seem to be convincing enough, and they have led philosophers to argue that in this case the wants in question are clear psychological states, but equally they may conflict with what the person who has the wants or desires actually needs.

It is certainly correct to suggest on the basis of a consideration of this kind of example that needs can be ascribed independently of a person's avowed wants and desires, and as we shall see below this point is crucial to arguments about false consci ousness vis à vis needs; but it is surely too strong to suggest that wants are therefore psychological states whereas needs are not, and this is so for a number of reasons. On some psychological theories - particularly those inspired by Freud - it is possible to ascribe wants and desires to someone independently of his own avowed wants and desires. A man may be thought to have unconscious or subconscious wants, desires and wishes which can be teased out by the psychotherapist and ascribed to the patient even though on the face of it they will conflict with his avowed wants. We say 'on the face of it' just because the ascribed wants or desires may well make more sense of his avowed wants than the man's own perception and justifications of his avowed wants. To say that wants are psychological states whereas needs may be ascribed independently of a person's avowals seems to beg the question as to whether there can be externally ascribed wants and desires.

Second, to say that needs are ascribed objectively to persons independently of their avowed wants and desires undermines a whole contemporary movement in social policy - the emphasis upon revealing 'felt needs' through participation programmes, community action and so forth. Walton (1969) places very great emphasis upon the 'felt needs' of those who are recipients of the social services as against needs ascribed to such people by experts - psychologists, social workers, medical practitioners, town planners, etc. - and Bradshaw (1972, p. 641) says of felt needs:

Here need is equated with want, when assessing the need for a service, people are asked whether they feel that they need it. In a democracy, it could be imagined that felt need would be an important component in the definition of need, but a felt need measure seems to be only used regularly in studies of the elderly and community development.

Again, to assume that there is a sharp difference between needs and wants in terms of the former being objective states, with the latter being subjective psychological states, would require us immediately to question the whole conception of felt need where the felt needs of the

recipients of the social services may conflict with the
needs ascribed to the recipients by social policy pundits;
and along with the questioning of this conception of need
would have to go a scepticism about the role of participation and community action within the welfare sphere, the
very rationale of which seems to be very often that those
who feel the needs are in the best position to say what
they are. Certainly this is central to the chapter on
'Community' in the Seebohm Report; in President Johnson's
poverty programme. We shall argue later that the valid
aspect of the argument about the objectivity of need can
be retained quite easily without insisting that needs are
not psychological states.

Finally, on this point it could be argued that to draw
too sharp a line between wanting as a psychological state
and need as an objective state of affairs mistakes the
character of psychological states. The contrast between
needs and wants in these terms seems to trade off the idea
that for something to be a need there has to be some kind
of external standard or norm that makes something a need,
whereas a want is exempt from this kind of restriction.
It is certainly true that a need does have to meet some
kind of accepted external criterion to be a need, and this
is precisely what was argued in the section of this chapter
that linked needs with ends. But this emphatically does
not distinguish a need from a want; a want or a desire is
not just a stirring in my bosom, a purely internal occur-
rence. We owe to Wittgenstein, and those who have followed him, the great advance in philosophical psychology
of rejecting as a total account of the character of psychological states that they are based entirely on the occur-
rence of an inner feeling. On the contrary, as we argued
earlier, wants are not just private, psychological occurrences: they are intentional in that they require objects
wanted. But more than this, the want is made intelligible
with reference to an end, and this reference is not going
to be merely a private standard of intelligibility: it
is going to be a standard shared by other members of my
society. Both wants and needs are going to involve
desirability characterizations, and these characterizations
are going to presuppose publicly accepted standards of
desirability.Richard Norman (1971) has made this point
particularly strongly: 'the intelligibility of a want is
essentially a matter of its relationship to public, supra-
individual standards and norms' (. 55). It begs too many
questions to assume that needs presuppose standards and
are therefore objective, whereas wants are internal psychological states. Both needs and wants presuppose norms and
standards of intelligibility. We want to suggest that

the differences between a want and a need is to be drawn
not in terms of one being related to an end and the values
to which these ends relate, but rather in terms of the
character of the ends involved.

NEEDS, MEANS AND GOALS

We are now able to take up the question posed earlier,
which is obviously crucial for fixing as rigorously as
possible the concept of need: namely, whether there are
any goals, purposes, functions, states of life, etc., that
all persons may be said to want and that would provide the
basic justifying mechanisms for the needs that the pursuit
of these goals would generate. 'Are there basic human
needs?' therefore turns into the question of whether there
are any basic human ends that are wanted by all persons,
with basic needs being the necessary means for the pursuit
and realization of those ends. In the same way as a
particular individual's wants and needs become intelligible
and legitimate as we see them against the pattern of a background of his more basic wants and interests, so the question can be raised in the most general way: 'Are there any
basic interests and purposes that all persons have?'; which
would explain and legitimate the use of a notion such as
basic, intrinsic or human needs. If there are such ends
generating such basic needs, then there would be a class
of things needed that, following Rawls in 'A Theory of
Justice' (1972), we might call primary goods which would
be the basic concern of social policy. Many philosophers
have suggested that when we are talking about basic human
or intrinsic needs we are concerned with ends that have to
do with harm (Miller, 1976, p. 130) or ailing (Wollheim,
1976, pp. 162ff.). If a person is held to have a need
for something, then it is assumed that he will be harmed
by his not having it, and his getting what he needs will
overcome this harm or will be a remedy for his co dition.
Peters, in 'The Concept of Motivation', puts this point
cogently (1958, p. 17):
> at a common sense level, the term 'need' is mainly
> normative. It prescibes one of a set of standard
> goals. It usually functions as a diagnostic term with
> remedial implications that something is wrong with a
> person if certain conditions are absent ... the im-
> plication is that there is a state of affairs which is
> or is likely to be damaging to the individual in
> question.

The assumption here is that there is a certain state of
human flourishing or welfare, and if a person fails to

achieve this state he will ail or will be harmed. Needs
are what are necessary to achieve this condition of flourishing, and getting what one needs to flourish or to
improve one's welfare will act as a remedy for one's condition. The necessary means to flourishing or welfare that
are needed on this view might be called basic or primary
goods. So are we able to specify in a non-normative,
neutral and empirical way what basic human harm or ailing
consists in, and by implication what a minimum level of
human flourishing or welfare is, understood just in the
sense of not being harmed? If we can do this then we
shall be provided with a non-contestable account of human
needs which can then be made the object of social policy
and a non-contestable list of primary goods that are the
objects of such needs - both lists being generated by the
basic human ends or purposes in question. If we cannot
fill in this list of basic needs by 'reading them off'
from an incontestable list of basic human ends, then it
would seem that any person would be able to classify any
single one of his demands as being a basic need so far as
he is concerned just by arguing that he would be harmed,
according to his lights, if his 'need' were not satisfied,
and we can see how easy it would be to deploy such an
argument. If we allow a sphere of psychological harm,
then an individual might argue that the frustration of a
particular desire would cause him harm and therefore,
according to his own conception of harm, his desire would
become a need and there would be at least some kind of
obligation on the part of others to meet his need and thus
prevent harm from befalling him. Can we say that there is
an uncontested account of human flourishing so that failure
to achieve this state constitutes objective harm to a particular person, irrespective of the particular views of
that person, or are such standards of flourishing and harm
a matter of personal moral outlook so that the needs engendered by such basic goals would themselves be legitimated
by entirely personal moral values?

    This question has been discussed a good deal in recent
moral philosophy. Some philosophers, notably Mrs Foot and
Professor Anscombe, have argued that there are some things
that will be seen as harm and as a failure to flourish whatever one's moral, political or ideological standpoint, and
the most obvious case of this is that of physical injury.
However, this assumption has been attacked by H.O. Mounce
and D.Z. Phillips in their influential paper, On Morality's
Having a Point (1965), and they cite two examples to show
that even physical injury cannot be considered an incontestable basic harm, and therefore that physical health
could not be seen as a morally incontestable basic need or

primary good.   One example they quote is the case of
Brentano the Philosopher, who regarded his blindness in
later life as a blessing rather than as an affliction
because it allowed him to concentrate on philosophy. Here
a physical disability is not seen as constituting harm -
what harm consists of in this view is going to depend
crucially upon one's ideals, aspirations and moral values.
In the second case the Catholic mother resists the claims
of the rationalist that she will be harmed by having further children because her conception of harm cannot include the idea that harm can accompany the birth of
children of God.

These cases do seem to give some substance to the idea
that harm is so indeterminate a concept that any unsatisfied state could be thought to result in harm and thus
could generate a need, and the point is given particular
weight by the fact that both of these examples show how
elastic and contestable even the case of physical harm
might seem to be, which of all the possible examples
seems to be the most concrete and determinate.   If needs
are to be seen in terms of harming and ailing, then anything might in principle become a need.   Conversely, a
person to whom a need is ascribed, because it is thought
that he lacks something and therefore ails, may well be
able to resist the ascription of the need on the ground
that he does not think that he is being harmed.   For some
cases of course it is possible to convince the person by
factual argument;   e.g., in the case of the man who does
not know that he has diabetes and resists the ascription
of the need for insulin.   Other cases, though, are more
intractable.   The Catholic mother's concept of harm may
not coincide with that of the rationalist doctor, and because the difference is a value difference the assumption
of the need for sterilization or contraception may be
resisted interminably.

Considerations of this sort would lead one to suggest
that the concept of need is essentially contestable just
because the ascription of need is related to a norm of
harm that is essentially normative and is going to vary
from morality to morality and from culture to culture. In
the case of social services, where welfare is provided on
the basis of need, it would follow from these considerations that, when the social services recognize needs, these
needs are not, so to speak, being discovered as empirically
detectable states that people are in;   rather, a norm of
harm and of being harmed is being assumed and people are
regarded as being in need relative to this norm of harm,
a norm that may be contested within society just as much
as outside it.   There may be those characteristically on

the left politically who will argue that what counts as
being harmed is being construed too narrowly in contemporary society, and that much more should be made over to
the welfare branch of the state to cater for those needs
that would be generated by an expanded notion of harm.
On the other hand, those characteristically of the right
may well argue that the norm of harm is already being
construed too widely, and that welfare services proliferate endlessly to meet newly 'discovered needs' when
in fact these needs are being fostered by a fashionably
wide view of what constitutes harm to individuals.   Is
there any way out of what seems to be an *impasse* of moral
relativism and contestability about human needs?   If our
ideas about human flourishing and human harm are going to
vary from one moral code to another then our ideas about
needs are going to be equally morally contestable, and
there will be very little room for empirical social inquiry into the needs of individuals and communities because such inquiries are always going to be informed by
morally contested norms.

One way around this difficulty, and one that, formally
at least, has a good deal of power, is to suggest that any
consistent moral code, whatever it might be, is going to
have to recognize certain kinds of capacity and needs
among persons that will have to be fulfilled if persons
are to be able to pursue the ideals enshrined in any
moral code.   If it is in the nature of any morality to make
certain assumptions about the capacities and powers of
persons considered as actual or potential moral agents,
then these capacities and states would constitute basic
needs - the necessary means to the realization of any moral
ideal, whatever it may be, or the necessary means to the
realization of any moral capacity, whatever it might be and
however it might be envisaged.   The argument of the next
chapter is that there are such assumptions made in any
moral code and that it is thus possible to produce a
morally neutral list of basic human needs.

3 Human needs, objectivity and morality

The argument so far shows that what counts as a need will
depend largely on one's general moral position. This is
not because there is no common element in the various uses
of the concept of need, but because the common element,
which is roughly the notion of something necessary for the
efficient achievement of some goal, is so abstract that
nothing is ruled out by it, and nothing is necessarily
included: anything at all can, so far as the logic of the
concept goes, be an object of need, and nothing has to be.
   Moreover, on one level the concept of need is morally
quite neutral: two Agatha Christie devotees can happily
discuss what the villain 'needed' to do to escape detec-
tion without at all approving of murder. But often 'need'
refers to something that, in the opinion of the speaker,
is necessary for a good or desirable end, so that it is
good, or even obligatory, to satisfy it. It is this use
of 'need' that is used to justify social policies and to
persuade people to adopt them on moral grounds. The problem is that, as we have seen, the justification can work
only if one shares the speaker's belief that the end in
question is desirable, i.e. if one partially shares his
values. Since societies and individuals notoriously disagree about values, it seems to follow that, though there
can be general agreement about the abstract definition of
need, when we come to the practical question of what is to
count as a need, i.e. as something that society ought to
accept an obligation to provide, we are left with conceptions of needs that are essentially contestable.
   But this conclusion may be too hasty. The disagreements
about values may not be as deep or as real as they appear;
even if the question as to what ends people ought to pursue
is disputable, it does not follow that the same is true of
the question as to what their needs are. This is because
there are some conditions necessary for doing anything at

all, for performing any action or pursuing any goal what-
soever. No matter what morality one adopts, these conditions will be necessary for carrying it out. Needs of
this sort must be acknowledged in all societies, whatever
their moral code or standards, and may fairly be called
'unqualified' or 'human' needs.

SURVIVAL AS A BASIC NEED

The most obvious of such needs is physical survival. To
put the matter a bit abstractly, the existence of moral
agents is a necessary precondition of moral activity. So
if human beings have moral duties at all, they have a need
to survive, which in its turn implies a duty to help each
other to survive and to preserve life. One can avoid this
conclusion by denying that we do have moral obligations;
but such a view, although it may be irrefutable, is not
actually held by any sane person, much as people may differ over what our obligations are.
    This argument depends on two purely logical principles
of ethics. The first is that a moral code must be consistent; it would be senseless to assert that there both
is and is not a moral duty to do a particular thing.
(There is often, within a given moral code, a problem as
to which of two general but conflicting duties should take
precedence in a particular situation: but in these cases
one is wondering whether or not a duty exists, rather than
asserting that it both does and does not.) The second
principle, which follows from the first one, is that what
one has a duty to do one has a right to do: if the code
prescribes that something ought to be done, consistency
requires that it should also prescribe that no one should
prevent it from being done, i.e. that the person(s) who
ought to do it have a right to do it.

BASIC NEEDS AND MORAL OBLIGATIONS

It is with the nature of this right and the corresponding
duty that the problem really begins. Is it a duty to
provide positive help for other people in the performance
of their obligations where this is necessary? If so, it
follows that, whatever one's moral position, one has a duty
to fulfil needs, where possible; and one of these needs
must inevitably be for survival. But many people have felt
and argued that this exaggerates our duties; that although
it is an admirable thing to help others, our only strict
duty is to do them no harm. On both views, there is a need

for survival; but on the first view this leads to the
conclusion that we are therefore obliged to help one
another to survive, while on the second view our only
obligation is not to kill. Indeed, one might take the
second thesis further, and argue that, since our initial
obligations are all negative, and we have no positive
duties to one another except those we impose on ourselves by voluntary contract, we cannot even infer that
we have a moral need for survival: we have only a right
not to be killed.

A recent very interesting expression of this type of
moral view is to be found in Nozick's 'Anarchy, State
and Utopia' (1974), which is referred to elsewhere in
these essays. Nozick deals not with duty but with what
a person may legitimately be coerced to do, so that he
might not deny the existence of a need to survive or an
obligation to meet that need, but he would certainly
deny that the state, or anyone else, can be justified in
enforcing the obligation. (On some definitions of duty,
this would automatically mean it was not a strict dity.)
According to Nozick (chapter 3, sections 3 and 4),

> no moral balancing act can take place among us; there
> is no moral outweighing of one of our lives by others
> so as to lead to a greater overall *social* good.
> There is no justified sacrifice of some of us for
> others ... to use a person in this way does not suffi-
> ciently respect and take account of the fact that he is
> a separate person, that his is the only life he has.

Hence a person may be compelled to respect the rights of
others and to do them no harm all of which involves mere
abstention from certain actions, and no sacrifice of his
time or resources; but he may not be compelled to benefit
them at his own expense, however slight the expense, and
however great the benefit to others.

Nozick's position accords well with some of our moral
intuitions. The negative obligations do seem to be the
most vital and essential: Kant rightly comments ('Groundwork of the Metaphysic of Morals', p. 423) that if the
general policy were to observe only these obligations -
not to kill, assault, defraud, enslave, etc.:

> certainly the human race could exist, and without doubt
> even better than in a state where everyone talks of
> sympathy and goodwill, or even exerts himself occa-
> sionally to practise them, while on the other hand he
> cheats when he can and betrays or otherwise violates
> the rights of man.

It is also a moral intuition that cost-benefit analysis
ought not to be applied to all human situations, and that
there are things that may not be done to a person, however

great the benefit to others: it is precisely this that makes many forms of utilitarianism so implausible, because they seem to require us to sacrifice individuals unjustifiably to the 'happiness of the greatest number'.

But to extend this to a principle that no sacrifice of any kind may be exacted proves either too much or too little. Nozick supposes either that (a) the performance of a negative duty never involves any sacrifice, or (b) that what sacrifice is involved is in this case justified, i.e. is one that people have a right to exact. Now the first supposition is false: very often one can refrain from action at no cost to oneself, but by no means always; and there are circumstances under which one can abstain from killing an innocent person or taking his property only at the cost of one's own life. So the actual consequence of maintaining that no sacrifices can rightfully be exacted, whether they are big or small, would be the conclusion that one ought not to be compelled to do or refrain from doing anything that involves one in personal invonvenience.

In its turn, this conclusion leads us not to Nozick's position, that the role of the state should be minimal, but to philosophical anarchism, to a view like that of Robert Paul Wolff, in 'In Defence of Anarchism', that the state has no moral right of coercion at all, i.e. no right to exist, since a state is by definition a coercive order. This position seems to be not only unacceptable to Nozick himself, but also inconsistent. If we admit the existence of moral duties at all, we must admit also the derived duty not to destroy, or allow the destruction of the lives of moral agents, and if some coercion is essential in order to prevent this destruction, it follows that we are obliged to use coercion. This is so even if our ultimate moral value is freedom, since there is more, not less, freedom in a situation in which people are prevented from killing each other than in one in which they are not, and the obstacles to action are fewer and less all-embracing.

There is, though, another argument for anarchism, which has been traditionally offered, for example, by Kropotkin. This argument accepts, at least by implication, that coercion would be justified if it worked, but maintains that the actual effect of the state organization and its use of force is to corrupt men's natural goodness and desire to help one another, and to bring into being the very evils it is supposed to have been created to prevent: 'The main supports of crime are idleness, law and authority' (Kropotkin, 1970, final paragraphs). To evaluate such a position is too big a task to be done incidentally: instead, we shall assume the moral validity of government

as such, and discuss needs in that context. But Kropotkin's point is still very important, for the following
reason. If the general argument is correct, a society
has a duty to satisfy needs, and a right, in principle,
to use coercion in order to achieve this. However, whether
coercion, or even public organization, should in fact be
used depends on the factual question as to whether it is
effective; even though the duty to satisfy needs may
belong to society as a whole, it does not follow that
society as a whole should carry it out, unless it can do
so more efficiently than private individuals.

But to return to Nozick. If Nozick is distinguishing
between positive and negative duties on the ground that
negative duties involve no sacrifice, he is mistaken; and
if he still holds, in the face of this, that sacrifices
should not be exacted by coercion, he will be led into a
version of anarchism that seems inconsistent. On the
other hand, if he maintains that the sacrifice is justified
in the one case but not in the other, he must give some
reason for this. But this seems to be impossible: one
cannot say that one is less important, or less of a duty -
or indeed that in principle failing to keep someone alive
is morally any different from killing him. The attempt to
distinguish in theory between the two sorts of duty seems
thus to fail, and with it any attempt at a moral code that
prescribes only negative duties.

But Nozick's thesis has some validity in practice. So
far, we have argued (a) that if one holds that a person
has a moral duty one must also hold that other people have
a duty to help him to perform it, if their help is required,
and not merely to refrain from hindering him; and (b) that
a consequence of this is that, whatever one's moral position, one must acknowledge a duty to help other people to
survive, since this is a necessary condition for performing any moral duty. But this 'derived' duty exists only if
one can perform it, and if its performance does not conflict with more important goals or duties. This can happen
with either positive or negative duties, but it happens
much more often with positive ones, which consume both
time and resources. One may thus agree with Nozick to a
limited extent, by conceding that there are more exceptions to the rule that one must help others to survive
than to the rule that one must not kill.

That these must be exceptions to both principles seems
fairly clear. It is actually impossible to adopt the principle of always preserving life, since there are circumstances under which one can save one life only at the expense of another: self-defence is one example, distribution of scarce resources is another, and the (mercifully

rare) situation where the lives of both mother and unborn
child cannot be preserved is a third. It is possible to
adopt the principle of never actually taking life, but
most moral codes recognize exceptions to this, such as
self-defence.

The problem here is that if it is not possible to preserve every life, and if life itself is of value partly
as a necessary condition for realizing other values, there
are particular circumstances where the protection of life
or of these values can be brought about only if some lives
are sacrificed, or even taken: 'sometimes a man has to
take upon himself the sin of killing so that there should
be less killing in the world and that the highest values
might be preserved' (Berdyaev, 1960, part 2, chapter 4).

Now this raises the following difficulty. If the preservation of the 'highest values' can require the sacrifice or even the taking of human life, there will be
circumstances under which survival is not, morally speaking, needed. But what these circumstances are will depend on what one believes the highest values to be. So,
although all moral codes must admit that survival is a
need, they will differ over when it is a need and when it
is not. And if this is so, are we not back with 'essential
contestability', as regards the nature of human needs in
practice?

There are two reasons why this is not so. One is that,
since values require moral agents, the circumstances
under which the sacrifice of the lives of moral agents
promotes these values must be highly exceptional; so
there will still be agreement that survival is a need
under normal circumstances, even though there will be
some disagreement over which circumstances are abnormal.
Second, the exceptions by and large concern political and
legal policy, rather than welfare policy - issues such as
when war is permissible, how it should be conducted,
whether there should be capital punishment, whether abor-
tion and euthanasia should be legal, etc.

Two issues, though, do appear to concern social policy.
The first is the case of the person who as a result of
serious illness or injury feels that he is unable to lead
a worthwhile life ever again, and that he needs to die
rather than to live. This raises a problem for the law:
should he be permitted, or helped, to end his life, or
not? It also raises a deep moral problem: there are many
honest and sensitive people who would say he was wrong,
and many equally honest and sensitive people who would
say he was right. But it is not really a problem for
welfare policy, which is concerned with the provision of
the means to meet needs. For this, on a social level,

must be dictated by the needs of the overwhelming majority:
the fact that a few individuals do not have these needs
can be ignored, since we are concerned only with giving
everyone the opportunity to satisfy them. Welfare policy
can aim at providing everyone with the means for survival
in so far as this is possible: it can leave it to individuals to decide whether to take advantage of these
means, and to the law to decide when one person must
take advantage of them on another's behalf.

Where there is a real problem for welfare policy is
with regard to the distribution of scarce resources.
Indeed, there are three problems. The first arises when
resources are insufficient to meet all needs, when there
is actually not enough food or not enough of a particular
medical resource to go round. There is then an unpleas-
ant moral problem as to how these resources should be
distributed. Often - though probably not always - the
best solution morally may be to leave it to chance, rather
than to presume to judge who should live and who should
die; but this may not always be possible.

In a developed society this arises only with regard to
medical care, and it is closely connected with the second
problem - when need-satisfaction has the first claim and
when it does not. There is a case for saying that the preservation of life, except in special cases, takes precedence over all other duties. But it would be possible for
a society to devote all its resources to prolonging life,
with the result that its members could do none of the
things that make life worthwhile. So how do we decide
what should be given to preserving or prolonging life, and
what to improving the quality of life?

It seems clear that at least food and shelter must be
provided by a society for all its members, if this is
possible. At the other end of the scale, it seems clear
that there is no obligation to provide costly medical
treatment whose success is uncertain or which can prolong
life but not under conditions that make it worthwhile.
But once a form of treatment can certainly save lives and
restore their value, and can be provided without diverting
resources from other life-saving treatments or destroying
the value of life, it seems reasonable to say that there
is an obligation to provide it. For example, it is beginning to be felt that we have now an obligation to provide
an adequate number of kidney machines, and that resources
should be diverted to this: and this feeling seems
morally right. On the other hand, we do not seem to have
an obligation to provide heart transplants.

THE REACH OF THE PRINCIPLE OF NEED

The third problem concerns the obligations of a rich
society towards a poor one. The first obligation of a
society is presumably to its own members, just as the
first obligation of an individual is to his own family:
we can all see the absurdity of Mrs Jellyby, in Dickens's
'Bleak House', whose children were unfed, unwashed and
in rags, while she devoted her time and energy to the
plight of the natives of 'Borrioboolah-Gha, on the left
bank of the Niger'. But popular morality has often gone
beyond this and maintained, consciously or unconsciously,
that the obligations to one's family, or tribe, or community, are the only obligations, and that one owes nothing to strangers. Today, for example, racial discrimination is rarely defended on grounds of supposed racial
inferiority, and much more often on the ground that it is
right to favour members of one's own race, even though
it is no better or worse than any other.
   But this position is in accord neither with our moral
intuitions nor with rational considerations. If we have
obligations at all, we have obligations towards anyone we
are able to help, since if human life is of value at all,
we cannot give rational grounds for saying that some lives
are of value and some are not. When there are conflicting
claims on time and resources, it is right that the claims
of those closest to us should take precedence: but we
cannot give any valid grounds for saying that these are
the only claims.
   An argument for this could be made if it could be
shown that not all human beings are moral agents, and that
only certain favoured races or classes are capable of
living the good life. But it is clear that, no matter
how the good life is defined, only individuals could be
supposed to be incapable of leading it. It is a matter
of empirical fact that there exists no racial or social
group all, or even many, of whose members are so handicapped, or uncontrolled, or corrupt, as to be disquali-
fied from being moral agents. Attempts to show the moral
or intellectual inferiority of particular groups always
rest on premises that are either false (e.g. the claim
that physical characteristics are evidence of moral
vices), or irrelevant (e.g. variations of average IQ between races, which tell us nothing about untested types
of intelligence and from which we can infer nothing about
individual members of the races concerned), or meaningless
(e.g. 'genetic inferiority').
   There may be individuals who are currently not moral
agents: they may be too handicapped, physically or

mentally, to be able to act purposively, or too uncontrolled or insensitive to be able to act morally, or so
corrupt that they always act wickedly. But we can never
know - in principle, and not merely in practice - whether
or not this incapacity is permanent or curable. It follows that even these rare individuals must be regarded as
potential moral agents, and that therefore our moral
obligations to them are the same as to the rest of
humanity.

So what can one say about the obligations of a relatively wealthy society? Its first obligation must be to
meet the needs of its members. But after that there is a
problem of deciding what attention should be given to
providing help for poorer societies and what to the
provision at home of things that are desirable but not
essential. To attempt to answer this involves us in a
larger problem, that of what is meant by the obligations
of a society as a whole. What does it mean to attribute
a duty to a group?

In the end, since only individuals can carry out
duties, it must be a shorthand way of referring to the
obligations of the members of the group. But what precisely are these obligations with regard to satisfying
needs? If a person needs help, and someone else, who has
no prior obligation, is the only person who can provide
it, the situation is clear: that person should provide
the help. The situation is also clear if it is the united
help of the whole group that is required: each person has
the duty to contribute his bit. But the usual political
situation is one in which various people need help which
any of several individuals or sub-groups could provide.
In these circumstances it seems wrong to say that everyone has a duty to help, since this is unnecessary. It
also seems wrong to say that no one has such a duty, and
that they are all entitled to refuse help. But if only
some people have the duty, how are they to be identified?

The answer to this may be that every member of the
group does have an obligation; but it is not an obligation to provide help - which would lead rapidly to too
many cooks spoiling the broth! - but to see that help is
provided (see p.   below). Sometimes the one entails
the other, if one has no means of knowing whether anyone
else will provide the help - if, for example, one witnesses
a crime from one's window, and has no way of knowing whether there are other witnesses and what they are doing. In
other circumstances it is possible for a group to confer,
and to agree on who will do what by way of seeing to what
needs to be done.

In the political situation, the duty of members of a
society appears to be to set up a system that will make
the satisfaction of needs possible. This does not necessarily mean that they are obliged to set up a state welfare system: this would follow only if a welfare state
is in fact the most efficient system for satisfying
needs, and achieves that end better than private enterprise. In general terms, one can say that every member of
a society has an obligation to support the setting up and
maintenance of institutions for relieving needs, but what
exactly this means in practice will depend on what is
possible and will work best in a given society at a given
time. This applies, it seems, also to the relief of needs
in poorer societies, once needs at home have been met.
But again, what is to be done depends on what is possible:
there is an obligation to give aid to underdeveloped countries, but only if the aid genuinely relieves need in
those countries.

But does not this bring us back to where we started?
We seem to be saying that for practical purposes what is
needed depends on the nature of particular societies:
'survival' has become an abstraction, and the practical
duty to ensure it where possible will take all kinds of
different forms and will be relative to one's society,
in other words, 'essentially contestable'! And matters
are made worse by the following consideration: if survival is a need because it is a necessary condition of
moral activity, survival cannot just mean merely staying
alive; it must be staying alive in a condition in which
one can act freely and purposively.

AUTONOMY AS A BASIC NEED

In other words, the basic needs are for survival and autonomy, where 'autonomy' means the freedom to act morally.
But while all moral codes will agree that autonomy is a
human need, this agreement seems purely verbal. Everyone will agree that people should be free, but they will
differ radically in their opinion of what they should be
free to do, so that there will be hardly any overlap in
their various conceptions of autonomy, and they will all
be relative to various systems of values.

However, it is still possible to distinguish a type and
degree of freedom, admittedly limited, which will be
needed regardless of these variations. It is not a freedom to do any particular thing, but a freedom from certain hindrances which, if they become too strong, make any
moral life impossible, and therefore must be removed. The

most important of these hindrances are, we think, three:
arbitrary power, ill-health and ignorance.

By 'arbitrary power' we mean a situation in which one
person (or group) is able to control the actions of another
in accordance with his personal whim or caprice. Such
control is different in two ways from controls imposed
by or in accordance with a system of laws or rules. In
the first place, it is unpredictable: the 'controlee'
does not know what he will be permitted to do and what he
will not. This ignorance is always either an actual or
a potential threat to purposive action, since it makes all
plans for the future subject to possible arbitrary interference; on any moral view, not only on some, it threatens
moral activity. This is because it interferes with action
in general: any particular restriction on behaviour may
be approved of by some people and disapproved by others,
but a restriction, even if merely potential, on all or any
purposive activity must be a hindrance to the moral life,
however it is coneived.

This susceptibility to arbitrary power can arise either
from the absence of a framework of social rules, or from
the existence of gaps in the rules; and both of these can
arise either both *de iure* and *de facto* or *de facto* alone -
rules may not exist, or they may exist but be ignored.
For the only way in which people in a group can plan for
the future without the threat of arbitrary interference is
by living under a set of rules that determines what they
are and are not entitled to do. The rules do not need to
be written, or to amount to a developed legal system; and,
in theory at least, they might be enforced only by moral
persuasion and not by punishment and coercion, as envisaged
by anarchists such as Kropotkin. They do not even need-
to be consciously thought of as rules, as long as in practice they are reasonably well understood and obeyed.

This total absence of law does not occur in principle,
but there are sometimes periods of disturbance in which
it occurs in practice, because law enforcement has become impossible; and occasionally this lawlessness becomes endemic. Indeed, though this is rare with regard to
whole societies, it is not uncommon over relatively small
geographical areas - the so-called 'urban jungles', or
actual jungles or other impassable areas. But what is
much more common is a gap in the law, so that the law fails
to give protection to everyone and from everyone. This
occurs, for example, with some forms of the institution
of slavery, although it is not a necessary feature of
slavery that the master is empowered to exercise arbitrary
control over the slave.

In the modern world, these theoretical legal gaps are
rare: most (though not all) societies give verbal acknow-
ledgment to principles incompatible with them. What is
extremely prevalent is a gap in practice; in particular,
one of three sorts. First, law enforcement agencies, whether governments, police or armies, may be unable (or
unwilling) to protect people from gangsters or warlords,
or a host of petty criminals whose cumulative effect is
similar. Second, the government and its officials may
systematically ignore the rules that are supposed to
govern their behaviour, so that arrest and imprisonment
do in fact take place in an arbitrary way, and without
any great reference to what a person may actually have
done: it is because of this misuse of procedure that the
USSR is able to combine an admirably liberal constitution
with intense arbitrary repression.

This amount of freedom - protection both from criminal
fellow-citizens and from criminal governments and officials - amounts in effect to Montesquieu's 'freedom to
obey the law'. It is compatible with great legal repression, but is still a degree of freedom for which people
in many parts of the world would be very grateful. But
although there is a need for a working system of rules
that prevents arbitrary use of power both by officials
and by ordinary citizens, it does not follow that every
social system that achieves this should be supported:
it is possible that a non-arbitrary system might be so
repressive as to be worse than an arbitrary one. This
is unlikely in practice as most totalitarian regimes
use both repressive legislation and illegal and extra-
legal methods of control - but it is not impossible.

On the other hand, a system that fails to achieve this
aim fully is not necessarily to be opposed: this will
depend on what the best way of improving matters in practice turns out to be. For this need, which interestingly
could be called either a need for freedom or a need for
order (at this level they entail each other and are not
opposed), can be fully satisfied only in a Utopia. What
should be done to bring a society nearer to this unat-
tainable ideal depends on circumstances - on whether the
fault lies with the officials or with general social attitudes of indifference to law-breaking by individuals or
governments (many people accept one and become furious
about the other), on what the possibilities are for
change, on the harm and unheaval any change may cause,
and on the likelihood of improvement. Conservative, reformist and revolutionary policies may all have their
place in the right circumstances.

But even a working non-arbitrary legal system is not
enough to provide freedom from interference based on whim
and caprice, unless people are also free from economic
constraints. If an economic system is such that capitalists, or party officials, or governments, or trades
unionists, are able in practice to decide whether or not
people have jobs, a great deal of arbitrary control can
be exercised. Freedom from this control involves freedom from total economic dependence on any one person or
group, whether the system in which this arises is capitalist, socialist or mixed. Once again, exactly what is
needed depends on circumstances, essentially on how a
particular system can best be modified, and in particular how total control can be taken out of the hands of
one group without being put into those of another.
   So it seems reasonable to conclude that, despite the
ethical dispute over the nature and limits of human freedom, there ought to be agreement among those willing to
adopt a consistent moral position that there is a need
for freedom from unregulated interference by one's fellow-
citizens, from arbitrary behaviour by officials and from
total economic dependence on others. How these needs
can be met will vary, but it will vary according to the
situation in a particular society: the same principle
will be at work, but what is possible in practice will
change. One factor in this situation will be the moral
beliefs of the society, but these do not, at this level,
alter the nature of the need or make its existence contestable: rather, they make certain ways of meeting it,
and other needs, possible or impossible; and they are
on a par with economic, geographical and historical
factors which have the same effect.
   Similar considerations operate with regard to the need
for freedom from ill-health or injury. If either is
sufficiently severe, it will interfere with the capacity
for purposive action: so once again any moral code must
acknowledge a minimal level of health as a need. But if
a need is something that ought to be satisfied, and if
'ought' implies 'can' (it seems senseless to suggest that
someone ought to do something that they cannot do), then
what this means in practice will depend on what is medi-
cally possible in a particular society (there can even be
diseases that are so endemic that they are unrecognized
as diseases). Also, the level of health required in order
to be able to operate may vary from individual to individual, and from society to society: it may well be the
case that people in poorer societies, as a result of custom, actually need somewhat less food than people in
wealthier ones, and also can keep going when in a less

healthy state. But these variations in what is possible
and in the (always woolly) borderline between what is
absolutely essential and what is only highly desirable
do not make the actual concept of physical health variable:
we are still essentially concerned with removing barriers
to purposive action.

The same can be said even of mental health, though
this is less obvious. Indeed, it is often thought now-
adays that no objective definition of mental health or
illness is possible, and that it must be relative to the
values of various societies. But while there is much that
is called mental illness, and to which the name is
appropriate only if one makes certain value-judgments,
there are also mental states that, like physical diseases,
interfere not merely with the ability to do particular
things, but with one's general capacity for action. These
include, for example, extreme depressive states, inability
to concentrate, delusions and hallucinations, phobias,
obsessions and compulsions, all of which, if they are
serious enough, prevent a person doing anything planned
or purposive; for example, someone who is subject to a
morbid compulsion to wash has not chosen an eccentric
way of life, but is being prevented from choosing to do
anything. Mental health, in the sense of freedom from
these states, seems to be a valid and reasonably objective
concept, though one relatively restricted in comparison
with how the term is sometimes used. In this sense, it
is a need that should be satisfied, if possible. Whether,
and when, we have the right actually to force someone to
be treated for either physical or mental illness is a
very difficult question, which will have to be left aside
here; but one can say that the opportunity for treatment
is something that society ought to provide if it can.

But there is one more aspect to freedom from ill-
health. An ugly environment, or one lacking in most
amenities, can, and does, work on the mind so that it
produces an incapacity for action rather like that produced by physical or mental ill-health. Exactly what it
takes to do this or to prevent it will vary much from person to person, but within a given society there will be
enough consistency for it to be possible to formulate
what essentially is needed: in our society some people
can dispense with pleasant and reasonably clean and
healthy housing, but most people cannot; and most people
would agree as to what is intolerable, ugly or dirty or
depressing; their ideals would be very different, but
their notion of minimum acceptability would probably be
similar.

Finally, the need for freedom from ignorance leads to a need for education. The nature of the education required will vary: the common factor is that it will involve attaining the skills and knowledge necessary in order to be able to operate in the society in question. In our society, literacy is probably such a necessity: in many other societies it has been unnecessary and unessential. But in all societies there will be a minimum of education essential to make operating purposively in that society possible; and whereas it is always disputable whether specific skills are needed, it cannot be denied that these general skills are required by everyone.

We may now summarize the argument of this chapter. If there are necessary conditions of moral action, irrespective of particular moral codes, there will be some things that must be classed as needs whatever one's moral position. These conditions include physical survival and autonomy, i.e. freedom from arbitrary interference, ill-health and ignorance; and members of any society have a duty to create a social system that will satisfy these needs as well as possible, and also a duty, if conditions and resources permit, to help the creation of such systems in other societies. The amount of time and resources given to this, instead of to other good aims, and the whole way in which it should be done will depend on circumstances. But this does not mean that the actual concept is a relative one: it means that the same aim will have to be pursued differently under different circumstances. What changes from age to age and society to society is not the general human need but (a) what is possible, given existing resources and (b) what will work, given existing social institutions, attitudes, etc. (under 'what will work'... etc. is included the radical alteration of those institutions themselves, if this seems, in a given situation, to be the best way of satisfying needs).

This means that a very important part of social policy, though only a part, could be decided without reference to overall views of what society should be like. The provision of what will satisfy human needs provides plenty of room for argument. But the argument ought to be a factual and empirical one, concerning the most efficient way of meeting these needs; normative arguments should appear only if this most efficient way conflicts with ends that are desirable on one normative view but not on another.

4

The moral basis of welfare provision

THE NATURE OF THE OBLIGATION TO PROVIDE WELFARE

Broadly speaking there are two views on the question of
the moral basis for welfare provision. One is that welfare is a matter of charity, generosity, humanity; of
giving, but not of strict obligation. The corollary of
this view is that the recipients have no moral right to
what they receive because no individual person can have
a right to another person's charity. The other view is
that welfare provision is a matter of strict obligation
for those who hold resources and that those who are in
need have strict moral claims on those better off in
society. Their needs create a right to welfare and a
duty on the part of the better endowed to grant welfare
benefits to meet such needs. However, as we shall see,
in this second case there is considerable disagreement
about how this putative obligation is to be analysed,
whether in terms of rights, justice or needs - but in
each case the upshot is much the same: that people have
a moral right to welfare provision. Each of these views
ultimately embodies a vision of human society and human
morality, and the discussion and evaluation of these
different conceptions of the normative basis of welfare
provision raises some of the deepest questions about the
nature of human society and moral obligations.
   At the same time this seemingly abstract issue in
political philosophy is at the very centre of concern in
the debate about stigma and about the role of the state in
welfare provision. If it is accepted that welfare is to
be seen as a form of charity and institutionalized generosity, then it would seem that the recipients of welfare,
understood on this basis, might well feel that their receipt of benefits could be stigmatizing. Indeed, one
way in which welfare beneficiaries do encapsulate their

sense of being stigmatized is to say that they are
receiving charity. If those in need have no right to the
resources of others, other than an appeal to their generosity or humanity, then it is difficult for them to
avoid being put in a subordinate status and dependency
upon the good will of others. Those who received such
benefits might be expected to express gratitude. While
gratitude is never the appropriate response to receiving
one's due, it is always the appropriate response to receiving gratuitous aid. Gratitude is the response to
charity and alms-giving, and not to wages and merited
awards. As so often in the history of political thought,
Hobbes put the point so clearly that it is impossible to
improve on it (1955, p. 99):

> As justice dependeth on antecedent covenant; so does
> gratitude depend on antecedent grace; that is to say
> on antecedent free gift ... the breach of this law is
> called ingratitude; and hath the same relation to
> grace, that injustice hath to obligation by covenant.

(For a good contemporary analysis see Lyons, 1969.) On
the other hand, if there is a moral right to welfare then
this situation of dependency and subordination need not
arise. The situation becomes one of equality, in which
those within resources are under an obligation to transfer
resources to those in need; those in need have the moral
right to such resources. Of course, in this situation
stigma may still remain because it is a well entrenched
view in our society that people have only a right to what
they have bought or exchanged. The idea that there is a
right of unreciprocated recipience is a profoundly anticapitalist one, and if there is a defensible view of
welfare provision to be presented in these terms then
stigma would become an educational rather than a theoretical problem.

In addition, the question whether there is a basic
moral claim or right to welfare raises issues about the
forms that welfare provision should take. If we take the
view that welfare is a work of benevolence and humanity,
then this might well favour some private, non-state form
of welfare provision. It is arguable that, even if one has
a duty to be benevolent, this duty does not pertain to
any particular person or to all persons in society. As
Hayek (1976) argues, 'This obligation can exist only
towards particular known people and though in a great
society it may be an obligation towards people of one's
choice, it cannot be enforced under equal rules for all'
(p. 165). We can choose to whom we shall be benevolent and
this requires that welfare provision should be privately
based outside the state sector. If the state has any role

to play at all in the field of welfare, it is only a very
residual one: to act as a safety net in situtions in
which private welfare activity has failed. On the other
hand, if the view is taken that there is a moral right
to welfare or that people have legitimate moral claims
to have their needs satisfied, then this requires some
kind of on-going institutionalized provision of the type
provided by the state in contexts where other legitimate
moral rights are claimed - for example the legal system
to assist the protection of various human rights in that
sphere.

This issue raises a fundamental problem of moral philosophy as well as being central to our understanding of
the welfare system and the processes of stigma.   There
does seem to be a clear distinction between justice and
benevolence; the former as a strict or perfect duty requires some kind of social or legal sanction to protect it,
and the beneficiaries of just claims have rights that are
enforceable; the latter as an imperfect duty always remains a matter of individual conscience and choice.   No
one in moral philosophy has put the distinction better
than Mill (1962, p. 305):

Now it is well known that ethical writers divide
duties into two classes, denoted by the ill chosen
expressions duties of perfect and imperfect obligation; the latter being those in which, though the
act is obligatory, the particular occasions of our
performing it are left to our choice; as in the case
of charity or beneficence, which we are indeed bound
to practice but not towards any definite person, nor
at any prescribed time ... duties of perfect obligation are those duties in virtue of which a positive
right resides in some person or persons; duties of
imperfect obligations are those moral obligations which
do not give rise to any right.... Justice implies something which it is not only right to do, and wrong not
to do, but which some individual may claim from us as
his moral right. No one has a moral right to our
charity or beneficence because we are not morally
bound to practise these virtues towards any given individual.

In what follows we shall probe some of the implications of
the view that welfare is a matter of institutionalized
beneficence and will attempt to make a case for saying
that, on the contrary, it is to be seen as a right.

This kind of issue leads us on to a much broader question which can be dealt with only very briefly here,
namely the relationship between welfare and political
legitimacy. If it is agreed that there is a right to

welfare, then this is going to bear upon the legitimacy
of government in the sense that the securing and protection
of right is regarded as a major legitimating principle of
government in general and of specific governments in particular. On this view the welfare institutions of the modern
state which exist to satisfy basic needs should not be seen
as 'optional extras' but as crucial to the whole legitimacy
of government. For example, Christian Bay argues as
follows (1968, p. 1):

> the only acceptable justification of government, which
> also determines the limits of its legitimate authority,
> is its task of serving human needs - serving them better
> than would be done without any government. The only
> acceptable justification of a particular form of govern-
> ment, which again also determines the limits of its
> legitimate demands on the individual's obedience and
> loyalty, is that it serves human needs better than other
> forms of government.

On the other hand, if the claim that there is a moral right
to welfare is made over to purely private charity or to
market forces, then the non-existence of a welfare branch
of government will have no bearing upon its legitimacy.

A great deal is at stake therefore in trying to work out
a coherent and true answer to the question. What if any
is the moral basis of the claim to welfare? Issues about
the stigma of recipients, the duties of the citizen and
the legitimacy of the state are all brought into play in
our attempt to answer the question.

A good many social and political philosophers are
hostile to the idea that there is an entrenched right to
welfare - whether this is based upon an explicit theory of
rights or whether it is vindicated by an appeal to justice
or by an appeal to need. A few examples will be quoted
from recent works of analytical social and political philosophy to give some indication of the flavour of the objections. Lucas (1966, p. 260) argues:

> The benefits conferred by the Welfare State are to be
> justified on grounds of Humanity, economic expediency,
> on Public Interest rather than Distributive Justice....
> Arguments for the redistribution of money incomes must
> be arguments of Humanity, economic expediency, or some-
> thing else; but not Justice.

Similarly, Acton (1971, p. 71) says:

> basic Welfare should not be removed from the market
> and provided for welfare out of taxation. Poverty and
> misfortune are evils but not injustices and the moral
> demand they make is for help on the ground of humanity.

On the issues of whether welfare should be as a human right,
Cranston (1973, p. 65) says:

a philosophically respectable concept of human rights
has been muddied, obscured, and debilitated in recent
years by an attempt to incorporate into it specific
rights of a different logical category.... What are
now being put forward as universal human rights are
social and economic rights.... I have both a philosophical and a political objection to this. The philosophical objection is that the new theory of human
rights does not make sense. The political objection
is that the circulation of a confused notion of human
rights hinders the effective protection of what are
correctly seen as human rights.

Arguments against the idea that the moral basis of welfare
provision can rest adequately upon a conception of basic
human needs is to be found in Nozick (1974, chapter 8) in
Minogue (1973, chapter IV and in Acton (1971, pp. 68-72).

WELFARE AND ALTRUISM

This question about the basis of welfare provision relates
to another and in some ways more elusive issue but one
that is of central importance both to the theory and practice of the welfare state. It is sometimes suggested that
state welfare provision ought to be regarded as a form of
institutionalized giving or altruism because in this way
it could be seen as providing the basis of a sense of community. Welfare benefits are outward and visible signs of
the desire of the majority to help their less fortunate
fellow men and in this sense are concerned with developing a sense of community and involvement of one person
with another. On the other hand, to suggest that the
provision of welfare is a strict obligation and implies
a correlative right on the part of recipients of welfare
to what they receive is often thought to inhibit such a
sense of community. Relationships characterized by
rights and duties seem to lack the involvement and spontaneity that mark exercises of gift-giving and altruism.
Indeed, in the history of social and political thought
those who have had the strongest commitment to the importance of community have frequently been the greatest
critics of visions of society based upon concepts of
right and obligation just because this would render human
relations mechanical and procedural and would not leave
room for the exercise of altruism, generosity and humanity,
as Flathman (1976) cogently argues: 'A recurrent strain
in communitarian thinking is that an emphasis on individual
rights fragments human relationships in a manner and to a
degree that renders genuine community impossible' (p. 184).

This kind of emphasis in thinking about the importance of
altruism and community in welfare contexts will be discussed in more detail in the final part of the book, but
at the present juncture it is worth bearing in mind that
Richard Titmuss's 'The Gift Relationship' (1970) is a
very powerful statement of this theme; indeed, he argues
(p. 212) that in much of social policy we are concerned not
with rights and obligations, but rather with

> stranger relationships, with processes, institutions
> and structures which encourage or discourage the in-
> tensity and extensiveness of anonymous helpfulness in
> society; with ultra obligations which derive from our
> characters and are not contractual in nature.

Titmuss derives the term 'ultra obligation' from Professor
Grice's 'The Grounds of Moral Judgement' (1967), and his
use of the term has a good deal in common with Mill's concept of imperfect duty. That is: no one has the right to
the performance of an ultra obligation. Indeed, Grice's
own example of an ultra obligation makes precisely this
point (1967, p. 155):

> When Sir Philip Sidney lay dying on the field of Zutphen,
> fatally wounded and parched with thirst, he was brought
> by another soldier a mug of water. Instead of drinking
> it for himself with thought for nothing but his own
> plight, he gave it to another man who lay beside him in
> a similar condition. This, most people would agree,
> is a morally good action of outstanding merit. But
> moral goodness is not a question of moment. The ques-
> tion concerns the concept of a right, and the right of
> the other soldier to receive water from Sidney. It is
> plain I think that he has no such right.

Grice goes on to suggest that character is an important
consideration in thinking about the basis of ultra obligations. In linking much of social policy with ultra obligations Titmuss (1970, p. 212) seems implicitly to deny that
those who are deprived have a right to the resources that
they are given via welfare policies. Indeed, the whole
emphasis on gifts in his writing seems to be a clear
affirmation of this. One has no right to a *gift*. The reason why Titmuss seems to wish to talk in this way is because of the importance to him of community and fellowship
which he seems to see as becoming attenuated in modern
society with its economic relations and relations of
rights and obligations. However, as we shall see, the
concept of community in Titmuss is an obscure one and
hardly more appealing than the supposedly procedural relationships that welfare based upon rights and duties is
likely to produce. In any case, the concept of community
seems to protean to be much use as a legitimating principle

in social policy. For the moment, though, it is enough to
note that the issues that this chapter has as its concern
strike at the very heart of our understanding of the welfare
state. Indeed, if welfare (or much of social policy) is a
matter of ultra obligation it is not at all clear that it
is legitimate to have a welfare *state* at all. Ultra obligations relating to charity and beneficience are surely
rendered ineffective when the state coerces contributions
by taxation.

   It is clear in the face of this critique that those who
propose the contrary theses - that there is a secure moral
right to welfare on the part of recipients and an obligation to provide it on the part of those who possess resources - have to be clear about the precise form in which
they wish to defend the theses, and there has certainly
been some confusion here. But broadly speaking there
appear to be three basic possibilities: the argument has
to be put forward in terms of justice, rights or needs
(Telfer, 1976, p. 107), and in the remainder of this chapter
these possible bases for welfare provision will be discussed
in some detail. Although there are no absolutely decisive
arguments, it will become clear that reference to the concept of need is basic and the roles of both justice and
rights are secured with reference to need.

JUSTICE AND SOCIAL WELFARE

The first difficulty to be confronted is whether justice
is a relevant consideration in this kind of context, and
there are two possible arguments to show that it is not.
The first is to maintain, as Acton (1971) does, that those
who are in need because they are poor, handicapped, lacking
intelligence, unable to cope with life, etc., are not suffering from an injustice, because this situation is no one's
fault but is rather the result of the arbitrary distribution
of nature. If we leave belief in God on one side, the differences that result from natural endowment are not injustices; they are rather 'natural facts'. If they are not
injustices, then it is absurd to appeal to a principle of
social justice to secure their rectification. The second
argument is analogous to the first. It holds that, even
within welfare contexts which we are talking about, harms
or deprivations that people endure that are clearly not
natural (in the sense of inherited or genetic) but are in
a sense 'social', they are still not injustices, because
they, no more than genetic harms, do not result from
deliberate actions. The best source of this argument is
Hayek (1976, p. 64):

It has of course to be admitted that the manner in which
the benefits and burdens are apportioned by the market
mechanism would in many instances have to be regarded
as very unjust *if* it were the result of a deliberate
allocation to particular people. But this is not the
case. Those shares are the outcome of a process the
effect of which on particular people was neither intended nor foreseen by anyone when the institutions
first appeared - institutions which were then permitted
to continue because it was found that they improve for
all or most the prospects of having their needs satisfied. To demand justice from such a process is clearly
absurd, and to single out some people in such a society
as entitled to a particular share evidently unjust.
In neither of these cases is an appeal to injustice relevant because the situation of the needy, the deprived, the
handicapped, those lacking in intelligence is not the
result of deliberate action. In the first case it is
just a natural and arbitrary distribution of nature; in
the second case it is the unintended and undeliberate consequence of an otherwise beneficial system. If no one is
responsible for bringing it about, no one can be blamed
for arranging it unjustly. The rain that falls on the
just and the unjust cannot be condemned for its lack of
concern for moral distinctions. Neither can a social
order be condemned as unjust if no one has planned and
controlled it. Hayek in his recent book, 'The Mirage of
Social Justice', has portrayed this view with the greatest
clarity, and it is perhaps worth quoting his account of it
at some length (1976, p. 68):

> we do cry out against the injustice when a succession
> of calamities befalls one family while another steadily
> prospers, when meritorious effort is frustrated by some
> unforeseeable accident and particularly if, of many
> people whose endeavours seem equally great, some suc-
> ceed brilliantly while others utterly fail.... And we
> will protest against such a fate although we do not
> know anyone who is to blame for it or any ways in
> which such disappointments can be prevented.... It
> is no different with regard to the general feeling of
> injustice about the distribution of material goods in
> a society of freemen. Though we are in this case less
> ready to admit it, our complaints about the outcome of
> the market as unjust do not usually assert that some-
> body has been unjust; and there is no answer to the
> question of who has been unjust. Society has simply
> become the new deity to which we complain and clamour
> for redress if it does not fulfil the expectations it
> has created.

On this view then, those who suffer deprivation, whether natural or social, are not suffering from injustice and have no moral claim on the resources of others in society by an appeal to the principle of justice. Of course it may be desirable to help the poor and the handicapped, but this is a matter of generosity, charity, benevolence or humanity, not justice. Welfare is a gift to be bestowed, not a right to be claimed.

Ultimately one's response to this argument will depend very much upon a general view of the social order and the possibility of its rational control. It is quite central to Hayek's argument that society is seen as a spontaneous order that does not arise as a result of centralized directions for the achievement of particular social goals. This conception of society in its turn is based upon an epistemological assumption, namely that, for any individual, that individual is going to be relatively ignorant of many of the factors relating to the attainment of his own ends, and that this ignorance relatively increases with the growth of human knowledge. If we wish to make the best use of our incomplete knowledge and to minimize the occasions on which we may have to be made to submit to another's will, a market society is to be preferred in which each individual pursues his own ends whatever they may be. There can be no overall plan or design to society because the amount of knowledge required to secure the plan is not available and there is no agreement on what the ends of such a plan would be:

it is due to the fact that we do not enforce a unitary scale of concrete ends, nor attempt to secure that some particular view about what is more and what is less important governs the whole of society, that the members of a free society have as good a chance successfully to use their individual knowledge for the achievement of their individual purposes as they in fact have.

In a spontaneous market or catallactic order each person can pursue his own ends without any agreement on the overall ends of human life being presupposed by the existence of such an order. Just because the market is a spontaneous order in this sense, marked by the relative ignorance of those who seek to secure their ends within it, questions about justice and injustice become meaningless. There is no overall distributing body against which such complaints can properly be made any more than there is an overall distribution of natural assets.

Because of human ignorance, and because of lack of agreement on ends, the market or catallaxy cannot be controlled in ways consistent with individual freedom. However, aspects of the argument may be doubted, and the

seeds of doubt may be found in some hints in Rawls's
'Theory of Justice' (1972) where he says (p. 102), concerning both the idea that natural endowments are neither
just nor unjust and the idea that initial starting places
are neither just nor unjust,

> The natural distribution is neither just nor unjust,
> nor is it unjust that men are born into society at
> some particular position. These are simply natural
> facts. What is just and unjust is the way that insti-
> tutions deal with these facts.... The social system is
> not an unchangeable order beyond human control but a
> pattern of human action.

This is the crux of the argument between Hayek and Rawls,
and those who believe in social or distributive justice.
For Hayek and for Rawls society is a pattern of human
action, but for Hayek, because of ignorance and lack of
agreement about ends it is and ought to be beyond human
control; for Rawls it is not. Later we shall see reasons
for dissenting from Rawls's own view on justice, but here
it is arguable he has an advantage over Hayek because it
is perhaps possible, although not in the way in which
Rawls suggests, to secure some agreement about ends to be
pursued - namely, basic need satisfaction. To take up an
argument used earlier and which will recur later, it *is*
possible to secure broad agreement about some ends, namely
those that are necessary conditions for achieving any other
ends. Hayek of course denies that we can reach agreement
on needs (or for that matter any other end). We have
argued however, that it is possible to produce a rationally
compelling account of basic human needs. If this is so,
then there seems no reason in principle why society could
not be organized to meet these basic needs as a matter of
strict obligation. It will of course be a view that is
still consistent with Hayek's moral pluralism, but it will
still be based upon the view that between plural moralities
and different views about the ends of life it is in fact
possible to pinpoint some necessarily agreed notion of
need, those needs the satisfaction of which is necessary
for the pursuit of any end whatever. So it is arguably a
precondition of Hayek's view that men should be free to
pursue their ends as spontaneously as possible, that there
should be an obligation to provide not merely the legal
framework that is a necessary condition for this, but
also those needs that are equally necessary conditions
for the pursuit of any end. In defending a market as a
social order in which men are free to pursue their own
ends in their own way, Hayek argues that there should be
enforcement of what might be called the 'rules of the
game', that framework of rules of mutual non-coercion that

that is a necessary condition for each man to pursue his
own ends. This state-imposed order is morally justified
because it is required as necessary for men in order for
them to pursue whatever their ends are; by parity of
reasoning it could equally well be argued that basic need
satisfaction is equally a necessary condition of securing
the pursuit of any end. Indeed, Hayek in 'The Constitution of Liberty' (1960) does concede to the state an obligation to meet absolutely basic needs, but he clearly
wishes to distinguish this from the suggestion that
'justice' is involved at all (p. 303):

> It is essential that we become clearly aware of the
> line that separates a state of affairs in which the
> community accepts the duty of preventing destitution
> and of providing a minimum level of welfare from
> that in which it assumes the power to determine the
> 'just' position of everybody.

There are two difficulties with this passage. We are
left entirely unclear about the source of the duty of the
community to prevent destitution - certainly more recent
thinkers in this tradition, notably Nozick, have not
allowed for any such duty. Second, it is clear that Hayek
would seem to mean by destitution absolutely basic need,
in which case the duty to meet absolutely basic need could
be seen as a principle of distributive justice - to each
according to his basic needs - despite Hayek's rejection
of the terminology of 'justice'. In addition, the idea
that there is a clear line that sets off a minimum level
of need satisfaction from 'just' provision is highly
questionable, even if basic need satisfaction is not to be
regarded as a principle of justice.

Clearly, therefore, justice is a relevant principle for
analysing the obligation, if such there be, of providing
for welfare, despite the argument to the contrary by
Acton and Hayek. However, there are many philosophers
who, though sympathetic to the claims of the poorer sections of the community, are convinced that the provision
of welfare cannot adequately be analysed in terms of the
principle of justice - not because justice is irrelevant
in the ways suggested by Hayek and Acton, but because just
distribution is logically or analytically tied to notions
of desert and merit rather than to need, and that appeals
to social justice when thinking about the distribution of
resources may be counter-productive for needy people because appeals to the principle sanction only distribution
according to merit or desert and not according to need.
There are several examples of such a view in the literature, but perhaps one of the clearest treatments of the
appeal to the principle of justice from this point of view

is Campbell (1974), who points out the extent to which the
notion of social justice is introduced into debates about
the role of the welfare state with the assumption that it
is: 'the moral basis of their claim that distribution
of scarce resources ought to be made in proportion to the
needs of potential recipients' (p. 1); and he goes on
to quote from Harold Wilson's statement of the principle
'from each according to his means, to each according to
his needs' and from similar views developed by Richard
Titmuss and Anthony Crosland on the same kind of lines.
However, Campbell thinks this kind of appeal is dangerous as a defence of a welfare system (1974, p. 1):

> I wish to argue that it is conceptually mistaken and
> tactically naive for welfare moralists to imply that
> need *per se* is a criterion of just distribution and that
> their case would be more clearly stated and therefore
> more securely based if they were to appeal to benefi-
> cence or humanity instead of to justice.

The basis of this claim that need cannot be by itself a
principle of distributing justice is (p. 1):

> that there is a close logical association between the
> concept of justice and that of desert or merit and
> association which ... rules out any simple and direct
> conceptual link between the principle that distribu-
> tion ought to be proportional to need and the idea of
> justice.

Campbell cites an impressive array of philosophical
authority for this claim and in particular J.S. Mill in
his essay on 'Utilitarianism' (1962) and Sidgwick's
'Methods of Ethics' (1907). The upshot of Campbell's
thesis is that (1974, p. 2):

> desert is a necessary criterion of justice in that no
> just distribution can properly ignore the deserts of
> the recipients where desert is taken to refer to any
> feature of personal behaviour, character or achieve-
> ment for which someone can properly be praised or
> blamed.

Of course, a distribution according to merit or desert
may well not favour the kind of distribution of benefits
and burdens that 'the welfare moralists' want. Those
who are in need may not be particularly meritorious, and
indeed, in the nineteenth century, particularly within the
Charity Organization Society, a good deal of time was
spent trying to work out ways of differentiating between
the deserving and the undeserving poor as a basis for the
distribution of relief. So a great deal hangs on Campbell's
suggestion that justice is necessarily linked with desert,
although he does shy away from the stronger theses that
desert or merit is a necessary and sufficient condition,

i.e. a definition of justice.

Certainly those whom Campbell regards as being mis-
guided in their appeal to justice to support welfare
measures have been well aware of different principles of
justice. Titmuss, for example, at the end of his post-
humous book 'Social Policy', says (1974, p. 141):

Among all the theories and principles relating to
social policy ... perhaps the three fundamental ones
centre round the historic principles of distributive
justice. They embrace four well known maxims:

1   To each according to his need
2   To each according to his worth
3   To each according to his merit
4   To each according to his work.

However, while Titmuss regards these as all defensible,
though competing, principles of justice, Campbell wishes
to argue that only a meritorian principle is defensible,
because of the tie-up of meaning between justice with
merit/desert. (In terms of Titmuss's list of principles,
2, 3 and 4 could all in fact be seen as desert principles.)

One of the basic grounds for this assimilation of
justice to desert would be its use in the context of
criminal justice, where clearly merit or desert has to be
shown before justice in the form of punishment is distributive. Only if the person has committed the crime does
he deserve to be punished; only if he has done a criminal
act does he merit punishment. In this kind of case merit
and desert are quite fundamental. Campbell therefore
wishes to cut through these arguments about distributive
criteria to argue that, logically or analytically, or in
terms of the very meaning of the word, justice has to be
allied with desert.

For those who wish to defend a need-orientated criterion
of distributive justice, there seem to be two ways of
coming to terms with Campbell's argument. The first is
to attempt to deny the linguistic point about desert considerations being bound up with at least part of the very
meaning of the word 'justice' and to drive a wedge between justice and desert considerations so that desert/
merit becomes one among a number of competing criteria of
distribution. The second alternative is to deny that
desert/merit provides a desirable criterion of distribution and that, even if the conventional use of the word
does indicate an analytical tie-up between justice and
desert, philosophical reflection can lead us to try to
displace this conventional conception of justice. On a
radical version of this kind of view it might even be
claimed that Campbell's conceptual claim is a way of providing legitimation for the form of distribution, charac-

teristic of a capitalist society - with the suggestion
that our language and conceptual structure is closely
bound up with the society of which we are a part. Within
a capitalist society it is not surprising that the way
in which we use the word 'justice' reflects the general
character of the reward structure within capitalism.
Indeed, this suggestion could be developed quite cogently
with reference to David Miller's 'Social Justice' (1976),
where, in the final chapter on Social justice in sociological perspective, he discusses the interweaving of a
desert-orientated criterion of distribution and the organization of capitalist society. In view of this, the theorist who believes that need does provide a sufficient
criterion of distribution may well argue that his thesis
is a revisionary one, that it does go against the moral
and 'political discourse of everyday life' within which
the connexion between justice and desert is deeply embedded (Campbell, 1974, p. 5), but he will in his turn
regard the social and political discourse as reflecting
a particular type or conception of justice rather than some
context-independent analysis of the concept of justice *per
se*.
    The purely linguistic point can however be discussed
as it stands. If it is true that desert is a necessary
feature of claims to just treatment, then this must follow
analytically from an explication of the concept of justice
as it is embedded in our language, and if this is so it
would render other varieties of claims to justice - for
example need or historical entitlement - meaningless.
Neither of these positions can be cogently maintained
without begging the question.
    A formal analysis of justice, as Campbell himself
notes, needs to make no reference at all to considerations
of merit or desert - for example, Rawls (1972) provides
what seems to be an unexceptionable characterization of
the formal concept of justice: 'institutions are just
when no arbitrary distinctions are made between persons
in the assigning of basic rights and duties and when the
rules determine a proper balance between competing claims
to the advantages of social life' (p. 5).
    This might be thought to characterize the basic con-
cept of justice, and of course this makes no specific
reference to merit or desert. Desert can be used as a
principle of interpretation of this basic concept - that
desert will be the basis for the assigning of basic
rights/duties and for arbitrating competing claims - but
this way of interpreting the concept is only *one* among a
number of possible ways of doing it - need, entitlement,
etc., are equally ways of interpreting the principle. If

Rawls's characterization does uncover the basic, primitive
or underlying concept of justice as it is used in our
language, then Campbell's thesis is mistaken. It may be
true that merit or desert is the usual way in which the
concept is given an interpretation or cash value, but there
is no entailment between the articulation of the basic concept of justice and this particular conception. The formal
analysis of justice does not yield a desert-oriented conception;   rather, it yields a formal specification which,
as Rawls argues, 'settles no important questions'. A
material theory of justice, one with a specific substantive
content, will have to be an interpretation of this formal
principle, but a number of interpretations are possible -
need, merit, entitlement, etc. - and all are contestable.
It is therefore to claim far too much to assert that there
is a necessary logical connection between merit, desert
and justice so that it would become a necessary condition
of the correct use of the term in everyday social and
political discourse. If there were, it would follow that
those who hold that there is a necessary connection between
justice and desert would have to hold that need-orientated
theories that take no account of desert are in fact unintelligible. Now many critics of need theories would argue
that such theories are indefensible, but not that they are
meaningless.

Particular material conceptions of justice will therefore be contestable - no particular one has a necessary
connection with the underlying concept of justice such that
it can be derived without further ado from a merely analytical treatment of the concept. It may be that in our
society a desert-orientated material conception of justice
is well entrenched, but this is explicable sociologically
and is not evidence for a logical connection.

Those who defend a need-orientated view might on this
analysis be seen as attempting to revise the entrenched
desert-based conception of justice, and this can be done
by attempting to suggest either that the notions of desert/
merit are so indeterminate as not to yield any tenable
principle of justice, or that no man ultimately deserves
anything because the features of his life that are the
basis of his 'deserts' are features for which he is not
responsible.

Oddly enough, there would be some agreement between
the need theorist and a market theorist such as Hayek that
distribution according to desert, although a well entrenched
principle, trades off a vague and indeterminate notion of
desert or merit. The suggestion here would be that in a
morally pluralistic society there is not likely to be wide
agreement over what features of human life are thought to

be particularly meritorious or deserving. It may be the
case that, in a small, closed, highly homogeneous society
characterized by a high degree of moral agreement, there
would be such agreements. Within our own pluralistic
society, such agreement is notably lacking – as Hume (1902,
pp. 192-3) says:

> So great is the uncertainty of merit, both from its
> natural obscurity and from the self conceit of each
> individual, that no determinate rule of conduct could
> even follow from it; and the total dissolution of
> society must be the immediate consequence.

Any agreed definition of merit or desert as a basis of
distribution is likely to have to involve the domination
of one group's view of what is deserving or meritorious
over the views of other groups in society; whereas in
fact activities that are supposed to be rewarded by the
desert principle appear to be incommensurable. How, and
in terms of what, is the activity of the concern pianist,
the bus conductor, the philosopher and the sewage worker
to be made commensurable so that a meaningful distribution
according to desert can take place?

However, this is not the fundamental objection that is
levied against the distribution of goods and services,
benefits and burdens on the basis of merit or desert.
The basic objection to this line of thinking is that the
abilities, capacities, powers and assets of individuals
do not support claims to deserve or to merit anything.
These are moral claims, which must be based upon a claim
to be responsible for the ability or asset in question.
However, it has been argued that such a claim cannot be
vindicated – that a person's intelligence, abilities,
capacities, powers, assets are not in the end features
of his life for which he is responsible; they are the
result of nature and nurture in some combination, and in
neither aspect is an individual responsible for what he
has become. Rawls (1972) makes this point particularly
clearly: 'No one deserves his greater natural capacity
nor merits a more favourable starting place in society'
(p. 172). Character depends in large part upon fortunate
family and social circumstances, for which he can claim
no credit, and he suggests that this is 'one of the fixed
points of our moral judgements' (p. 311). In a comment
upon this idea, Stuart Hampshire (1972, p. 36) has both
sharpened the argument and taken it much further:

> But one may ask: Is there anything whatever that,
> strictly speaking, a man can claim credit for, or he
> can properly be said to deserve, with the implication
> that it can be attributed to him, the ultimate subject
> as contrasted with the natural forces that formed

him.... I think it would be better to think of naturally
acquired advantages as unearned and undeserved....
On such a view, the notions of desert and merit would drop
out as irrelevant because talents would be regarded as
naturally explicable and explicable in terms of nurture,
and in neither case is an individual responsible for the
features of his life in question; and where responsibility evaporates,desert has no role to play. These
factors are arbitrary from the moral point of view.

This would be the absolutely fundamental objection to
desert as a distributive principle. However, there is
something deeply counter-intuitive about the argument,
despite Rawls's claim that it is a fixed point of our
moral judgment. A man's initial genetic endowment is
clearly outside his control, as is his early upbringing -
but at the same time this view would require us to reject
the idea that at a certain point in their lives people
are able autonomously to develop the talents that they
do have, however contingent their possession of them may
be. The Rawlsian theory would have us reject this view
because 'character depends in large part upon fortunate
family and social circumstances for which he can claim
no credit (Rawls, 1972, p. 104), and he goes on to suggest
(pp. 311-12) that, because

The initial endowment of natural assets and the contin-
gency of their growth and nurture is arbitrary from
the moral point of view ... the effort a person is
willing to make is influenced by his natural abilities
and skills and the alternatives given to him. The
better endowed are more likely, other things being
equal, to strive conscientiously.

These arguments clearly provide a block to any claim
that autonomous choice plays a role in human development
at all. Now there is something seriously wrong with this
line of reasoning, at least in terms of the ends that it
is trying to serve. The whole argument is couched in
moral terms - natural talents are arbitrary from the
moral point of view: but it is very far from clear what
kind of role a moral point of view is going to play in a
vision of human society that involves such a root-and-
branch rejection of human autonomy when it even rejects
character as something for which autonomous choice is in
large part responsible. Such a changed conception of
human nature would have a very major disturbing effect on
an overall view of morality. A line of argument developed
by Peter Strawson (1974) (among others) and Morris (1968)
has drawn attention to the ways in which tacit commitments are built into our terms such as 'responsibility',
'guilt' and 'resentment', suggesting that the application

of these concepts to people involves treating them, under
appropriate conditions, as persons having the capacity
to deliberate, choose, form intentions and act as autonomous agents. If these concepts were displaced from our
language - which would seem to be a natural consequence of
Rawls's theory - we should, as Connolly says, 'strip
ourselves of the ability to view each other as members
of a moral community' (1974, p. 71). Indeed, the whole
account here seems to run along very oddly with Rawls's
other insistence that self-respect is a primary good. As
Nozick (1974) says on this point, 'one doubts that the
unexalted picture of human beings Rawls' theory presupposes and rests upon can be made to fit together with the
view of human dignity it is designed to lead to and
embody' (p. 214). These considerations about need and
desert are therefore not sufficient to provide a knock-
down argument against a desert-orientated principle of
distribution. The exact consequences for morality of
rejecting human autonomy in this way seem so unclear that
the argument has to be found wanting.

One other argument that could be used here to reject
the idea of desert/merit-based distribution is that it is
both impossible and morally wrong to attempt to disentangle the contributions made by individuals to the total
social product. Any particular action in the productive
process is going to require, in a modern, complex industrial
set-up, a scheme of social co-operation in order to be performed, and within this co-operative framework it is very
difficult to work out who deserves more than others in
the sense that his particular contribution to the whole
process is decisive. It may have been the case in very
simple peasant/agrarian societies that individual contributions to the process of agricultural production could be
disentangled, but a consequence of the division of labour
is that there is no straightforward way in which individual contributions can be disentangled. The *locus
classicus* of this view is Kropotkin's book, 'The Conquest
of Bread' (1926), in which he studies the organization of
a coal mine - the miner, the engineers, the cagemen, the
boy who helps him and so on - and he comes to this conclusion (p. 163):

> All those who are engaged in the mine contribute to
> the extraction of coal in proportion to their strength,
> their energy, their knowledge, their intelligence and
> their skill - ... But how can we appraise the work of
> each one of them...?

The resources, the means of production, etc., open to men
are the results of centuries of co-operation (cf. Sraffa's
(1971) dead labour in 'The Production of Commodities by

Means of Commodities') and the relationships of production
are so intertwined that personal, decisive contributions
cannot be filtered out (p. 10):

> The means of production being the collective work of
> humanity, the product should be the collective property
> of the race. All things are for all men, since all men
> have need of them, since all men have worked in the
> measure of their strengths to produce them, and since
> it is not possible to evaluate everyone's part in the
> production of the world's wealth.

For Kropotkin desert is both redundant and inappropriate.
We cannot disentangle individual shares within the productive framework, and even if we could, we would not be able
to say with any degree of certainty that a particular
person's activity within production was more basic than
anyone else's. Assets and abilities are common and what
they produce is a common commodity.

In this section we have tried to establish that *contra*
Campbell and others there is not a logical tie-up between
the concept of justice and that of desert such that a need-
orientated criterion of distribution, independent of desert
or meritorious considerations, would be meaningless. A
desert-orientated view is one position or interpretation
of what justice is, and it is contestable. As we have
seen, it makes certain assumptions about human autonomy
and natural assets that have been discussed, however in-
adequately, by Rawls and Hampshire; and it is compelled
to see the relationships of production in highly individualistic terms so that it is clear who does what, what
role this plays in production and what moral claim this
discrete and disentangled activity gives rise to in the
reward structure.

The appeal to social justice then has to be interpreted in terms of the possible candidates cited by Titmuss
and others such as Nozick's entitlement theory, but there
does not seem to be any independent, external standard
that can be appealed to in order to secure some arbitra-
tion between this opposing and competing principle. As
Rawls says (1972), 'The various conceptions of justice are
the outgrowth of different notions of society against the
background of opposing views of the natural necessities
and opportunities of human life' (p. 9). Rawls himself
believes that there is what he calls an Archimedean point
which will allow a particular conception of justice (his
own) to be objectively vindicated. However, as we shall
show later, there are good reasons for rejecting this view
and with it the whole search for an absolutely secure
foundation for the moral claim to welfare provision via a
conception of justice just because the appeal to justice is
so contestable.

So far as the particular problem of this chapter is
concerned, the examination of justice leaves us with a
range of competing principles - merit/desert/worth/entitle-
ment/need - each of which appears to be capable of any degree up to a point; so perhaps it might be thought that
a more secure basis for the right to claim welfare, for
it to be given in a more than supererogatory way, is via
a theory of rights rather than a theory of justice.

HUMAN RIGHTS AND THE RIGHT TO WELFARE

There is certainly some plausibility in suggesting
that the state provision of welfare should be seen in
terms of rights rather than in terms of justice. In the
first place, if there is a right to welfare on a par with
other human rights then this would seem to bypass problems
about stigma and the possible casualness and supererogatory
nature of benevolence and charity. If a person has a right
to welfare, then there is no reason of principle why the
exercise of the right to welfare should be any more stigmatizing than the exercise of any other human right - for
example in the sphere of legal or political rights. At
the same time as treating welfare as a right on the part
of the recipient avoids the problem of stigma, so conceding that there is a right to welfare would seem to avoid
the suggestion of casualness, personal choice and supererero-
gation which would be characteristic of welfare provision
if it was provided only out of charity, generosity or benevolence. If there is a human right to welfare, then, subject to certain provisos (which will be dealt with later),
it looks as if there would be a strict obligation to
provide welfare, and as if this would be a state responsibility on a par with the responsibility to secure other
human rights. The securing of these rights cannot be
left to private agencies, markets or chance, or personal
benevolence.
    In addition to these advantages for the welfare theorist
of regarding welfare as a right, this view has been entrenched in the United Nations Universal Declaration of
Human Rights. In the Declaration on Human Rights economic
and social rights are regarded as equal with some traditional civil and political rights such as rights to life,
freedom of movement, speech and opinion and a right to a
fair trial.

Article 22 states that:

> Everyone as a member of a society has a right to social
> security, and is entitled to realisation through
> national effort and international co-operation and in
> accordance with the organisation and resources of each
> State of the economic, social and cultural rights indi-
> spensable for his dignity and the free development of
> his personality.

Article 23

1   Everyone has the right to work....
2   Everyone without discrimination has the right to
    equal pay for equal work.
3   Everyone who works has the right to just and favour-
    able remuneration for himself and his family an
    existence of human dignity, and supplemented, if
    necessary, by other means of social protection.

Article 24

> Everyone has the right to a standard of living adequate
> for the health and well being of himself and his family,
> including food, clothing, housing, and medical care and
> necessary social services, and the right to security in
> the event of unemployment, sickness, dissolution, widow-
> hood, old age or other lack of livelihood in circum-
> stances beyond his control.
>   Motherhood and childhood are entitled to special care
> and assistance. All children whether born in or out of
> wedlock shall enjoy the same protection.

Article 26

> Everyone has the right to education. Education shall
> be free at least in the early and fundamental stages.
> Elementary education shall be compulsory. Technical
> and professional education shall be made generally
> available and higher education shall be equally acces-
> sible to all on the basis of merit.

On this kind of basis welfare is a human right to be
claimed against the state and a strict obligation to be met
by the state. These rights extend the rights of citizenship

from the purely civil, legal and political sphere to that
of the social and economic. Accordingly these rights will
be called social rights.

However, there are major objections over the whole
idea of this extension of the notion of human rights to
social rights. These objections are largely twofold:
first, that social rights are radically unlike 'traditional' human rights and should not be grouped together;
second, that these social rights could not really be con-
ceded without endangering the human rights of other people
in society. For the first set of objections we shall look
particularly at Cranston's 'What Are Human Rights?' (1973)
and at Human Rights Real and Supposed in 'Political Theory
and the Rights of Man' (ed. Raphael, 1967); for the second
set of objections we should look particularly at Nozick's
'Anarchy, State and Utopia' (1974).

HUMAN RIGHTS AND SOCIAL RIGHTS

In his denial that social rights are human rights Cranston
(1973) does not mince his words because he sees at stake
both philosophical clarity about human rights and political
questions about legitimacy (p. 65):

a philosophically respectable concept of human rights
has been muddied, obscured and debilitated in recent
years by an attempt to incorporate into it specific
rights of a deficient logical category. The traditional
human rights are political and civil rights such as the
right to life, liberty and a fair trial. What are now
being put forward as universal human rights are social
and economic rights.... I have both a philosophical and
a political objection to this. The philosophical objection is that the new treaty of human rights does not
make sense. The political objection is that the circulation of a confused notion of human rights hinders the
effective protection of what are correctly seen as human
rights.

In this chapter we shall be concerned primarily with the
philosophical objection because the political objection
follows from it. If there are no social rights, no right
to welfare, then clearly the assumption that there is will
muddy the waters in the discussion of human rights; on
the other hand, if there is a defensible and meaningful
notion of social rights then the political objection will
no longer hold.

What are the philosophical grounds, then, for Cranston's
argument that social and economic rights are in a distinct-
ly different class from traditional human rights? He

suggests in fact three tests for genuine human rights -
practicability, paramount importance and universality -
and he argues that social and economic rights fail each of
these tests. On the face of it, the philosophical basis
of these tests seems to be clear enough. The test of
practicability follows from the fact that rights bear a
clear relationship to duties. If there is a right to X,
then there is a duty to facilitate X, and so it must be
possible and practicable to facilitate X. One cannot
have a duty to do what is logically impossible or what is
in a given situation impracticable; similarly, one cannot
have a right to something that is impossible or not practicable. The second list is straightforward: for something
to be a human right then it must be a right of a person
as such and not a person within a particular role, and
consequently the universality of a right is a necessary
condition of its being a human right. Finally, he suggests
that a right has paramount importance. If something is a
universal right to be claimed by all persons, then this
right has to concern features and states of human life that
are of paramount importance. On Cranston's view social
and economic rights fail these tests and therefore do not
satisfy the necessary conditions for human rights. In the
next section we shall investigate why they fail, and this
investigation will be instructive for, as we shall see,
Cranston's tests are shot through with ambiguities.

THE TESTS OF RIGHTS

If, as Kant plausibly suggested, 'I ought implies I can',
then the claims that rights embody must be capable of
being met; otherwise there is no obligation to meet them.
Cranston argues that traditional human rights such as the
right to life, freedom of speech and opinion, freedom of
movement, etc., easily pass this test because the claims
that they embody are very largely claims on the forbearance of others. These rights are impinged by the interference of others, and they are largely satisfied when
other people do not interfere, and forbear. Because these
rights do not embody claims on resources, the test of
practicability seems easy to meet, even for the poorest
of governments: 'Since those rights are for the most part
rights against government interference with a man's activities, a large part of the legislation needed has to do
no more than to restrain the government's own executive
aim' (Cranston, 1973, p. 66). On the other hand, Cranston
argues that social and economic rights are not rights of
forbearance so much as rights to resources. Government

has to provide something in the case of social and economic rights rather than forbear, as in the case of what he
regards as genuine human rights. It may then be the case
that governments may not have access to the resources to
provide for the social and economic rights of its population (Cranston, 1973, p. 67):

> The government of India, for example, simply cannot
> command the resources that would guarantee each one
> of our 500 millions inhabitants of India a standard
> of living adequate for the health and well being of
> himself and his family....

Because rights of forbearance are always practicable,
since they do not involve the distribution of scarce
resources, they therefore belong to a different logical
category from human rights such as the right to life,
liberty, etc.

However, there are some grounds for probing this argument in some detail. A great deal, of course, depends
upon the meaning of 'practicable' in this context, and
here, as David Watson has pointed out, Cranston (1973)
takes a very strange example to indicate what he means by
'practicable' (p. 66):

> It is not my duty to do what is physically impossible
> for me to do. You cannot reasonably say that it was
> my duty to have jumped into the River Thames at Rich-
> mond to rescue a drowning child, if I was nowhere
> near Richmond at the time that the child was drowning.

However, the impossibility here is a logical one - a person cannot be in two places at the same time (our ability
to identify persons is bound up with their spatio-temporal
position) - so it is inconceivable that this action could
be done in the sense that it would be meaningless to say
X in Manchester at time t_1 should have saved Y drowning
in Richmond at t_1. If this is what is meant by practicability, then clearly it is practicable for social and
economic rights to be implemented in the sense that it
makes sense, it is not logically impossible, to envisage
them being implemented. However, this is clearly not what
Cranston has in mind here. He means contingent impossibility - that at the present time it is not possible for
many countries to provide for the satisfaction of social
and economic rights because they do not have access to
the resources, capital wealth and so forth to implement
these rights. Yet a genuine right is something 'that
can, and from the moral point of view must, be respected
here and now'.

Now there seem to be three possible answers to this
sort of difficulty. The first is to consider in more
detail his claim that traditional human rights to life,

liberty, etc., because they are largely rights to forbearance, do not require resources and therefore are always
practicable. But it is far from clear that this is the
case. Traditional rights - life, liberty, property, etc.
clearly require forbearance on the part of others to be
met. However, such forbearance cannot just be legislated
into existence - a right not to be killed (the right to
life) will require protection by police forces, defence
forces, etc., all of which are going to involve capital
expenditures. Similarly, the right to a fair trial 'by
an independent and impartial tribunal' (article 10) is
going to involve expenditure on a legal system; article
21 claims a right to some form of representative political
institutions and for political participation which again
involves the expenditure of capital on legislatures,
elections, etc. The securing of what Cranston is willing
to regard as genuine human rights therefore will require
not just negative forbearance but also positive expenditure. In this case practicability is going to be a more
serious test for traditional human rights than Cranston is
prepared to admit. And, granted that we are talking about
'practical' practicability and not just logical practicability, it is going to be a matter of socioeconomic
judgment, a judgment that may well be contestable. It
does not seem, therefore, that the stringent standard of
practicability suggested by Cranston, which would allow it
to be a human right if and only if it can be satisfied
now, is appropriate. It is surely more appropriate to say
that governments ought to respect all of these rights so
far as they are able to 'in accordance with the organisation and resources of each state' (article 22). This
would apply to both 'traditional rights' and economic and
social rights. If Cranston's criterion of immediate practicability is accepted, then it is not clear how even the
right to life can be a right, for as Raphael says, 'no
amount of legislation or of police forces can prevent all
murders'; and yet as Cranston argues, a right is something
that from the moral point of view has to be respected now.'
The ambiguity here is over the word 'respect'. Does it
mean that the right has to be fully practicable and implemented now, in which case Raphael's argument is persuasive;
or does it mean that governments must do what they can to
secure these rights? If so, then clearly economic and
social rights may be rights equally with traditional
rights just because even these rights cannot be fully
satisfied now.
     The second test of rights proposed by Cranston is uni-
versality. A human right has to be a universal moral
right, and he argues that social and economic rights are

not universal in the appropriate sense. A universal moral
right is one that human beings have as human beings and
not because they fulfil a particular social role, or have
a particular colour of skin or a particular set of religious beliefs. The right to life, for example, is held
to be a genuine universal moral right - just because it
is a right of human beings as such. However, Cranston
argues that this is not the case in regard to social
rights, and he quotes article 24 of the UN Declaration
which claims that holidays with pay is a universal human
right. On this he says (1973, p. 67):

> This so called human right to holidays with pay plainly
> cannot pass. For it is a right that is necessarily
> limited to those who are *paid* in any case, that is to
> say to the *employé* class. Since not everyone belongs
> to this class, the right cannot be a universal right,
> a right which in the terminology of the United Nations
> Declaration 'welfare' has.

A right to holidays with pay is not a real human right
because it is claimed only by some human beings in a particular position, because they fulfil a certain role, that
of being an employee. Those who fall outside of this role -
children, mentally deranged persons and capitalists -
cannot claim this as a right because they do not belong
to the appropriate type of role or social position.

However, there are some difficulties with this view.
It does seem clear that universality is a candidate for
a central necessary test for any claim to be a human
right. Indeed, historically many natural right theories
depended upon state of nature arguments - the condition of
human beings before civil authority or power and before
any determinate organization of human society with specific roles and functions. The trouble with the criterion
of universality as Cranston has proposed it is that it
does not clearly demarcate (as he wants the test to do)
economic and social rights from civil and political
rights (the traditional rights). On this, David Watson
(1977) argues that the traditional right to a fair trial
or due process of law will not pass the test (p. 39):

> this so-called human right to a fair trial plainly
> cannot pass the test of universality. For it is a
> right that is necessarily limited to those persons
> who are on trial in any case, that is to say the
> accused class; since not everyone belongs to this
> class, the right cannot be a universal right, a right
> which everyone has.

The same is true *mutatis mutandis* of rights to leave one's
country, freedom of religion and peaceable assembly - in
all these cases those rights are limited to those who be-

long to the particular group in question. In the first
case the right would exclude the comfortably settled, in
the second the activist and in the third the apathetic.

No doubt Cranston would reply to this that, while not
everyone in society at any one time belongs to one or
other of these particular groups, they could in fact become a member - and that the rights relate to possible
rather than necessarily actual states and features of
human life. However, this argument would apply equally
well to social and economic rights: not all people are
employed, not all people are destitute, not all people are
at any particular time in need of education; but equally,
all these are possible states of life which any person
could find himself in. So perhaps universality, which
does seem to be a genuine criterion, that to be redeployed
to relate not just to the situation that all people every-
where are in now but to those possible situations in
which they could find themselves. Alternatively, if we
wish to use Cranston's notion of universality, then
possibly the right to life is the only one that clearly
passes the test - children and imbeciles presumably would
not have rights to non-interference and property of their
own, in which case these are not universal rights.

However, it might be thought that reinterpretation of
universality makes it possible for a list of human rights
to proliferate endlessly. Becoming a mastic asphalt
spreader is a human possibility, although not a state of
life that all men share; and yet, if my reformulation of
the thesis of universality is correct, then it would seem
that, because it is a human possibility, there could be
human rights attached to being a mastic asphalt spreader.
However, this implausible possibility would be ruled out
by Cranston's other criterion, that human rights must be
of paramount importance. Cranston argues that this criterion is 'less definite, but no less crucial', but he
really gives no attempt to provide a criterion of paramount importance, other than in terms of one or two examples (1973, p. 67):

> It would have been my duty to rescue the drowning
> child at Richmond if I had been there at the time;
> but it is not, in the same sense, my duty to give
> Christmas presents to the children of my neigh-
> bours.... Common sense knows that fire engines and
> ambulances are essential services, whereas fun fairs
> and holiday camps are not.

In terms of these examples, it would seem that the basis
for a judgment about paramount importance would be that a
person's life is at stake and that this must be universally important. The reason for this presumably is that,

whatever anyone regards as important, he must recognize
human life to be important because without living human
beings the notion of their having importance or being
more or less important has no meaning. In order to achieve
any important end, whatever he may think it is, a man must
recognize that the preconditions of achieving those ends
are of paramount importance and the most obvious of these
is life. However, while the right to life may be taken
by Cranston to be equivalent to the traditional right of
the prevention of arbitrary killing, it could equally
well be taken to encompass economic rights too – people
die as effectively from starvation as they do from murder,
and in this sense social and economic rights could pass
the test of paramount importance just as much as rights
against homicide. Indeed, Cranston's own examples of
fire engines and ambulances may give something of a hostage
to fortune to his critics on precisely this point. Raphael
(1967) is surely correct here when he says: 'Tom Paine
evidently understood the natural right to life as implying
not only laws against homicide but also laws to provide
bare subsistence. Will anyone say that he was wrong in
terms of paramount importance?' (p. 87). It might be
possible for Cranston to meet this point by a doctrine of
acts and omissions. A law against homicide fulfils the
right to life because it requires others to forbear, to
omit to do something (namely to kill me); on the other
hand, the right to subsistence requires someone to act to
give it. However, we saw earlier that this distinction
is very difficult to maintain because the prevention of
homicide is secured not only by passing legislation mea-
suring forbearance, but also by institutions such as
police, prisons and gallows, which do require positive
actions on the part of government and considerable capital
expenditure.

This point perhaps gives us a clue about the current
relationship between 'traditional' rights and social
rights, and it is that social rights – to employment,
education, social security, etc. (subject to the proviso
that they are being met as far as is practicable) – in fact
provide a good deal of essential means to the exercise of
traditional rights. Rights to life and liberty may require certain things – among them health and education to
make them exercise a reality – not just negative forbearance on the part of government. As Raphael (1967) says,
'If a man is subject to chronic unemployment in a depressed
era, he will not thank you for the information that he has
the basic rights of liberty' (p. 87). Indeed, this kind
of perspective goes back not only to Tom Paine and Louis
Blanc, whom Raphael quotes, but also to T.H. Green, whose

influence upon the early development of the welfare
state was enormous, and there are perhaps echoes of this
influence in R.H. Tawney's 'The Acquisitive Society' (1961)
(Tawney was a pupil, and Edward Caird was also a disciple,
of Green, who was Master of Balliol from 1896 to 1908:
'Political rights afford a safeguard and significance to
civil rights ... economic and social rights provide means
essential to the exercise of political rights' (p. 121).
Traditional civil and political rights may not be capable
of being either secured or acted upon without social and
economic rights.

In terms of the analysis proposed by Cranston, therefore, there does not seem to be any great difficulty in
regarding welfare as a right to be claimed against society -
so far as the capital resources of society permit - and
clearly there will be difficulties of economic judgment
here. Such rights would require that welfare, so far as
it can, should be provided as a matter of obligation on
the part of society as a whole and not left to the charity
of individuals. Second, it can be claimed as a right, and
therefore should not depend upon the beneficence or generosity of society, and therefore should not be seen as
stigmatizing.

One further difficulty for the welfare right theory not
discussed by Cranston is that traditional human rights
assign duties and obligations to individuals who are to be
regarded as morally culpable if they do not respect the
right or perform the duties claimed under the right. Thus
the right of X to life entails a duty on the part of
other people not to kill him; the right of X to free
speech implies a duty on the part of other individuals
not to interfere with X's exercise of that right (subject
to conditions such as that X's exercise of his right does
not preclude someone else with an equal right to exercise
his right to free expression). Those who fail to respect
these rights and fail to perform these duties are morally
culpable. However, it is not at all clear against whom
social and economic rights are claimed. While each and
every individual has a duty to respect X's right to life
and free speech, this cannot be the case with X's economic
and social rights. No single person can have the strict
obligation to fulfil the economic and social rights of
other persons. As Narveson says, 'One could work twenty-
four hours a day at the relief of suffering and could
impoverish oneself contributing to charity, but it is felt
that to require one to do this would be going rather too
far' (1967, p. 235).

While I have a general moral duty not to harm and interfere in the lives of others, and others have a right to

claim such forbearance from me, I cannot have a general
and strict moral obligation to provide resources to re-
lieve the suffering of all who suffer, and they in turn
have no right to my resources for such relief.

If this is so, then it would seem that welfare could
not be a right just because the right could not be claimed
against any particular person; no particular individual
could be blamed for the non-fulfilment of the right, and
no specific individual would be responsible for any claim
to compensation falling due as the result of the failure
to implement that right. It would seem that again it
would be best to see welfare as a matter of humanity,
generosity, altruism and therefore imperfect duty, to
which there would be no corresponding right.

It might be thought that the answer to this would be
that the right to welfare is a right to be claimed not
against individuals, but rather against society as a
whole, or more specifically the government, and this is
in part the answer that Narveson gives in his interesting
utilitarian discussion of this question. However, this
still does not go quite as far as the welfare right theorist wants to go. As Narveson himself says (1967), this
move would still make the right in question an imperfect
one, because if we go back to Mill's distinction (1962,
p. 305) - an imperfect duty is one that is directed
against no particular person - the case we are now considering is closely parallel to this, and the right to
welfare would become a right against no one in particular
and thus would by parity of reasoning be an imperfect
right. In the same way as no specific right corresponds
to an imperfect duty, so an imperfect right could not
imply any specific duty on the part of anyone. To be
forced into this position would be just about the same as
having to recognize that there is no right to welfare.

However, it is possible, following the lead of Narveson,
to take matters further than this. Consider what Narveson
says (1967, pp. 235-6):

> But a duty has to be someone's duty. It can't just be
> no one's in particular. Consequently the thing to do
> is to make it everyone's duty to do something, even if
> that 'something' is a matter of seeing that someone
> else does it. Those who are put on the business end,
> such as the police, medical people, firemen, etc.,
> should, of course, be compensated for going to the
> trouble of performing these activities. The simplest
> solution is simply to make these professions supportable
> by the public.

If this is accepted, and we think that there are good reasons for accepting it, then the strict or perfect duty of

individuals would not be that of the personal provision of
resources to deprived individuals, but rather the support
of institutions, welfare agencies, social workers, etc.,
that attempt to meet social needs. As a strict duty
this could then be required by government through taxation
to support the meeting of social need. In this way we
could still see the welfare state in terms of rights and
duties rather than in terms of institutionalized altruism.
To see the human right to welfare as implying a duty to
support government welfare measures would be equivalent to
seeing due process of law as a human right. A specific
individual has not the duty to provide such due process,
but rather the duty to see that the procedures of due
process are in fact carried out. The perfect duties corresponding to the rights of welfare are not then the personal provision of resources and services to individuals,
but rather the duty to support governments and institutions that are organized to meet such needs.

However, the bases of these rights have not yet been
explained and it will be argued that a theory of rights
has to be based upon a theory of needs of the sort set
out in chapter 3.   But before this is attempted one further complication surrounding the idea of the right to
welfare has to be investigated, namely Nozick's claim that
welfare provision, whether instituted on a basis of justice
or on a basis of rights, in fact undermines perhaps the
most entrenched conception of a right that we have - human
inviolability: the right to be treated as an end in oneself and not as a means to the ends of others.

RESPECT FOR PERSONS, INVIOLABILITY AND THE RIGHT TO WELFARE

> Act in such a way that you always treat humanity, whe-
> ther in your own person or in the person of another,
> never simply as a means, but always at the same time
> as an end.

Thus Kant provided his second formulation of the categorical Imperative in 'The Groundwork of the Metaphysics of
Morals' (1974), and this provides Nozick, in 'Anarchy,
State and Utopia (1974), with his basic moral presupposi-
tion. Nozick sees the principle as being a principle of
human inviolability and he assumes that such a principle
of inviolability involves the idea that each individual has
rights that impose limits on how he may be treated and
dealt with by others (p. 30):

> Side constraints upon action reflect the underlying
> Kantian principle that individuals are ends and not
> merely means; they may not be sacrificed or used

for the achieving of other ends without their consent.
Individuals are inviolable.
Nozick regards such a principle as generating property
rights. If individuals are inviolable they have rights to
what they earn, to what they have acquired - to what they
have mixed their labour with - so long as, following
Locke, in the acquisition of property they have left 'as
much and as good for others', or they pay compensation
for those who cannot acquire property after the acquisi-
tions of others. To have a property right requires that
the person who has the property right to X shall determine what shall be done with X (Nozick, 1974, p. 171).
This right cannot be violated without infringing on the
principle of inviolability. In Nozick's view any institutional procedure for redistribution to the worst-off members of society or the needy, whether justified in terms
of social justice or of 'rights', cannot fail to violate
this basic principle. This is so for several reasons. In
the first place, we cannot coherently appeal to some
conception of the social good in order to justify the
violation of an individual's rights involved in the redistribution of his property to others (Nozick, 1974,
pp. 32-3):

Why may one not violate persons for the social good?
Individually, we each sometimes choose to undergo some
pain or sacrifice for a greater benefit or to avoid a
greater harm.... Why not *similarly* hold that some
persons have to bear some costs that benefit others
more for the sake of the overall social good? But
there is no *social entity* with a good that undergoes
some sacrifice for its own good. There are only individual people with their own individual lives. Using
one of these people for the benefit of others uses him
and benefits the others. Nothing more.... Talk of an
overall social good covers this up [intentionally?].
Nozick operates with a severely individualist approach to
the understanding of the social order, an approach some
of the deficiencies of which are discussed in this book.
Here this individualism is crucial for rejecting any
appeal to the claims of society. There are only individuals with their rights and their own pursuit of their
goods; anything else is both mysterious and sinister.
    Second, any kind of redistributive pattern to transfer
goods and services from those who have them to those who
have not - the needy, the deprived - treats these things
in an entirely ahistorical way, as if they had come from
nowhere, out of nothing, manna from heaven. Goods are
made, created by human effort and human labour, and they
can be redistributed consistently only with the rights of

the one who made the goods if he consents to it;   otherwise the basic right - that of inviolability - is
infringed (1974, p. 160):

> Whoever makes something, having bought or contracted
> for all other held resources used in the process
> (transferring some of his holdings for these co-
> operating factors) is entitled to it. The situation
> is *not* one of something's getting made and then there
> being an open question of who is to get it. Things
> come into the world already attached to people having
> entitlements over them.

Production and distribution are not two separate issues
for Nozick any more than they were for Marx, but for
Nozick the reason why they are not separate issues, unlike
for Marx, is that production gives men property rights
in what they have created. Consequently, if the created
object is redistributed either as it is or by taxation
individuals property rights are being violated. Again, a
good deal of the plausibility of this thesis depends upon
Nozick's direct individualism - the idea that individual
contributions to production could be filtered out and
matched with equally determinable property rights in the
objects created in production.

Finally, he argues that any patterned principle of
distribution that sanctions the redistribution of goods
from those who have created them to those who have not,
whether based upon social justice or upon social and economic rights, would be equivalent to giving the state,
the agent of redistribution, a property right, or part
property right, in the individuals whose assets had been
redistributed (Nozick, 1974, p. 174):

> Whether it is done through taxation or wages or on
> wages over a certain amount, or through seizure of
> profits, or through there being a high social pot so
> that it's not clear what's coming from where and what's
> going where, patterned principles of distributive jus-
> tice involve appropriating the actions of other per-
> sons.... If people force you to do certain work or
> unrewarded work for a certain period of time, they
> decide what you are to do and what purposes your
> work is to secure apart from your decisions. This
> process whereby they take this decision from you makes
> them a *part owner* of you. Just as having such partial
> control and power of decision by right, over an animal
> or an inanimate object would be to have a property
> right in it.

Such a consequence Nozick holds to follow from any plan to
redistribute to the needy, and he comments that 'these
principles involve a shift from the classical liberal's

notion of self-ownership to a notion of (partial) property
rights in *other* people (p. 172). And this shift is of
course incompatible with the Kantian principle of respect
for persons.

If welfare is institutionalized in state activities,
distributing it as a right or in accordance with some
principle of distributive justice, then there is going to
be an entrenched clash of rights between what Nozick
regards as the absolutely basic right of inviolability
and welfare rights (1974, p. 173):

> Proponents of patterned conceptions of justice, however,
> often will face head-on clashes (and poignant ones, if
> they cherish each party to the clash) between moral
> side-constraints on how individuals may be treated
> and then patterned conception of justice that presents
> an end state or other pattern that must be realised.

The historical entitlement conception of justice for
which Nozick argues is the only conception compatible with
the principle of inviolability. This implies that when
holdings have been acquired justly (justice in acquisition) -
that is to say when unowned natural resources have been
acquired by mixing one's labour with them - they have been
justly acquired if there is left enough and as good for
others; or if compensation is paid when the appropriation
of an unowned object worsens the position of others. If
this condition is satisfied then an individual is entitled
to his holdings and has property rights in them; those
property rights are violated by any compulsory redistribution. However, there can be justice in transfer when an
individual freely chooses to bestow some of his holdings
on others, and this is in fact for Nozick the only way
compatible with the theory of rights that welfare may be
provided in society by generosity, philanthropy, beneficence - by freely transferring resources on those who are
in need. But this is supererogatory; it is not a strict
obligation, and it is false to argue that the needy have
a right to the receipt of such transfers (Nozick, 1974,
p. 151):

> A distribution is just if it arises from another just
> distribution by legitimate means. The legitimate means
> of arriving from one distribution to another are speci-
> fied by the principle of distribution in transfer.
> The legitimate first 'moves' are specified by the prin-
> ciples of justice in acquisition.

If we wish to inquire whether a particular distribution is
just we have to inquire *how it came about* - how the holdings were acquired and how they were transferred (if they
were). Because transfers operate *inter alia* via bequests,
it also follows that the justice of the distribution of

holdings in a particular generation is dependent not just
upon the transfers that have been affected within that
generation but also upon how the holdings within that
generation come about from bequests from previous generations. The right of bequest for Nozick is a central part
of justice in transfer. Consequently, children have to
put up with the consequences of their parents' successes
and failures and the character of their bequests to them.
There can be no process of rectification at the start of
each generation because this would infringe the right of
bequest and thus of justice in transfer. The only role
that rectificatory justice has is when initial holdings
have not been acquired according to the criteria of appro-
priative right or when transfers have not been freely
made.
    The importance of Nozick's theory for the purposes of
the discussion central to this book is that he denies that
the idea of a right to welfare, or a duty to meet needs,
however analysed, can be compatible with what he would
regard as a central and deeply entrenched moral principle -
treating people as ends in themselves. Any institutionalized welfare system that is not based upon the free consent of each individual whose holdings are being transferred involves a violation of fundamental rights. This
characterization of the consequences of taking inviolability seriously is very important, because very often in
fact the welfare system is itself justified in terms of
making concrete institutional form the principle of respect for persons.
    However, there are some difficulties with Nozick's
views, some more manageable than others. One obvious
assumption that is made is the idea of self-ownership,
or possessive individualism, which is a dominant characteristic of the classical liberal tradition of political
thought. It is really beyond the scope of this book to
deal with this fundamental assumption of Nozick's (interested readers could refer to 'The Political Theory of
Possessive Individualism' (1962) and 'Democratic Theory:
Essays in Retrieval' (1974) by C.B. Macpherson), but there
are equally what might be called middle-range difficulties
in his theory that might be worth considering.
    Nozick does accept a principle of rectification which
will involve redistribution if the current distribution
came about illegitimately, that is if in acquisition unowned resources were not acquired according to the principle of justice in acquisition, or if transfers have
been made illegitimately - because of coercion, etc. This
rectificatory redistribution will not violate the property
rights of those who hold goods because they hold goods

illegitimately. Those who benefit from the redistribution, in fact, would seem to have a right to the redistribution because the existing maldistribution that is being
rectified infringes their property rights. So if at any
particular time a distribution is found to have come about
illegitimately, then it can be rectified and those who will
benefit presumably have a right to this redistribution.
However, what Nozick says in detail here is extremely
interesting (1974, p. 231):

> Perhaps it is better to view some patterned principles
> of distributive justice [i.e. such as distribution
> according to need (RP)] as rough rules of thumb meant
> to approximate the general results of applying the
> principle of rectification of injustice. For example,
> lacking much historical information and assuming
> (1) that victims of injustice generally do worse than
> they otherwise would and (2) that those from the least
> well-off group in society have the highest probabili-
> ties of being (descendants of) victims of the most
> serious injustice are owed compensation by those who
> benefited from the injustice ... then a rough rule of
> thumb for rectifying injustices might seem to be the
> following: organise society so as to maximise the
> position of whatever group ends up the least well off
> in society.

Maximizing the position of the worst-off groups on this
basis is not an act of charity; it is a rectification of
an injustice to property rights that have been infringed,
and as such it does not infringe the rights of the better-
off who, on this rule of thumb, are likely to have some of
their holdings unjustly. To this extent, therefore,
Nozick is willing to see the needy and the deprived position improved by state action *and* as a matter of duty, and
thus of right for the needy and the deprived. However, it
is also clear that he does not see such an extensive rectification as an on-rolling activity. It will be an overall
once and for all rectification with subsequent rectifica-
tions being made only in specific cases - at least, this
would seem to be the implication of the very final sentence
of this paragraph: 'although to introduce socialism for
our sins would be to go too far, past injustices might be
so great as to make necessary *in the short run* a more
excessive state to rectify them' (p. 231). This kind of
root-and-branch rectification is not to occur afresh in
each generation because this would require continual on-
going and extensive state activity which Nozick explicitly
denies. It is a once and for all rectification to take
society back to a kind of an approximation to a just starting point after which only specific, determinable injustices

in acquisition or transfer would require rectification.
After the initial return to a just starting point, subsequent generations would inherit the consequences of previous transfers of holdings made by their predecessors.
However, this view requires considerable justification
because, as A. Goldman has argued (1976, p. 824):

> The deepest moral problem with such an operation is
> that it allows or rather forces some to start in life
> with nothing but economic handicaps and prospects of
> misery and deprivation ... we cannot see why children
> should be held responsible for the sins and omissions
> of their ancestors or why they must remain almost
> inevitably locked within material and deprivation be-
> cause of their initial environments.

After the wholesale rectification discussed earlier, this
would subsequently be exactly the situation, and there
would be no role here for justice or for rectification
unless it could be shown that the parents or other ances-
tors of these deprived children were the victims of injustices in transfer after the wholesale rectification. Any
attempt to rectify the cycle of deprivation either would
mean transferring holdings from others to these children,
and thus would go against inviolability, or would involve
equalizing the starting places of each generation by redistribution by taxes on inheritance. This, however,
would infringe the right of bequest which is part of justice in transfer (those with holdings have the right to
leave them to whom they choose). However, as Hillel
Steiner has pointed out (1975), it is not at all clear how
rights of bequest can be involved in violations because it
is not clear how a deceased person's rights and liberties
can be infringed. This is crucial, although it does appear
highly esoteric, because of course for Nozick it is not the
right of inheritance that is being infringed: there is no
right of inheritance because such a right would give the
prospective inheritor a property right in the prospective
bequeather. The transfer of holdings from generation to
generation, and thus the way in which children suffer or
enjoy the consequences of their parents' foresight, depends
entirely upon the right of bequest. Not that it would make
much difference for Nozick to concede this point, because
if in fact bequests were taxed away those who wished to
leave their children their wealth and property would merely
make this property over to them as gifts prior to their
deaths. A gift tax would not involve the problems for
Nozick that a tax on post-mortem bequests would, and on
his view it would be clearly an infringement of justice in
transfer assuming that the holdings to be given away were
justly acquired in the first place and were given freely.

These unequal starts in life for children, however,
depend on the idea of bequest being a right of transfer and
gifts of justly acquired holdings being legitimate and free
from redistributive taxation. Granted this, the wealth and
property of parents can legitimately be transferred with
differentiating consequences for subsequent generations.

However, this would still leave a central aspect of
Nozick's analysis entrenched. After the various rectifica-
tions have been effected, then those who become needy not
as the result of injustices and illegitimate transfers
have no rights against those with holdings. Their relief
will depend entirely upon philanthropy and charity.

RESPECT FOR PERSONS AND EQUALITY OF RESPECT

The basic difficulty that has to be faced is whether the
Kantian principle of respect for persons as ends is inconsistent with requiring the better endowed to help those
in need by giving up some of their holdings or marginal
amounts of their earnings. Clearly, for Nozick the principle basically requires forbearance - not to harm, mani-
pulate or interfere with others. Each individual has
property rights which are infringed if the state requires
that resources should be given to the needy as a matter of
right.

One of the ways of probing the exact implications of the
principle of respect for persons is to note that for Kant
it was an alternative formulation of the Categorical Imperative in which the idea of acting under rules equally applicable to all is insisted upon. In his discussion of the
first formulation of the principle, Kant takes up the
question of interpersonal relationships in the context of
a discussion of beneficence. He takes the case (1974,
p. 90) of a man who is:

> himself flourishing, but he sees others who have to
> struggle with great hardships (and whom he could easily
> help; and he thinks 'what does it matter to me...').
> Now admittedly if such an attitude were a universal law
> of nature, mankind could get on perfectly well.... But
> although it is possible that such a universal law of
> nature could subsist in harmony with this maxim, yet
> it is impossible to *will* that such a principle should
> hold everywhere as a law of nature. For a will which
> decided in this way would be in conflict with itself,
> since many a situation might arise in which a man
> needed love and sympathy from others and in which, by
> such a law of nature issuing from his own will, he would
> rob himself of all the hope of the help which he wants
> for himself.

A rational man may will ends that require co-operation of
others with him if he is to secure those ends, and if so
he has to will the means to those ends - the help of
others - and if this is universalized then he will will
that men help one another to achieve those ends, which
requires co-operation. On this kind of basis then it would
seem inconsistent with the Kantian premise to argue that a
man has no duty to help those in need because in a similar
situation he might be so deprived and needy that he could
not achieve whatever ends he might have without the help
of others to satisfy his needs. The principle of respect
for persons, as an alternative formulation of the Categorical Imperative, would be consistent with such a principle
of social co-operation. However, it does not actually
require it, because the position need not be the only one
open to a rational man. As Robert Wolff (1973) points
out, it would be possible for a man never to set for himself an end whose achievement appears to require the co-
operation with others and to forswear any ends he has
adopted as soon as it turns out that such co-operation is
needed (1973, p. 171). In addition, the actual upshot of
Kant's discussion is unclear - it does not imply that such
help in realization of ends should be seen as a right as
opposed to a claim; that it should not necessarily be
seen as a strict obligation rather than as a matter of
beneficence. Certainly it is possible to read Kant as
implying a principle of help as a right, but in the case
of Goldman (1976, p. 831) this goes beyond the text:

> We undoubtedly not only would want to be helped or to
> be answered favourably when begging for help, but would
> want to be able to demand help as a right so that the
> need for begging with its additional degradation would
> not arise. We would want not to await the beneficence
> of others as a dog might do but to be able to demand
> satisfaction of basic needs as a right of human
> beings....

As Goldman articulates the case, it is made to appear
rather intuitive - a matter of what 'we' would or would
not require in certain circumstances - and it could be
argued that it may or may not be in the spirit of Kant's
position. However, the argument could perhaps be made a
bit tighter than Goldman presents it. If all Kant's argument shows is that general benevolence is a coherent universal principle for a rational agent to will, then an
individual clearly would not have a right to benevolence.
Also, it is not clear that an agent willing only general-
ized benevolence would have any expectation that others
would help him. Benevolence for Kant is an imperfect
duty - it is something that it is desirable to do, but it

is not obligatory for any particular individual to render benevolent help to any other particular individual in any specific amount. Consequently, if a rational agent is going to will a principle of co-operative help as Kant suggests, it might well be that he would will it as a right and as a correlative strict duty on the part of those who help, because otherwise a particular individual could have no confidence that people's benevolent impulses would be directed towards him. On this interpretation, then, Goldman might be correct in arguing that the Categorical Imperative willed by someone who sought ends requiring co-operation would will such help as a right and would recognize a corresponding duty to help others in the pursuit of their ends, and this could be a basis for rejecting Nozick's view that no entrenched principle of need satisfaction as a right is consistent with the Categorical Imperative of which the principle of respect for persons is held to be an alternative formulation. However, this still leaves two issues entrenched. First, there is the difficulty posed by Wolff of purely individual ends which do not require co-operation. Is there any reason for thinking that the pursuit of such ends is impossible? Perhaps so: it is not an argument that the ends in question have to be co-operative, but rather that the pursuit of any ends, public or private, might require others' help. For example, the fulfilment of the basic needs of life and autonomy are central for the pursuit of any end, private or public. A man could hardly forswear any end that required co-operation if in fact he could not pursue any end at all, if he was unable to supply his basic needs by himself. In this sense, therefore, perhaps reflection on Kant's example on his own terms might provide a basis for rejecting Nozick's claim that a recognition of need satisfaction as a right is inconsistent with the principle of respect.

However, one obstacle remains. While Kant takes the view that the principle of inviolability is just another formulation of the Categorical Imperative - an assumption on which the argument above trades - many philosophers, and perhaps Nozick, would want to reject this. In order to make the Kantianism of Nozick less oblique it would really have to be shown that the same kind of conclusion could follow from a direct consideration of the principle of respect for persons and inviolability, and perhaps this can in fact be done.

Even if Kant's formula about treating men not merely as a means but as an end is held to be independent of the first formulation of the Categorical Imperative, there are still grounds for arguing that the principle of respect

for persons requires a commitment to co-operative need
satisfaction. In his discussion of this principle, Kant
again takes the example of beneficence (1947, p. 98):

> Now humanity could no doubt subsist if everybody
> contributed nothing to the happiness of others but,
> at the same time, refrained from deliberately impair-
> ing their happiness. This is, however, merely to
> agree negatively and not positively with humanity as
> an end in itself unless everyone endeavours also, so
> far as in him lies, to further the ends of others. For
> the ends of a subject who is an end in himself must,
> if this conception is to have its full effect in me,
> be also, as far as possible, my end.

The exact interpretation of this passage is, of course,
open to question, because any interpretation will be an
attempt to reach substantive moral conclusions from a
purely formal premise about consistency. However, it can
be suggested, though not conclusively shown, that a principle of need satisfaction could be derived from this
passage and that Nozick's argument about the kinds of
rights and claims consistent with the respect for persons
principle is not the only one. Nozick's account clearly
seems to fall under Kant's point about taking the principle
in a purely negative way – of not interfering, not violat-
ing and manipulating individuals – but equally, Kant
asserts that there is another aspect of commitment to the
principle which has moral legitimacy, namely that respecting another person as an end implies trying as far as it
lies within one's power to facilitate the efforts of
others to achieve their ends. Of course there are some
ends and some means to them of which I may morally dis-
approve, and it could be no part of my respecting another
person that I should seek to help him to achieve his end,
say, of being a successful thief. However, it was central
to the argument of the previous chapter that there are
certain means – survival and autonomy – that are necessary
conditions for the achievement of any end, whatever it
might be, so that whatever ends he has an individual has
to have these means of achieving them.

It might be argued against this view that it secures
only benevolence; but here again the argument from the
previous considerations relating to the Categorical
Imperative becomes important. Benevolence is not a perfect duty, and if all Kant's argument about a positive
commitment to the principle of respect secured was benevolence, then it would not do the work he wants it to do.
I can only be serious about my respect for other people's
ends in so far as I am equally serious about their means –
in this case, their needs.

Clearly all of this is highly controversial, as was the
argument in the previous section, but I hope that it has
at least weakened the idea that Nozick's entitlement
theory of justice is the only one compatible with the
principle of respect for persons. It does seem equally
possible to claim that the principle could equally require
the idea of need satisfaction as a right. However, in
order to support this argument reference again had to be
made to the argument in chapter 2 about basic needs and
then reference to ends, and in the next section it will
be argued that in fact a good many of these intractable
arguments about justice and rights can be bypassed if
these notions of basic needs is made central. Indeed, it
is this notion that, it will be argued, supports a coherent and logically defensible theory of rights.

NEEDS AND RIGHTS

It was suggested in chapter 3 that, whatever moral disagreements there may be, those who have developed moral
outlooks, however different, that command certain ends or
require certain duties to be performed are logically
committed to a conception of basic needs. Ends (however
different) and duties (however varied) can be pursued and
performed only by human beings acting autonomously; and
therefore any moral view to be coherent must recognize the
maintenance of human life and the development of autonomy
as basic obligations. Of course, as was previously argued,
what these obligations imply for the level of satisfaction
of these needs is going to be a matter of moral controversy,
different groups pitching their views about the nature of
satisfaction involved at different levels. But none the
less, despite this difference, the need for life and autonomy provide the logically basic human needs that have to
be recognized by any logically self-consistent moral point
of view. Those needs provide the basis of the obligation to provide welfare. The satisfaction of these needs
cannot be a duty of charity or benevolence, or any other
work of imperfect duty or supererogation. The obligation
to satisfy these particular needs has to be a strict
obligation because it is impossible to make sense of
there being other obligations that could outweigh the
obligations to meet these needs just because those whose
needs in this sphere are not met are not able *ex hypothesi*
to pursue any other obligations, whatever they may be, or
any other ends. On this view, therefore, there is a strict
claim to welfare (understood as basic need satisfaction
according to some morally specific conception of satis-

faction) and a strict obligation to supply welfare in this
sense, assuming that it is possible to do so. The possibility here cannot be denied by an appeal to other social
ends, or other social obligations, because, as we have
already argued, these ends themselves require basic needs
to be satisfied.

On this view welfare is an entitlement, and its provision is a strict duty, and this provides the proper
basis for regarding welfare as a right. To call this
entitlement to need satisfaction a 'right' does not really
make any difference to the argument, although it does provide an important rhetorical device for those who wish
to press the claim of need fulfilment. Joel Feinberg has
something highly instructive to say about this (1970,
p. 255):

> I accept the moral principle that to have an unfulfilled
> need is to have a kind of claim against the world even
> if against no one in particular.... Such claims based
> on need alone are permanent possibilities of rights,
> the natural seed from which rights grow. When manifesto
> writers speak of them as if already actual rights, they
> are easily forgiven, for this is but a powerful way of
> expressing the conviction that they ought to be recog-
> nised by states here and now as potential rights and
> consequently as determinants of present aspirators and
> guides to *present* policies. That usage is, I think,
> a valid exercise of rhetorical licence.

A proper view of human, universal rights would ground
them in a theory of basic human needs of the sort outlined in chapter 3. These needs for survival are to be
satisfied by various types of forbearance - in the case of
survival by forbearing against killing; in the case of
the need for autonomy by forbearing against interference -
but at the same time they are also to be satisfied by
various sorts of resource provisions without which the
needs recognized negatively by forbearance cannot be
satisfied. Of course, the level of satisfaction in question is going to be a matter of normative dispute, but
this does not render the whole conception ineffectual any
more than disputes about what sorts of provision will
actualize the right to participate in government makes
this right ineffectual.

In order to act legitimately, in the sense of satisfying
basic moral duties laid upon it, governments have to recognize the basic duty of need satisfaction; and thus the
provision of welfare, not necessarily in the form of present welfare states, is a basic aspect of political legitimacy and not just some kind of optional extra within the
general political framework. It follows from this also

that government cannot be wholly want-regarding (to use
Barry's distinction); it has to be ideal-regarding in
recognizing the duty to satisfy basic needs and, as we
saw in chapter 3 needs may, but equally may not, be cor-
related with felt wants. The task of government is not
to 'take as given the wants which people happen to have
and concentrate attention entirely on the extent to which
a certain policy will alter the overall amount of want
satisfaction' (Barry, 1965, p. 38). Because people can
be said with perfect propriety not to want what they
need, and because there are ways, outlined in chapter 3,
for delineating a class of basic needs which lays basic
obligations on governments, legitimate governments have to
be ideal-regarding. However, this does not mean that
there is no relationship at all between want-regarding
and ideal-regarding considerations. It will be recalled
from chapter 3 that the class of basic needs was defined
in terms of the necessary conditions that have to be
satisfied in order for *any* ends to be pursued, so it
could be said at this point in the argument that the role
of government in attending to the ideal-regarding principle
of need satisfaction is acting so as to facilitate subsequent effective want satisfactions. Indeed, Barry, in
developing his distinction between ideal-regarding and
want-regarding principles, argues that those actions of
government that affect the 'distribution' among people of
satisfying wants are themselves want-regarding. What
we are arguing is that the satisfaction of basic needs is
a precondition of securing want satisfaction, and that
these needs cannot necessarily just be treated as wants
just because some people may not in fact *want* those things
that in fact they need.

    This thesis does not entail that legitimate governments
should pay no regard to people's wants - their ends and
their desires to achieve them - or that government should
indulge in a radical root-and-branch criticism of the
articulated wants of its citizens. On the contrary, the
thesis is a rather narrow one, at least in principle: that
there are basic needs - for survival and autonomy - and
that the government has a duty to satisfy these prior to
and in order to arrange the maximal form of want satisfaction.

    It could be argued that such a proposal is politically
illiberal - people's preferences should be taken as basic,
and it is not the role of the government to assume a
characterization of basic needs. In reply to this however
two points need to be made. First, people's preferences
may themselves be seen to be at least in some part functions of other social factors - production, advertising,

a sense of the range of opportunity open, etc. To this
extent wants may not be so clearly and completely self-
directed as classical liberals might suppose. In addition, however, it is important to realize the restricted
nature of the thesis being argued. It is basic needs
that government has a duty to satisfy through welfare
institutions, and these have been defined in such a way
in chapter 3 that they do provide a firm basis for
ascriptions about what people really need irrespective of
whether they want/deşire those things - the way in which
we are to see both wants and their satisfaction outside
of this sphere is beyond the scope of this book, and indeed the authors themselves might disagree. What is
argued, and is the basis of the argument, is that there
is a right to basic welfare (the fulfilment of basic
needs), and that this right has both positive and negative
aspects - distribution of resources and holdings as well
as forbearances. However, once there is institutional
embodiment of the principle subsequent wants could be
satisfied in a number of different institutional settings -
the economic market, for example, or in a socialist planned
economy - but these are outside of the scope of the argument.

Part Two

Needs, welfare and political processes

Liberalism does not make the content of preferences
the test of fairness in distribution. On the contrary,
it is anxious to protect individuals whose needs are
special or whose ambitions are eccentric from the fact
that more popular preferences are institutionally and
socially reinforced, for that is the effect and justification of the liberals' scheme of social and political rights. Liberalism responds to the claim that
preferences are caused by systems of distribution,
with the sensible answer that in that case it is all
the more important that the distribution be fair in
itself, not as tested by the preferences it produces.

Ronald Dworkin

5   Needs, interests and power

NEEDS, INTERESTS AND POLITICS

The foregoing discussion provides a useful set of parameters for thinking about needs. It seems, in the light
of the arguments advanced in the previous chapters, that
it is false to suggest that there are no states of the
person that could be called basic or human needs and to
suggest that all needs are entirely morally relative and
the products of a particular moral code. In addition, we
can infer from our account of basic needs that there is a
general obligation to provide resources to meet needs.
However, it is still true to say that there is considerable room for doubt and dispute over what will in fact
satisfy the basic needs for survival and autonomy. Frequently this will be an empirical issue to be settled
between individuals whose moral outlook is the same,
but it would be dangerous to assume that even within a
given society moral and political values held by different groups and individuals are likely to be in agreement over what is going to be an adequate standard of
satisfaction of basic need. Indeed, most of the political disputes about the provision of welfare are likely
to be disputes of this kind, and the pressing of a particular view about the interpretation of need satisfaction
raises issues about power in society and how different welfare policies for the provision of need are put on to the
political agenda. This is so for the following reason.
There must be a relationship between basic needs and interests; while it may be true that a person's interests
are linked with his opportunities to get what he wants
and therefore may vary widely, just because wants may
vary, it must still be the case that for any person
autonomy and survival are generally basic interests
(even if the individual is unaware of this) just because

the satisfaction of these interests is a necessary
condition of pursuing want satisfaction, however an individual's wants are to be construed. Only in so far as
my basic needs are satisfied can I pursue any other wants,
and in this sense basic need satisfaction must be a basic
interest for every person. Only in so far as these basic
interests are satisfied can I attempt to further my other
interests. One way of making this point in the language
of traditional political theory is to say that basic
needs constitute a person's real interests, not in the
sense that a person is possessed of some kind of real self
or real will, which are just forms of mystification, but
rather that there are certain needs or interests which are
logically basic in the sense that their satisfaction is a
precondition of pursuing any other interests.

The linking of needs to interests, though, broadens
the terms of the discussion in that it gives it a much
more clearly political dimension. It is in the political
area that persons seek to articulate and press their
interests on to the political agenda, and others may try
to thwart them. The possibility of articulating interests
and getting them on to the political agenda raises issues
about the nature of power in relation to the specification of interests and needs. These themes will be explored
in this chapter.

As we have seen, while the specification of logically
basic needs and the obligations to which they give rise
can be analysed at one level in a way that avoids morally
and politically contested issues; nevertheless, these
basic needs only allow us to deduce in very general terms
the kinds of obligations that would be laid on society
in terms of welfare provision. Some more specific content
has to be given to the fact that basic needs include needs
for food, shelter, education, medical care, etc., and it
is just at this point that differences both moral and
political are likely to arise. All parties in a society
may well recognize, or can be brought to recognize, the
same basic needs, and recognize that these needs lay some
obligations upon them; but there may still be major disputes about what more specifically these obligations amount
to and how extensive are the resources that have to be
allocated to provision for need satisfaction. This is
true even in the case of things like hunger and shelter,
which are clearly required to meet the basic need of survival. But it does not follow from this that there is any
clear obligation to meet a specific level of satisfaction
of such needs. This point is made implicitly by Basil
Mitchell (1971) in the following passage (p. 215):

Everyone has a biological need for shelter, but when we campaign for Shelter this is not all that we have in mind. We want reasonable standards of housing, and this means *inter alia* some minimum provision for privacy, some access of recreation grounds, etc. In tackling the housing problem we aim to provide not just houses but homes where our standards are already culturally determined.

The recognition of need therefore lays obligations on those who recognize such needs, but it is not clear how extensive these obligations are. On the one hand it might be thought that in many cases this could be settled on the lines suggested in a previous chapter, that is on a purely empirical basis; but equally plausibly, it can be argued that, unless there are unproblematic definitions of the levels of satisfaction required by the recognition of basic needs, then the obligation to satisfy such needs is defective just because those with the obligation will never know when they have discharged it.

This is a crucial point both for theory and practice: for theory in that some critics have argued that needs cannot give rise to rights or human rights just because with traditional human rights it is reasonably clear how far the duties and obligations enjoined by those rights extend, whereas if need satisfaction is indeterminate and likely to be subject to ideological controversy, then the obligations involved may be thought to be so indeterminate as to be irrational. The point is also important for practice, in the sense that some critics, notably Enoch Powell in 'Politics and Medicine' (1966), have pointed out that new advances on medical technology may enable more and more lives to be saved and thus satisfy the need for survival. But does this mean that the state has a responsibility and a duty to provide such technology to all of those whose lives may be saved by it? Here is a matter of crucial importance: to try to determine the standard of satisfaction to which the recognition of need entitles an individual. Another way of putting this point would be to argue that basic needs are always going to have to be interpreted in some way within a particular society and thus in a sense are going to become social needs. Thus the question posed above becomes, what kinds of obligations are there to meet social needs, that is needs with specific standards of satisfaction attached to them, and how are social needs determined and specified within a society? The former question was discussed in chapter 4; the latter question will be considered in the remainder of this and the subsequent chapter.

THE OBJECTIVITY OF SOCIAL NEED

To take the view that social needs can be defined objectively within a particular society assumes a very high
degree of consensus about social norms as these are involved, as we have seen in the specification of need. Of
course, there was during the 1950s and early 1960s a
period in which it was widely thought that some kind of
consensus on social values had been achieved, at least
within Western industrial society. This was the period
in which Daniel Bell wrote 'The End of Ideology' (1960).
Alasdair MacIntyre (1971) has summed up the assumptions
behind this kind of claim in The Ideology of the End of
Ideology (pp. 3-4):

> The central message of this thesis was that in the
> advanced industrial societies of the West ideology was
> at an end because fundamental social conflict was at
> and end ... practical politics must now be a matter of
> pragmatic compromise with an agreed framework of basic
> and not so basic values. This agreed framework depended
> upon a consensus which had been arrived at by means of
> the institution of the welfare state and of the poli-
> tical and economic domestication of the working class.
> The rival and competing interests which had been allowed
> competition within the official political order would
> no longer breed disruptive conflict; and the presenta-
> tion of ideological world views which might inform a
> politics of passionate conflict would henceforth be out
> of place in advanced industrial societies.

In such a situation, the consensus norms of society would
give a relatively unproblematic definition of social need
and hence of the objectives of the welfare state and of
the rights that individuals would be able to claim against
the state. On this sort of basis an account of social
need would draw upon the same value basis held by both
the dominant groups in society and those who were in need.
The civic culture was thought to be relatively homogeneous
in terms of values and thus there would be no basic problem
involved in accounting for social needs as defined and
specified by such norms.

This assumption is now much less plausible than it was,
and in the case of Daniel Bell this criticism has been
made on exactly this issue of social needs and their
definition. Bell was chairman of the Panel on Social
Indicators set up in the USA in 1966 by the Department of
Health Education and Welfare on the instigation of President Johnson. The aim of the Panel was to produce a
document, which eventually appeared in 1968 as 'Toward a
Social Report', which was designed to measure the

performance of society in meeting social needs - the assumption being that these needs could be defined without difficulty with reference to consensus norms. In 'The Coming of Post Industrial Society' (1974) Bell argues as follows (p. 329):

> No society in history has yet made a coherent and unified effort to assess those factors that for instance help or hinder the individual citizen in establishing a career commensurate with his abilities, or living a full and healthy life equal to his biological potential; an effort to define the levels of an adequate standard of living and to suggest what a decent social and physical environment ought to include. The document *Toward a Social Report* is the first step in the effort to make that assessment.

However, this attempt to secure the definition of social need in a consensus way was very severely criticized at a conference organized by the Social Science Research Council in 1968. It was argued by critics of the document that no adequate social theory had been worked out to sustain this position. As one of the critics, Andrew Shonfield, wrote in 'Social Indicators and Public Policy' (1971) (see also Rule, 1971):

> The American faith as revealed in *Toward a Social Report* still rested very heavily on the assumption of a very definite, though sometimes inarticulate, consensus on the major issues of public policy. The readings on the dials could be simple but their significance massive because here everyone agreed over a broad range of social policy about what was desirable and undesirable.

A similar, rather undemocratic, account of the definition of social needs is given by P. Thoenes in 'The Elite and the Welfare State' (1966, particularly pp. 148, 161). At a more philosophical level, Braybrooke's idea of welfare shaped by a census notion in 'Three Tests for Democracy' (1968b) embodies much the same assumptions about agreed norms for social needs, and indeed he carries this point over to argue that ordinary citizens without any particular expertise in either psychology or social administration are able to ascribe social needs to their fellow citizens.

However, Hamilton (1965), Miller (1958) and Parkin (1972) have all produced studies that attempt to show that there is a marked moral pluralism in contemporary Western societies and that the boundaries of these plural moralities are those of social class. This factor is absolutely crucial in this context. Social needs are, on the whole, going to be ascribed to and articulated by members of subordinate groups in society - those who in some way or

other have been pressed to the floor of need within the
socio-economic framework. If there are significant differences in the values of the groups - the dominant
groups who ascribe the needs and the subordinate groups
who articulate them - then each group's conception of the
range of social need may vary with these values. The
norms that define legitimate social need for one group
need not be entirely congruent with the norms of another
group, and so not only the values but also the accounts
of need in question, and thus preconceptions of what constitutes a social problem and what is a legitimate objective of the social services, may be very different.
    This need not in any way be a straightforward dis-
agreement. It may be that the extent of need as ascribed
by policy-makers may be narrower than the felt needs of
those to whom needs are ascribed, and certainly this does
occur and it is one of the rationales of community work to
represent felt needs to policy-makers whose conception of
need may be narrower or in some way different from those
who are the recipients of social service provision. On
the other hand the reverse can hold. In this kind of
context those involved in the formulation of social policy
may well have a wider conception of need than the clients
of social services - perhaps because their view of what is
possible to achieve via social service provision is wider,
but also because of the brute fact that many of those who
are in need seem to be the least aware of their needs.
In 'Relative Deprivation and Social Justice' Runciman
(1972) showed that the poorest section of the population
are hardly aware of their poverty, and as Forder (1974)
says of the study of St Anne's in Nottingham by Coatès
and Silburn, 'the phenomenon of poverty among wage-
earners seems to be self-feeding, in that, the lower a
man's wages, the more deprived he appears to be, the less
aggressively he will construe his needs' (p. 52). Differences in values and differences in what appears to be
possible are going to make differences between conceptions
of need between various groups in society, and it is of
the utmost importance that it should not be assumed at
the outset that there is an agreed consensus over norms or
even the possibilities in a situation.

CONSENSUS, CONFLICT AND THE CONCEPTION OF NEED

Broadly speaking, it is possible to divide up the possible
range of disputes over the definition of social needs into
three main areas.

First of all there is the area of consensus, which
involves a broad acceptance of the general framework of
society, its economic structure and its socio-political
system, distribution of power, status, benefits and burdens. Social needs are then derived from agreed norms of
consumption, etc. Within such an agreed framework, however, there are two possible ways of approaching needs
which may lead to tension but not to dissent fundamental
enough to destroy the consensus. In the first place,
needs may be defined by various administrative experts
acting within the values encapsulated in the general socio-
political set-up, and on this kind of view the definitions
of need may well be thought of as a fairly technocratic
enterprise - the kind of approach to be found in 'Toward
a Social Report'. Particular social services may then be
set up in response to these expert definitions of need.
However, it is of course possible for such technocratic
definitions of need to fail to meet an individual's conception of his own needs or his felt needs, and certainly
this kind of criticism is often encountered in writings
from both the Left and the Right; on the Left because
people should in some sense play a major or determining
part in what they need; on the Right because expert
definitions of need are likely to create bureaucracy, be
paternalistic and generally embody adherence to the maxim
that 'the man in Whitehall knows best' (see Seldon, 1968).
The social services, if set up with reference to expertly
ascribed needs, may well deliver resources incorrectly
just because they fail to match felt needs. However,
while the Left and the Right may accept this, they differ
radically on the solutions involved. Seldon for example
argues that we should abandon talk about housing 'needs',
whether ascribed or felt, and so abandon the provision of
houses as an aspect of welfare policy and return it to the
market, where people's 'felt' needs may be turned into
effective demand. On the other hand, those who wish to
retain talk about needs and the rights that they consider
follow from it are more inclined to insist that there
should be established machinery which would allow an individual's own conception of needs or felt needs to be articulated as a counterweight to, if not actually displacing,
expertly ascribed needs. Two recent reports on community
work, 'Community Work and Social Change' (1968) and
'Report of the Committee on Local Authority and Allied
Personal Services' (1968), have both recognized this and
have regarded the presentation of the felt needs of social
service recipients to policy-makers as an important job
for the community work. Similarly, in 'The Client Speaks'
by Timms and Meyer (1970) a strong argument was developed

which related the sources of misunderstanding between the
client and the social worker about the needs of the client
in his situation to cultural differences between the clients
and the social workers.

It was precisely these possible differences between the
expertly ascribed descriptions of need and the felt needs
of potential recipients of social services that underpin
descriptions of the community workers' role, or at least
part of the their role, as being that of representing the
felt needs of groups to social service departments which
might not otherwise be taken account of. On this view
community work would be seen as a way of opening up communication within the same value framework. The community
worker acts not in such a way as to challenge the general
normative structure of society, but to secure the most efficient identification of need *within* that structure. This
is clearly revealed in the report, 'Community Work and
Social Change': 'It is precisely at this gap [i.e. the
communication of need] that community work comes to interpret to the local authority how the services appeal to the
consumer' (1968, p. 31). New modes of communication represented by the grass-roots representative function of
community workers have to be developed if needs are to be
defined more adequately, and this will include the dissemi-
nation of knowledge about the social services and the attempt to open up to those whose needs are being identified
the possibilities facing them. Very often needs may not
be expressed just because people's perceptions of what is
possible may be diminished or inhibited.

Perhaps the most worked-out policy operating with these
kinds of assumptions has been the American Poverty Programme, in which the poor were supposed to define and
articulate their own needs through participation in community development programmes - but again, the assumption
was that felt needs could be defined within the existing
socioeconomic framework.

These and other movements in social policy, whether we
regard them as window-dressing, mystification, a subtle
form of social control or a real extension of power over
social resources for those who use them, represent an
extension of the idea at least of participation, and thus
of respect for the felt needs of consumers. Even if these
developments are interpreted as measures designed to give
the appearance of control without the freedom that comes
from real control, the idea that the customer knows what
he needs better than the expert must be gaining ground as
an idea, for the tactic of increased participation to be
an appropriate one for authority to employ.

Granted this approach, the failures of the social
services are seen to be the results of a communications
gap; it is not envisaged at all that people's perception
of their own needs could act as a fundamental challenge
to the existing social and political order. Nor is it
suggested that the political and policy-making procedures
and the ways in which these are operated may prevent certain definitions of need being opened up for political
and policy discussions. Questions of power and the political context of need definition are bypassed, and everything is left as basically a problem in communications.
On this view the political and policy-making procedures
are neutral and will respond to felt needs when these
are sufficiently articulated and presented or put on the
political and policy-making agenda. This conception of
community work and its relationship to the political process has been well characterized by John Dearlove (1973,
p. 148):

> Those who argue that groups should use the proper
> channels perpetuate a myth that the only obstacle to
> policy change and a favourable response lies in a
> communication blockage between governors and governed:
> if the policy-makers are given information they will
> respond favourably to a demand grounded in genuine
> social need. It is true that the forces which encour-
> age the selective use of information are likely to
> mean that political decision makers are ignorant of
> many problems and needs, ignoring the existence of
> interests and forces for maintenance, and assume a
> reasonableness and possibility for give and take which
> is often quite lacking. Democratic rhetoric encour-
> ages the public to believe that reasonableness and
> consensus are possible.

The possible discrepancy between expertly ascribed needs
and felt needs not only raises problems about the definition of need in question but also questions the extent to
which it is possible for disadvantaged groups, even with
the help of community workers, to get their own felt
or articulated needs attended to or on to the agenda of
politics or recognized as legitimate needs, and in this
sense issues about the definition and articulation of
need are inseparably bound up with issues of political
power, and the extent to which it is possible for disadvantaged groups to gain access to a political hearing.

It is at this point that a far more radical approach to
the problem of the articulation and ascription of need
gains a foothold. The conception of need that we have
just been examining assumes that the discrepancy, when
there is one, between felt needs and ascribed needs is a

problem of communication and that issues of power play no
great part in the formulation of the difficulties. However, a more radical view may well embody one or both of
two conceptions of need and its relationship to power that
are not allowed under the consensus model. One of these
possibilities is that the power structure of society is
such that some demands or interests based upon felt need
are going to be suffocated at birth or argued out of the
policy and political arena, and that something like community work, helping to articulate such needs, will do
nothing fundamentally to challenge this power structure,
reflecting as it does, on this view, a system of privilege
that may well be challenged by the articulated needs of
active disadvantaged groups. The second possibility is
that, not only will the existing structure of power prevent felt needs from being articulated within the political
arena, but also, the power structure that is both legitimated by and reflected in all kinds of meaning systems -
moral norms, institutions, social rituals, etc. - may so
mould individuals that they are in some sense unaware of
their real needs or the depths of their poverty and deprivation (cf. Runciman, 1972, and Coates and Silburn, 1974).
The first of these possibilities, while radical, is still
reformist and would probably sanction community action
programmes to challenge the power structure with the needs
that the poor and the disadvantaged feel themselves to
have; the second view is more radical and assumes that
people may have needs of which they are unaware, and be in
poverty the depths of which they are unaware of, just
because the conception that they have of themselves and
their opportunities within the existing society is so
restricted by the power and organization of advantaged
groups whose privileges and opportunities would be challenged by the deprived and the needy if only they were
aware of the extent of their need and deprivation. These
two possibilities and their problems will be examined in
some detail.

THE MOBILIZATION OF BIAS AND THE ARTICULATION OF NEED

The first view, as we have briefly indicated, operates on
the assumption that the political and policy-making process is not neutral, that it does represent vested interests, and that its lack of response to those in need is
not just a matter of a failure of communication so much as
a desire to prevent these needs being recognized as legitimate just because the recognition of such needs would
considerably weaken the privileges and undermine vested

interests. Political and social procedures may not be
nautral; they may encapsulate and embody the interests of
some group or groups of people within society who are able
to use the political and social machinery to prevent the
airing of some issues or to neutralize such issues once
they are aired. Schattschneider has characterized this
situation as follows (1960, p. 71):

> All forms of political organisation have a bias in
> favour of the exploitation of some kinds of conflict
> and the suppression of others because organisation is
> the mobilisation of bias. Some issues are organised
> into politics while others are organised out.

The actual organization of a political system or policy-
making process on this view is not neutral, but rather, to
quote Bachrach and Baratz, 'develops a mobilisation of bias,
a set of predominant values, beliefs, rituals and institutional procedures (rules of the game) that operate systematically and consistently to the benefit of certain
persons and groups at the expense of others' (1970, p. 43).
To assume that the reason why the felt needs of groups are
not met is because of a communications gap neglects these
characterizations of the political system, for on this
view the issue is not one of communication but of power.
It might be thought that the exercise of power can take
place, and indeed be identified, only in contexts in which
actual concrete decisions are made that overtly and decisively affect someone's or some group's interests - for
example when in a social service department, local
government or national government an actual decision is
made not to regard a particular group as being in special
need and thus as having no special claims on resources.
Clearly this is an important, empirically detectable,
paradigm case of the exercise of power: an actual observ-
able decision is made that affects the declared felt needs
of a particular group. However, it is equally arguable
that power can be exercised just as decisively but in
covert and much less easy to detect ways. A simple
example based upon and quoted by Bachrach and Baratz may
illustrate this. Members of staff in a university department have tried to work for the reform of the courses
defined by the department and the professor has resisted
these reforms, partly because he dislikes change, partly
because the proposed changes might adversely affect re-
cruitment to his own courses. At no time however has the
professor made an explicit decision to veto the proposed
changes; rather, a whole range of delaying procedures
have been introduced into the structure of the discussion -
the professor has involved issues about academic freedom;
subcommittees have been set up; reforming proposals have

been regarded as running contrary to the spirit of the
university charter; the proposals would require long and
arduous meetings of the faculty board to change regulations;
it is suggested that the proposed changes in courses are
so radical that they would change the identity of the subject and possibly those who are proposing the change would
be more at home in a different department. After a long
period in which some or all of these points are made inter-
mittently, those who are proposing the changes lose heart
and drop them, even though they still take the view
professionally that the proposed changes are in the interest
of the subject. In this kind of context no overt decision
has been taken to oppose or veto the changes; all that has
happened is that procedures, rituals, appeals to the ethos
of the institution and to the 'identity' of the subject
have all been used in such a way that the proposals have
been effectively defeated, and more than this, the experience may have been such to make the performers feel that
it is not really worthwhile to try to push for other
changes in the department in the future. Although no
decision has been taken, procedures, rules of the game and
the values supposedly expressed in the institution have
been mobilized to defeat the proposals, and we may assume
for the sake of the argument to prevent other radical
proposals being made in the near future. In this sense
power has been exercised, albeit in a latent way. Whereas
Dahl and the pluralist have tried to equate power with the
making of key decisions, Bachrach and Baratz have tried to
argue that, even where decisions are not made, power may
still be exercised (1970, p. 44):

> A non-decision, as we define it, is a decision that
> results in the suppression or thwarting of a latent
> or manifest challenge to the values or interests of
> the decision maker. To be more explicit, non-decision
> making is a means by which demands for change in the
> existing allocation of benefits and privileges in the
> community can be suffocated before they are even
> voiced; or kept covert; or killed before they gain
> access to the relevant decision-making arena; or fail-
> ing all of these things, marred or destroyed in the
> decision implementing stage of the policy process.

In their book Bachrach and Baratz try to show that non-
decision-making, although in a sense a non-event, may
still be empirically detected, but of course not as easily
as an actual, public, overt decision. They distinguish
the following possible areas in which power is exercised
but in the absence of an overt policy decision:

(a) A case when force or intimidation is used to stop
     a demand or claim to need being made.

(b)   A kind of positive and negative thinking may be used
      to prevent an issue being voiced - the removal of
      some valued privilege which the potential voicer has
      or a privilege which he will be given if he plays
      the game.

(c)   A case in which the norms or procedures of the
      political system may be used to kill demands. An
      example of the first case would be an attempt to
      stigmatize a demand against the background of
      broadly shared normative agreement - for example,
      branding a demand Trotskyite, or militant; an
      example of the second case would be where an
      established rule of procedure has been broken -
      for example, the withholding of payment. In both
      these cases those who claim need may be stigma-
      tized so that their claim can be safely ignored.

(d)   If demands are made and articulated they can be
      referred to committees or commissions for pro-
      longed study or by steering them through time
      consuming and ritualistic procedures which are
      built into the political system. These kinds of
      procedures may well be effective in the case of
      those whose deprivation makes it unlikely that
      they will have the skills or knowledge of organi-
      zation to be able to navigate themselves effec-
      tively through these procedures.

(e)   Power may also be exercised through the use of
      symbolic appeals - for example, in terms of eco-
      nomic stringency the claims of the deprived may
      be bypassed by appeals for all of us to pull
      together, forget our grouses and 'back Britain' or
      whatever; or conversely, such claims to depriva-
      tion may be symbolically stigmatized - the use of
      the word 'stigma' is potent, hence by designating
      the consequences of a particular claim to need
      being acted upon as a 'scroungers' charter'.

(f)   Administrative or legislative devices may be used
      to bypass claims to need - for example, a parti-
      cular group of tenants who are suffering severe
      deprivation may be denied remedy because landlord-
      tenant relationships are private, or battered
      wives may not receive help because what goes on
      in the matrimonial home between husband and wife
      is regarded as being not a suitable sphere for
      legislature or administrative help.

Although the link between non-decisions and the exercise
of power is a very difficult one, it is surely too strong
to argue as some critics do that as non-overt 'occurrences'
non-decisions and their consequences in terms of the exer-

cise of power are unverifiable and therefore speculative.
The second face of power - that linked with non-decisions -
seems to fit too closely to an everyday experience in institutions and organizations for it to be dismissed as a total
fiction. Nevertheless, however intuitively plausible this
conception of power may be, a good deal of work does still
require doing on its empirical detectability before one
can begin to feel happy with it as a tool in social and
political analysis.

However, leaving aside its status within social and
political science, this conception of power and characterization of the social order that it yields is of the
utmost importance for coming to terms with issues about
needs and deprivation. If one takes the view that this
conception of power is radically mistaken, then of course
the problem of decision-makers responding to felt needs
is only one of articulation and communication; on the
other hand, if one is at all impressed by the mobilization
of bias thesis, then this picture of the way in which
policy-makers respond to needs is much too simple-minded.
Claims to need may be thwarted, stigmatized or admini-
stratively mangled, and in this way kept off the political
and policy agenda. Or they do not reach the level of
being pressed for just because those in need do not think
that it is worth it because of the anticipated reactions
of those who exercise power. At the same time, the needs
ascribed to groups, as opposed to those articulated by the
groups concerned, may well be only those needs that are
consistent with the political and administrative bias in
favour of the generally existing distribution of benefits
and burdens in society. The expertly ascribed needs may
also be part of the same mobilization of bias as Bachrach
and Baratz see as characteristic of the political systems
generally, and just because these ascriptions are backed
up by experts - the social worker, psychologist, town
planner, etc. - ascriptions consistent with this bias will
carry much more weight than the possibly more radical and
less expert emphasis upon felt needs.

In addition, this conception of power would lead one
to be sceptical of at least some forms of political participation that may be recommended as a way in which disadvantaged groups can get their view of their needs put
into the agenda. Certainly Bachrach and Baratz seem to
regard what they term 'co-operative participation' (1970,
p. 206) as yet another way in which the second face of
power appears. Co-operative participation occurs when
numbers of deprived groups are encouraged to participate
in policy-making but within parameters set by those groups
who exercise power - so that their claim to need is

going to have to be interpreted in the light of prevailing values (p. 207):

> Citizen participation is cooperative in nature when
> the activities of non-elites in decision making and
> policy implementation are channelled towards the pre-
> conceived goals of higher authorities. From the
> latter's view to permit the object of cooperative
> participation is to wake the participants' interest
> and enthusiasm and sense of identity with the goals
> of the enterprise in question. The technique can, of
> course,be made to secure the interest only of those
> who set the objectives.

Co-operative participation - perhaps community work involves elements of this - does not challenge the structure
of power and the existing distribution of benefits and
burdens in society, but, on the contrary, it may well
provide procedures for practical socialization in which
the values of those who hold the power in society are
learned and internalized by those who are involved in the
participation. In this way people may learn to identify
their needs or modify their identification of them as a
result of internalizing the goals, norms and conventions
of the existing social and political order through par-
ticipatory schemes. Indeed this point seems to be acknowledged by Bachrach and Baratz in the case of participation
schemes of which they approve (1970, p. 207):

> if effective inroads on the poverty problem are to be
> made, experts in the field - at least during the for-
> mative period - possess sufficient powers of manipu-
> lation to control the situation, in order to select
> the range of suitable policy options and to allow for
> experimentation and innovation (within certain pre-
> scribed boundaries).

If existing social and political organizations do involve
the mobilization of bias, then it would seem that more
extensive participation in the rules of the game, far
from counteracting or challenging the bias, may on the
contrary lead political dissidents to come to learn and
identify themselves with the values and expectations
expressed in the social and political organizations.
Indeed, not only this, but participation schemes may well
develop their own rules and procedures which on the lines
suggested by Bachrach and Baratz may well inhibit or
strangle the original point of the participation process.

To summarize the argument so far, the view that the
felt needs of the poor will find a response within the
social and political process when proper channels of
communication are opened up depends upon a particular
characterization of power and its relationship to the

political system, namely the view that institutions are
neutral and only have to receive the appropriate inputs
of information for a response to be forthcoming. However,
there are other ways of characterizing power and political
and social procedures, which see them as serving the values
of the dominant groups in society as Schattschneider says:
'Whoever decides what the game is about decides also who
and what can get into the game'(1960) - and on what terms.
On this view, as Parkin says (1972, p. 83):

> those groups in society which occupy positions of the
> greatest power and privilege will also tend to have the
> greatest access to the means of legitimation. That is
> to say the social and political definitions of those
> in dominant positions tend to become accepted and
> enshrined in the major institutional orders, so pro-
> viding the moral framework of the entire social
> system.

This kind of characterization of the social and political
system would sanction an approach based upon challenge and
conflict - or community action programme - rather than one
that relied upon opening up the existing system to greater
preoccupation by underprivileged groups without at the
same time undermining the role of those with privileges
in the working of social and political organizations.

CONSCIOUSNESS, HEGEMONY AND THE DEFINITION OF NEED

To see the political system in relation to the recognition
of need in the way first discussed is very radical, but
equally it is possible to carry this argument much further.
The position that has just been discussed assumes that
people do know their needs - their felt needs; their difficulty is getting these needs acted upon once they are
turned into demands or claims either because of the mobilization of bias in the political system, of the fact that,
although people do have the needs, they do not turn them
into demands because from experience they know that the
social and political order will fail to be responsive.
However, a much more radical view would be that people are
in fact unaware of their needs, or that the needs that
they do articulate are in some sense false - people are
encouraged to need certain things as opposed to others,
whereas those needs that are not recognized are the more
important ones. The argument is that in the first case
the deprived suffer from false consciousness - they are
not aware of the depth of their real need - and in the
second place the whole society is thought to embody false
consciousness in the sense that the conceptions of need in

that society - the social needs sanctioned as legitimate
in that society - embody false assumptions about human
beings. For both of these cases it is assumed that there
is a kind of external vantage point from which needs can
be assessed which is independent in the first case of what
particular individuals or groups may think about them and
in the second case of what society as a whole regards as
a legitimate level of need. These assumptions raise very
deep philosophical and epistemological difficulties, which
have to be faced before the view can be fully assessed,
because the standpoint is of the utmost importance for
looking at the role of welfare in modern society; not
only may conventional, socially legitimated needs embody
false assumptions about need, but also these assumptions
cannot, on this account, be counteracted by an appeal to
the felt and socially unrecognized needs of the deprived
because they may equally not realize the extent of their
need.

If we concentrate attention on the latter case first we
can continue the argument like this. What people see as
their needs and what they envisage as being reasonable
satisfactions of those needs are going to rest upon some
sense of what is possible; my definition of my needs and
their satisfaction is going to rest in an important way
upon my view of what it is possible and legitimate and
reasonable to demand in a particular social and political
context. As we have already seen, both needs and wants
are necessarily related to norms and these norms are in
turn going to embody assumptions about social and political possibilities as MacIntyre says (1964, p. 7):

> They do not exist in a vacuum waiting for an object.
> What we desire depends entirely upon what objects of
> desire have been and are presented to us. We learn to
> want things. Our desires have a history and not just
> a biological, natural history, but a rational history
> of intelligible response to what we are offered.

The next step in the argument is to go beyond this and
suggest that for the underprivileged and the deprived their
conception of what is possible and therefore the extent to
which they construe and press their needs is going to depend
upon their social values and their conceptions of the
political and social organizations - in short, upon their
degree of political and social knowledge. At this point
in the argument two possibilities are open. One is to
suggest that the needy and underprivileged, just because
of their lack of education and their rather restricted
view of the social and political possibilities, are apt to
underestimate their degree of need; the other, more
radical, view is to suggest that the values that these

groups have and their conceptions of the political are in
fact going to be defined for them by the dominant socio-
economic groups in society - that their view of their needs
is not thwarted and inhibited just by rather contingent
factors such as their degree of education, etc., but
because their view of what they need is the product of a
social system that works against the possibility of satisfying their real needs. In both of those cases a degree
of false consciousness is being ascribed to those in need
so that they mistake and underestimate the degree of their
need, but in the first case this false consciousness is
regarded as being the result of their subordinate status,
while in the second it is regarded as being a structural
and insidious feature of an alienating social system. In
both cases there is the assumption that the degree of
real need can be ascertained independently of the revealed
'needs' (desires) of those to whom the real needs are
ascribed, and clearly this assumes that there is some external standpoint from which the extent of need can be
estimated which is independent both of revealed or felt
need and of socially ascribed needs. However, the precise
nature of this claim to an objective standpoint is rather
different in the two cases, the first case being a much
more modest account of false consciousness than the other;
the kind of objective standard of assessment of need is
equally more modest and, theorists who hold this view would
argue, more empirical (Runciman, 1970, pp. 219ff). It is
important therefore to look at both of these accounts of
how false consciousness enters into the construal of need
and the different kinds of epistemological assumptions
that are made in each case.

EMPIRICISM AND FALSE CONSCIOUSNESS

The modest, hopefully empirical, approach is best characterized by 'Relative Deprivation and Social Justice'
(Runciman, 1972). In this book Runciman hopes to show
that an ascription of false consciousness can be made on
a broadly factual basis by attempting to construct a
framework of social inequality or three independent dimensions - namely class, status and power - and certainly most
of the evidence assembled to support this framework is
empirical. It is based upon an historical account of
social change from 1918 to 1962. The other side of the
coin is his investigation of people's subjective attitudes
to inequality - their own perception of their deprivation
and thus the extent of their own perceived needs. If we
grant that his account of inequality is objective, then

Runciman argues that those who are deprived do not actually perceive the true extent of their deprivation because they do not perceive the true extent of inequality. An examination of the phenomena of inequality and of the attitudes of those who appear to be deprived to those phenomena tends to lead to the suggestion that their sense of grievance is too inhibited; they are not aware of the real extent of their deprivation and their need - they suffer from false consciousness (p. 293):

> To criticise the relative deprivation which a person says he feels is not ... to dispute what he sees his reference group as having. It is to say that he is in some sense misguided in his choice of want; and it is for this reason that some notion of 'false consciousness' becomes relevant.

Clearly, this is the kind of notion that is brought into play when a person is said not to be fully aware of his poverty or his deprivation. In this way the ascription of deprivation and need goes beyond the individual's own perception of it, and clearly, as we have seen, it is possible to say this kind of thing about need. A man may really need insulin but may not desire it because he is ignorant of his diabetic condition; in the case of need that is under consideration we have to say that a man has greater social needs than he recognizes because he is ignorant about the facts of social inequality. However, in the former case the condition of being a diabetic is in the same sense objective and empirically detectable and there is an empirically established relationship between diabetes and insulin so that taking the latter controls the former. Because of this, the ascription of the need for insulin in the light of the man's diabetes is justified by these empirically detectable relationships. To justify the ascription of false consciousness to individuals about the true extent of their needs would require us analogously to claim that inequality can be measured in an empirical way and, second, that the forms of inequality in question actually *justify* a greater perception of need than is in fact present. That is to say, in order to attribute false consciousness in this sphere we need an objective measure of inequality and an objective assessment of the appropriate level of feelings of deprivation that these inequalities should inspire.

On the face of it there is no particularly intractable difficulty about the first of these requirements. There are clearly difficulties of a technical sort as to how data are to be compared and classified, the inferences to be drawn from statistics; but none the less it is not impossible to document in a way that would command wide

agreement on inequalities of income, inequalities in educational provision, medical care, wealth, social status -
although this latter case might be much more controversial. There will of course be a range of possible social
and political conclusions to be drawn from such evidence,
but it does seem possible to regard the evidence itself
as objective. However, where the difficulties over objectivity appear, as Runciman says (1972, pp. 3-4):

> Once the structure of a society has been examined and
> its patterns of inequalities mapped out, two questions
> at once arise, either of which leads in turn to the
> other: first, what is the relation between institu-
> tionalised inequalities and the awareness or resentment
> of them? And second, which, if any, of these inequali-
> ties ought to be perceived and resented - whether they
> are or not - by standards of social justice?

Again, the question of the actual extent of the awareness
of inequality as empirically set out can be assessed using
empirical techniques, and this Runciman seeks to do via his
survey. But this leads to the core of the problem - the
survey shows that those who are most disadvantaged have
least perception of inequalities, and to say that they
ought to perceive their subordination more clearly, resent
their position more strongly and construe their needs more
aggressively seems to make a moral and not an empirical
judgment, and one that trades on the notion of false
consciousness that people are not aware of the real depth
of their inequality and their real needs. The quotation
cited above shows that Runciman considers that the problem is closely bound up with issues of social justice, and
it is worth quoting at some length his own way of introducing issues about social justice into his discovery of
the variation between perceived and actual inequality
(Runciman, 1972, p. 292):

> Is it legitimate to speak of people's perceptions of
> inequality as distorted or to describe disproportionate
> awareness of inequality as 'envy' or is there no cri-
> terion which could be brought to bear by which the use
> of any such term could be better justified than any
> other? Some social theorists would reply that
> questions of this kind are not only unnecessary but
> unanswerable. In the first place, they would say that
> there are no 'scientific' grounds on which another
> person's wants or aspirations can be assessed and it is
> no business of the academic observer to express his
> personal approval or disapproval of them. In the second
> place some would argue that a notion like justice has
> no meaning beyond what is felt to be just at a parti-
> cular time and place so that it is meaningless to

bring it to bear on what people feel about the inequalities to which they are subject ... as I shall try to
show, a modified version of the contractual theory of
justice can demonstrate in principle what kinds of
grievance could be vindicated as legitimate.

A theory of social justice will then, on this view,
provide the objective standpoint that will enable a
diagnosis of false consciousness about needs, and deprivation to be made (p. 296):

Only a theory of justice, therefore, can provide an
adequate assessment of relative deprivation and in so
doing restate the 'false consciousness' argument in
an appropriate form.... The perception of inequalities can be shown to be unfounded ... if people resent
inequalities which are not unjust, they are illegitimately resenting them; and if they accept or are
aware of inequalities which are unjust, then they are
waiving, as it were, a right to resent them.

Social justice, consciousness and false consciousness
about deprivation and need are very closely related on
this view. The reason why a theory of justice is so
important is that, when attitudes towards inequality are
being assessed, those who are subject to the assessment
are going to have vested interests of some sort of another,
either for changing or for maintaining the existing
structure of the society, and the ascription of false consciousness is going to be bound up with these vested
interests. Those who are especially privileged in the
existing structure of inequality and who take the view
that inequalities represent ineradicable differences in
human capacities and powers will resist the ascription of
false consciousness to those who are in a subordinate
position - 'if they are not resentful', they may say,
'this is the result of their understanding of the social
order and they are contented with their lot'; on the
other hand, if those in the subordinate position construe
their needs aggressively this may equally be related to
their vested interest in change. Without an external
standard of social justice by which social arrangements
can be judged, the likelihood is that ascriptions of
false consciousness about needs are going to be ineradicably subjective. In order to render these descriptions
objective it is necessary to produce a theory of justice
that goes behind vested interests (Runciman, 1970, p. 220):

Once the members of a society *have* interests - and they
cannot but have them from the moment that society is
formed - they cannot be expected to agree on principles
by which conflicts between these interests are to be re-
valued. But if we suppose that such principles have had

to be established before anyone could know what their
interests might be, their agreement is altogether less
implausible.
A contractual theory of justice, which purports to derive
the principles of justice that would be agreed by rational
men acting in ignorance of their specific interests, aims
to provide just this Archimedean point that will allow
objective principles relating to the distribution of benefits and burdens in society to be formulated, on the basis
of which the false consciousness argument could be employed
objectively. John Rawls in his 'A Theory of Justice' (1972)
has provided a version of this kind of contractual approach
which claims to be able to derive principles of justice
from a situation of ignorance about specific vested interests. Rawls's argument is discussed extensively in another
essay in this volume and criticism will be found there, but
the major critical point established in that chapter is
that Rawls's grand philosophical design does not work to
establish a neutral Archimedean point. While the contracting parties in his original position may be ignorant of
their specific interests and features of their own
bodies - lack of physical handicap, intelligence which
could become the basis for specific interests - they are
supposed to know certain general facts about human society:
'they understand political affairs and the principles of
economic theory; they know the basis of social organisation and the laws of human psychology' (Rawls, 1972, p.
137). But these 'general facts' are at least contestable,
and for a marxist for example certain kinds of explanations about the structure of social and political organization may themselves embody particular interests. Such
explanations may be ideological, in the sense of encapsu-
lating assumptions about social groupings and the structure
of politics that serves the interests of a particular
dominant class in society. In the original, contractual
position a rational decision about the just structure of
society has to be made on the basis of this general knowledge, but unless this knowledge - social, political,
economic science - is shown to be non-culturally specific
and non-ideological, the hope for an objective account of
justice, that will serve as an Archimedean point for the
ascription of false consciousness, will be an illusion.
    Such a conception is not going to embody a Rawlsian
Archimedean point from which we can see the human situation from all temporal points of view (1972, p. 587).
Not all questions about false consciousness are answerable questions; on the contrary, the ascription of false
consciousness is not like the GP saying 'He needs insulin
although he does not know it and therefore does not want it';

it is rather an ascription from within a particular moral/
social/political standpoint or ideology, and ideologies
that are contestable. False consciousness and its possibility varies according to one's social and political
perspective: for the classical liberal-utilitarian it can
hardly occur at all (cf. Smart and Williams, 1973; Barry,
1965; and Lukes, 1974). For the radical and marxist,
false consciousness is an endemic feature of a particular
kind of social order in which particular ideological illu-
sions which lead to the wrong or mistaken identification
of one's needs are nurtured and serve the interests of
the dominant class - the encouragement to see deprivation
and social need as a localized, community basis, as
opposed to a structural or class basis, for the marxist
serves the interests of capitalism just because it disguises and conceals the systematic nature of inequality.
To see inequality from a class perspective, as opposed
to a localized community perspective, is to break through
the barrier of false consciousness (Parkin, 1972, p. 90):

> In a way, becoming class conscious, at least in the
> ideal-typical sense, could be analogous to learning a
> foreign language: that is, it presents men with a new
> vocabulary and a new set of concepts which permit a
> different translation of the meaning of inequality
> from that encouraged by the conventional vocabulary
> of society.

However, as Parkin says, 'becoming class conscious', and
therefore breaking through the barrier of false consciousness, 'must often amount to what is eventually a normative
transformation'. This is precisely the point: what constitutes false consciousness, what is seen as breaking
through its barriers, is going to involve assumptions -
its ascription cannot be a straightforward, empirical,
answerable question.

In the situation that we have been discussing, however,
false consciousness is still being construed in a restricted way: granted the facts about the inequalities in the
distribution of social goods, those who are in the subordinate position ought to construe their needs more aggressively; the fact that they do not is accounted for by the
phenomenon of false consciousness. However, there are
ways in which false consciousness can be construed much
more widely than this. Some philosophers, notably Herbert
Marcuse, have argued that the whole conception of what
will satisfy a man's needs in a particular society may be
false - that the whole range of norms relating to human
needs are fundamentally mistaken. This conception of the
extent of false consciousness is radically different from
the first case: in the former situation under-privileged

groups are thought to suffer from false consciousness
in that they construe their needs too narrowly *vis à vis*
the accepted need defining norms of society, but in the
latter case false consciousness - an illusory and mistaken
sense of what a man needs - is thought to be embodied in
the norms relating to need that are widely accepted in
society. In the next two chapters these issues will be
discussed in more detail.

6   Objectivity, social justice and social policy

There are two central, important and intractable logical
difficulties that seem to face debate in the area of
social policy. First, people can disagree about the
important features of a social situation, both in description and evaluation. This is hardly surprising, since
it is the framework wherein one structures phenomena that
tells one which are significant, and no framework is logically compelling. The other way of looking at it is to
argue that any explanatory (or evaluative) account (so
long as it is organized and is not circular) must begin
somewhere. What if we differ on some basic premise?
These are not derived from any further premise (otherwise explanation would go on for ever) and cannot be
empirical (since they are used to order data). At this
stage argument reaches an impasse in rational discourse,
both in analysis and evaluation.

These difficulties rarely intrude on the discussion of
social policy, since the existence of traditions that
take a particular standpoint for granted stands in the
way. There are in common use at least four ways of coping
with the problem that we may agree neither on the key
facts, nor on the explanation, nor on the evaluation of
a state of affairs. First, one may plump for a particular framework on grounds of elegance, or explanatory power,
or convenience, or prejudice, or interest. A good example
of this approach is contained in 'Coventry Community
Development Project's Final Report' (1975, part 1):

Our conclusions are controversial and (in a traditional
sense) they cannot be 'proved' from the work we have
done. Their correctness, or otherwise, has to be
judged by the cogency of the analysis and its capacity
to explain observed contradictions; the consistency of
the strategies which flow from the analysis; and the
effectiveness in practice of the lines of action suggested or tried out.

Second, one may ignore the fact-value disjunction: thus
a world of middle-range theory, comfortably unaware of the
morass on which it is founded. Much case-study analysis
in social administration is based on this sort of approach.
A recent publication (Hall *et al.*, 1975, pp. 4-5) states:
> Having completed our case-studies we have, with refer-
> ence to our broad conceptual framework, tried to formu-
> late middle-range propositions about how and in what
> particular circumstances certain issues attain pre-
> dominance over others.... We are, of course, conscious
> that these propositions leave much still unexplained....

Third, there is the phenomenological perspective,
embracing the diversity of analysis as the ultimate level
of understanding. Carrier and Kendal (1973, p. 221) claim:
> This alternative approach directs our attention to the
> questions of whose definitions of reality are embodied
> in 'welfare legislation', whose particular concepts of
> 'society and social problems' are involved in the
> policy-making process.... Recognition is then given to
> the different frames of reference, different perspec-
> tives of reality ... different versions of the issues
> at stake....

Finally, there is the quest for the security of a framework that is uniquely cogent - digging for bedrock on which
to lay foundations. This approach has a finality in argument that makes it especially attractive to writers on
social policy. If it seems reasonable to maintain, with
Rawls (1972) that 'justice is the first virtue of institutions' (p. 3), and we can find an unequivocal method of
establishing what is meant by justice; we have a secure
basis for critical evaluation. This chapter examines the
use of Professor Rawls's theory of justice as fairness
made in studies of social policy by Runcimen, Pinker, and
George and Wilding.

The theory is powerful and influential. It is unquestionably the most important development in theorizing on
social justice for some time. It is also, we believe,
flawed. How to explain its success? Discussion of the
theory will be followed by a critique of the role it plays
in reinforcing a particular view of society, and of solving
certain problems that are forced on students of social
policy in contemporary welfare states. Close analysis of
'justice as fairness' in theory and in application will
perhaps reveal the role it has been called upon to play
in ideology.

THE RESPONSE TO THE THEORY OF 'JUSTICE AS FAIRNESS'

The series of papers that culminated in the masterpiece
'A Theory of Justice' (Rawls, 1972) has certainly had
tremendous impact. In a select bibliography of critical
studies covering the brief period from 1971 to early 1975,
Daniels (1975, pp. 348-50) lists sixty articles and one
book. Moreover, the report has reverberated beyond the
cloisters of academic philosophy. The 'New York Review
of Books', the 'New York Times Book Review', 'The Times
Literary Supplement', 'The Nation', the 'Observer Review'
and 'The New Statesman' all carried commendatory major
reviews. Hampshire (1972) wrote: 'I think this book is
the most substantial and interesting contribution to moral
philosophy since the war' (p. 34). 'The Times Literary
Supplement' described the book as 'the most notable contribution to the tradition of Western political philosophy
since Sidgwick and Mill'. Daniels suggests a number of
reasons for this unparalleled impact.
     First, Rawls represents 'a welcome return to an older
tradition of substantive rather than semantic moral and
political philosophy' (Daniels, 1975, p. xi). However,
this does not mean that he abandons 'the sophisticated
apparatus and techniques of the professional philosopher'.
The argument of the book relates moral concerns to the
theories of the social scientist, particularly the eco-
nomist, the social psychologist and the student of welfare.
Thus its special relevance to the student of social policy.
Most important, the goal of the book is to commend a particular (and impressive) theory of justice - to produce a
persuasive and coherent framework for it: 'Moral philosophy is socratic: we may want to change our present considered judgements once their regulative principles are
brought to light.... A knowledge of these principles may
lead to further reflections that lead us to revise our
judgements' (Rawls, 1972, p. 49; see also p. 53). In a
spirited return to what had seemed to be the bankrupt
tradition of liberal political thought, 'A Theory of
Justice' poses questions that are central to all contemporary political philosophy. Even Crick (1972) describes
it as 'profoundly wrong, but perfectly relevant' (p. 602).
     The influence of the theory on writers on social policy
extends far beyond the three principally considered here.
Titmuss (1974, pp. 149-50), Harvey (1973, chapter 3),
Crosland (1974, p. 1), Smith (1977, *passim*) and others
have stressed its importance. This chapter will consider
the job that the theory does in justifying a particular
moral standpoint and hence a particular approach to welfare.

First, let us consider the theory as a structure of concepts rather than as an ideological weapon.

RAWLS'S THEORY

This discussion of some of the major aspects of a complex,
erudite and highly subtle work must necessarily be brief.
Rawls presents his approach as an alternative to either
utilitarian or intuitionist accounts of justice. The
utilitarian position generally maintains that justice is
an accommodation of two principles - one concerned with
the maximization, the other with the distribution of the
good. The classical formulation is 'the greatest good of
the greatest number'. As such, the theory has arguably
had great influence on the uneasy balance between prag-
matism and liberal reform that constitutes the intellectual tradition of British social policy. One problem
is the relation between the two propositions - the trade-
off between equality and the sum of welfare. Rawls however attacks utilitarianism on the grounds that 'it does
not take seriously the difference between persons' (1972,
p. 27). One man's meat is another man's poison - so how
can we know when we're maximizing the good, and what is to
count as equal distribution?

Intuitionism is the assertion that the propositions that
define justice are simply (and unaccountably) known to us.
This may be true. It does not advance the debate without
some means of discriminating when intuitions happen to
clash.

The object of 'A Theory of Justice' is to propound and
justify a particular definition of the term 'social
justice'. Rawls avoids the pitfall of attempting to formulate more or less convincing principles of justice. This
procedure simply lays one open to broadsides from those who
happen to use the word differently. Instead, principles
are derived by thought-experiment through a process that
sets them on a footing independent of the author's values.
We are asked to imagine a hypothetical situation so engineered that the principles that men would choose in it
cannot appeal to us as anything but principles of fairness.
Rawls claims (1972, p. 11):

> They are the principles that free and rational persons,
> concerned to further their own interests, would accept
> in an initial position of equality as defining the
> fundamental terms of their association ... we are to
> imagine that those who engage in social cooperation
> choose together in one joint act the principles which

are to assign basic rights and duties and to determine
the division of social benefits ... the foundation
charter of their society.

It is on the account of this position that the compelling
nature of the theory rests. An approach founded foursquare
on an appeal to 'free and rational' choice seems to offer
a foothold in the morass of relativism. The theory has
provoked widespread interest outside academic philosophy
in a way that other approaches to justice have not. Hare's
'Freedom and Reason' (1963), which, as Barry points out
(1973, pp. 13-14), reflects many features of Rawls's
approach, or Miller's (1976) thoroughgoing and in some
ways more sophisticated attempt to relate moral to social
theory (especially chapter 1), are scarcely mentioned by
writers on social policy. Rawls's presentation of the
original position is of crucial importance. How does
it go?

The details are spelt out in accordance with the principle of attaining 'reflective equilibrium' between theory
and judgment. The principle, in this context, requires
that the outcome of a moral theory should agree with our
considered moral judgments. Thus, a valuable method of
proceeding is to adjust the basis of the theory until it
produces results that accord with judgments. Moral opinion may itself be modified as a result of this creative
interplay with a convincing theory. The upshot is that
Rawls is fully justified in imposing any conditions that
his readers will accept in constructing his hypothetical
thought-experiment in such a way as to achieve the desired
conclusion. The recipe for the original position is care-
fully designed to produce the principles of justice.

THE ACCOUNT OF THE ORIGINAL POSITION

The theory asks us to imagine that men abstracted from
their social roles meet together to formulate the social
order - the distribution of relative rewards and deprivations between social positions - that they would regard
as acceptable. These hypothetical negotiators have no
idea what position in the society they are constructing
they will themselves come to occupy. Essentially, the
conditions are those of enforced impartiality. Rawls
argues that agreements freely negotiated under these
imaginary circumstances - compulsory fair play - would
necessarily fulfil the canons of what we mean by justice.
A man who doesn't know who is going to occupy the social
positions among which he distributes advantages can
scarcely be accused of making choices biased in anyone's

favour - and an unbiased judgment is surely fair. Thus
principles of justice derive from rational agreement, and
it must in principle be possible to predict the kind of
rational agreement the unbiased negotiators would make.
The theory is a theory of social contract, yet the ultimate
basis of the contract we imagine people would arrive at is
in their universal human rationality. This sets Rawls
firmly in an idealist tradition. As Hampshire points out
(1972), 'there seems in Rawls to be an illegitimate (and
Kantian) contrast between the essential rational man and
his accidental trappings' (p. 36). The attraction of the
theory is analytic, but its product is an engine for the
critique of values in the social order. If to achieve
this end we strip man of everything but his rationality
in order to be able to predict the moral principles that
would be decided on, the question arises of how reasonable
it is to expect to deal in principles at all. 'Everything
turns on what can be extracted from the concept of
rationality. But here "Catch-22" pops up again, for what
can be extracted can only be what is put in' (Barry, 1973,
p. 27; cf. p. 22). Rawls's attempts to grapple with this
problem lead both to difficulties in the specification of
the original position, and to problems in anticipating
the kind of judgments rational men might reasonably be
expected to make in it.

   First, it is tempting to suggest that men denied access
to knowledge of their own interests in society by the
'veil of ignorance' should know absolutely nothing about
the society under negotiation. Ignorance guarantees
impartiality. However, with the tool of reason, but no
grist other than hypothetical debating positions, men
might settle on all manner of distribution of advantage
and disadvantage. The order chosen might simply not work
at all, or the results of a given structure might be different from what our ignorant arbiters anticipated. Those
who thought cash incentives important to secure economic
growth and maximize the welfare cake would argue for a
different structure of rewards than those who didn't.
Both views cannot be correct. To generalize, so long as
relevant assumptions about the workings of social organizations are accepted, any social order could be fixed upon
as optimal. The rules we concoct to describe the operation
of a social system are at the same time limits to the via-
bility of redistribution. Does anything go as social
justice?

   Rawls concludes a lengthy discussion of the problem
(1972, p. 137):

   It is taken for granted that [the primitive nego-
   tiators] know the general facts about human society.

They understand political affairs and the principles
of economic theory; they know the basis of social
organisation and the laws of human psychology. Indeed
the parties are presumed to know whatever general
facts affect the choice of principles of justice.

Here is a problem. The 'knowledge' of the social and behavioural sciences on how people work in society is not
undisputed fact, like a laundry list or (some would say)
the knowledge interpreted by physical science. Key issues
are essentially disputed - which is why we became interested in the construction of a theory of social justice
to assess different interpretations of the facts relevant to understanding social policy in the first place.
The debate on incentives, growth and welfare is not only,
as the recent furore over the 'cuts in the social services' attests, a red-hot contemporary issue; it is an
issue that has recurred in discussion of state welfare
since its emergence in industrial society. On the macro-
level, Althusser and Talcott Parsons, both major struc-
turalists, would wish to insert rather different recipes
for the working of the social order behind the veil of
ignorance. No compelling rational process for preferring
the one to the other has been found. There is a problem
about deciding what knowledge should be made available to
the negotiators in the original position without assuming
what we want to prove.

The second problem is to do with how closely we can
restrict the range of decisions that the hypothetical contractors might conceivably arrive at. Even given an undisputed social science, what is to stop the disputants,
as students of games theory (or rational gamblers), from
constructing social orders in which some are benefited
grossly at the expense of others? Rawls argues (1972,
p. 149) that the parties

have no incentive to suggest pointless or arbitrary
principles. For example, none would suggest that
special privileges be given to those exactly six feet
tall, or born on a sunny day.... No-one can tell
whether such principles would be to his advantage.

However, the odds are such that it is eminently rational
to desire a world in which a large group of drones is
supported by a smaller group of helots - or in which a
large *rentier* middle calss is relatively advantaged at the
expense of a smaller, efficiently exploited working class.
The chances are that such principles would be to the advantage of any given individual. So much for rationality!

The force of this argument extends beyond the illustra-
tions of rational societal choice. If 'rational' means
'self-interested' the question of what is to be counted

as in a person's interest, and of how we can anticipate
the judgments of interest of rational negotiators, must
be answered. It is hard to see why it doesn't make sense
to construct any social order on a gambler's throw, if you
should choose to, since how you calculate the odds must
depend on how you evaluate the desirability of occupying
one social position as against another. The relative
weighting of social position is not quantifiable by a cal-
culus of universal rules, but depends on preference. In
this sense, there is nothing irrational about backing your
fancy. Tastes differ - as Rawls himself points out in his
critique of utilitarianism.

The theory of primary goods and the 'thin theory of
the good' that underlies it are designed to restrict the
range of choice of the original negotiators. Rawls asks
the question, how can the contractors 'decide which conceptions of justice are most to their advantage? Or must
we suppose they are reduced to mere guessing?' (1972,
p. 142). The solution is to inject into rationality a
notion of human wants: 'primary goods ... are things
which it is supposed a rational man wants, whatever else
he wants' (1972, p. 92). Can the primary social goods
that will direct the decisions of men who do not know what
positions in society they will themselves come to occupy
be satisfactorily specified? Such a list presupposes the
asocial view of man that divorces his appraisal of social
benefit and disadvantage totally from his social environment. Barry (1973, pp. 27-9) demonstrates that Rawls's
claim that 'other things being equal, human beings enjoy
the exercise of their realised capacities, and this enjoyment increases the more the capacity is realised, or the
greater its complexity' (1972, p. 426) is inherently implausible, as an account of an underlying principle to all
men's lives. There is nothing incredible in the rumour
that Wittgenstein sometimes preferred western comics and
horror movies to philosophical speculation.

An earlier attempt to specify 'primary goods' seems
more appealing. This is the claim that all men value
highly 'rights, liberties, opportunities and powers, income
and wealth' (Rawls, 1972, p. 92) - a list later extended to
include 'self-respect and a sure sense of one's own worth'
(p. 396). Few would disagree that this is true of most
advanced Western capitalist societies - though not of substantial minorities within those societies. However, that
is not the point. The problem is how such a theory of the
good enables us to predict what rights and liberties, what
structure of opportunities, what range of powers, what
income distribution and, most problematic of all, what
trade-off between the primary goods in those situations

where they come into conflict the primary negotiators
would find acceptable. We do not need to use examples
from unfamiliar societies, such as that of the Kwakiutul
Indians, where honour is considered far more important
that wealth (a marked contrast with the America of, say,
Nixon) to show that the universal rational judgment does
not exist. Hippies and shift-workers presumably display
rather different preferences between leisure and income.
Which is irrational? It is hard to see how Rawls' theory of
primary goods can provide a way of discriminating between
such judgments - unless it simply expresses a particular
set of values. Otherwise, the argument would have to be
like a perpetual motion machine, grinding the energy of
values from the circular process of pure reason.

We shall pass over a number of other criticisms of the
theory which are largely irrelevant to my interest in its
application to the study of social policy. The reader is
referred to Nozick's discussion of the limitations of the
notion of distributive justice (1974, chapter 4), to
Barry's Rawls primer (1973) and to Daniels's useful collection of essays (1975).

Rawls derives two basic principles of justice (1972,
pp. 150-1): 'a principle establishing equal liberty for
all, including equality of opportunity, as well as an
equal distribution of income and wealth' and the principle
that 'inequalities are permissible when they maximise, or
at least contribute to, the long-term expectations of the
least fortunate group in society'. Agreement on the
former is explained by the argument that 'it is not reasonable for [any individual] to expect more in a division
of social goods, and it is not reasonable for him to accept
less...', on the latter as rational insurance less the
worst befall. However, it seems eminently reasonable to
allow more social goods to some and less to others - and
be blowed to insuring against the chance of being worst
off, so long as the chances of being better off seem
acceptably high. Acceptability depends not only on a
rational and predictable science of probability, but also
on the relative weighting of prize and penalty. This is
a matter of judgment. To make the model work, we have to
know for certain how people judge - and we don't.

The impact of these criticisms is to argue that the
theory cannot be stated in such a way that it does the
job that students of social policy want done - founding
principles of justice on the peculiar ultimacy of reason.
The tinkering necessary to produce a satisfactory theory
of justice involves the assumption of undisputed social
science and the circularity of basing justice on values
concealed within an interpretation of rationality. None

the less, as Barry (1973, pp. 166-7), Miller (1976, pp. 49-50), Crick (1972, p. 602), Hampshire (1972, pp. 34-9) and Lukes (1974, pp. 183-4) point out, Rawls's theory is an excellent summary of how the concept of justice is typically used in what has been a major Western cultural tradition. 'In the end the "Archimedean point" for judging the basic structure of society that Rawls seeks eludes him.... Rawls' achievement, which is considerable, is indeed to have produced a theory of justice – a theory of liberal, democratic justice' (Lukes, 1974). How has the theory been used in the analysis of social policy?

Runciman uses the theory as a yardstick to assess the justification of inequalities in British society and the perception of those inequalities by citizens. Pinker uses Runciman in order to demonstrate that a particular approach to the evaluation of social policy based on the judgments of ordinary citizens can be made to work. George and Wilding use the theory of justice to underpin the contention that social policy has failed to achieve expressed objectives because 'radicals' have ignored its potential as a lever for political change. All three share a common desire to establish the centrality of particular values in social analysis. The net effect of such a use of Rawls has been to reinforce a tradition of analysis that minimizes class conflict perspectives. This coincides with the development of political and economic systems that necessarily tend to emphasize consensus on social goals and on methods of attaining them.

RUNCIMAN

In the most profound study of values and inequality in the postwar period, Runciman (1972) is concerned to plot the extent of false consciousness. Do people feel the sense of grievance that evidence on inequalities between groups in society would suggest they should? A framework of social inequality structured along the three independent dimensions of class, status and power is presented. Runciman in fact refers the categorization to Weber (Runciman, 1972, p. 44). However, Weber writes of class, status and party, and maintains that 'classes, status-groups and parties are phenomena of the distribution of power within a community' (see Gerth and Mills, 1948, p. 181). This raises the question of the validity of Runciman's assumption that the categories he uses are on the same logical level. Social inequality may well be a more complex phenomenon than his diagram suggests.

Evidence on existing inequalities and on perceptions
of them is assembled from a historical study of social
change covering the period from 1918 to 1962 and a questionnaire survey carried out in 1962. In effect, Runciman
constructs an 'objective' three-dimensional map of class,
status and power inequalities, and corresponding subjective
maps from the viewpoint of individual citizens from different social groups. By comparing the two, he is able to
show that (on the assumptions implicit in his use of empirical data) people do not perceive the true extent of
social inequality.

However, we need a further element to enable us to discuss how far a sense of grievance is justified by existing inequalities, the element that a 3D metaphor of the
distribution of social inequalities tempts us toward. An
ideal map of what the topography of advantage ought to be
is supplied by Rawls's theory. The status of the work is
thereby altered from a commentary on phenomena to an assessment of injustice. Runciman concludes that the range of
inequality is far greater than Rawls's standards would permit. The sense of grievance at inequality is less than
what is justified. False consciousness is charted fact.

If Rawls's theory of justice does not deliver the goods,
we are left with a simple chronicle of phenomena to interpret how we will. The problem of false consciousness
remains: any evaluation of social policy that describes
people's moral perceptions as out of tune with reality is
vulnerable to the demand that it justify its standpoint.
Lukes describes the picture of 'a just society with the
social and economic lineaments of twentieth century
Britain' based on Rawls's theory of justice with which
Runciman concludes his discussion, and comments (1974)
'one striking feature of this picture is its essential
contestability ... yet Rawls' aim is to eliminate this
very contestability.... Rawls' "thought-experiment" cannot
establish the truth of the theory which it advances'
(pp. 182-3).

Thus there are problems in using the theory of justice
as a touchstone to transmute the shifting sands of what
people feel about social inequalities to the firm bedrock of charted false consciousness. Pinker approaches
the problem of explaining the persistence and mapping the
dimensions of false consciousness from the opposite
direction, by questioning how far the theorist's description of social reality accords with the criterion of
popular perceptions. Rawls and Runciman furnish the pivot
for turning theory on its head.

PINKER

The exposition in 'Social Theory and Social Policy'
(Pinker, 1971) is so close-woven that the structure of the
argument becomes clearer when traced in reverse order -
from conclusion to premise. Chapters three and four contain the kernel of the argument. We shall discuss four
before three.

Pinker (1971) argues: 'Titmuss's great contribution
has been to identify stigma as the central issue, and to
define the main practical task of social policy as that
of finding ways to differentiate welfare provisions without stigmatizing recipients' (p. 136). His project is to
elaborate the theory of stigma, and to maintain its fundamental importance. A model of stigma in the welfare state
is presented in the closing sections of chapter four,
based on the detailed analysis of a wealth of evidence
from social anthropology, social psychology and theories
of gifting. It is interesting to recall Crick's (1972)
comment that '"justice as fairness" is too simply a set
of unconditional, asocial transactions between individuals' (p. 602) and Pinker's (1971) derivation of a 'model
of welfare' from 'a major premise akin to a psychological
proposition' (p. 170) - namely that in systems of exchange
it is always less prestigious to receive than to give.

Unlike most other theorists in this area, Pinker fails
to develop a clear distinction between felt stigma - a
psychological feeling of devaluation - and stigmatization - the social process whereby certain individuals are
devalued. The question at issue is limited to 'why
stigma is experienced, and what are the conditions ...
under which it is most likely' (Pinker, 1971, p. 136).
Felt stigma is attitudinal, stigmatization structural;
the former is the reflexive refusal to accept equal
citizen status, the latter the transitive denial of this
status to another. An approach that minimizes consideration of stigmatization is doubly surprising, in view of
Pinker's repeated use of phenomenological frameworks
derived from the work of Berger and Luckman (1967), which
turn on the necessary interdependence of social and
individual levels of analysis in social science. In
fact, footnote references to Berger and Luckman's book
outnumber references to any other work in this chapter.
The result is that analysis of the role of stigma in
society, and investigation of the social interests served
by the existing pattern of stigma, are limited. Society
reduces to the sum of individuals; social phenomena, to
the sum of individual perceptions. The sociology and
political science of stigma is reduced to the social
psychology of stigma.

The two aspects of stigma are mutually independent.
Goffman (1968) discusses the way in which the victim of
felt stigma avoids stigmatization by concealing his
'spoilt identity' from society (chapters 1 and 2).
Equally, Rose (1973) describes how claimants' unions
deny felt stigma in the attempt to transfer the social
process of stigmatization 'from the poor individual to
the rich society that condones it' (p. 413).

If felt stigma and stigmatization are confused, it is
possible to interpret stigma solely in terms of the location and definition of individual dependency in society.
Capitalist work-ethic values deny the citizenship of the
person who fails - and is seen to fail - to pay his way,
the argument runs. In so far as he internalizes these
values, the victim will himself deny his equality, himself take on the garb of stigma. Such an approach diverts
attention from the role of stigma, considered at the level
of social fact rather than social meaning. Piven and
Cloward (1971, p. 177) argue that stigmatization facili-
tates exploitation:

> Harsh relief practices also maintain work norms by
> evoking the image of the shamed pauper for all
> (especially the able-bodied) to see and shun. And
> so it is, if the justification given for welfare
> practices is usually moral, the functions these
> restrictions serve are typically economic.

Dearlove (1974, p. 24) claims that:

> Applications for welfare benefits are 'degradation
> ceremonies', and it is hardly surprising that the poor
> do not apply for their rights because it places them in
> situations where they are judged, evaluated, tested for
> eligibility; and where their honesty and character are
> cast in doubt. Rules and regulations do not float
> free of the economic and social structure, and the
> system of welfare benefits enforces and polices the
> work system.

Jordan (1973), Kincaid (1973) and Coates and Silburn
(1974) maintain that the stigmatic operation of the welfare system serves to divide groups whose true interests
are identical. This perspective has been reinforced by
the detailed empirical studies of the National Community
Development Project (for instance: Community Development
Project Interproject Editorial Team, 1977, pp. 38-42;
Community Development Project London, pp. 50-7; Taylor-
Gooby, 1977, pp. 7-8).

To take these phenomena of stigma into account, a theory
that discusses the balance of power in society, and has a
place for the interpretation of policy in terms of whose
interests are served and why, is useful. However, such an

approach would take us beyond the notion of stigma as
itself the 'central issue' - the place where discussion
of social policy begins. It would also take us beyond
Pinker's 'model of social welfare', which is exclusively
concerned to identify three factors that account for the
incidence of felt stigma. To locate stigma and stigmatization in society, we need a model of society. To understand how Pinker restricts the discussion of stigma to
the analysis of values and their internalization, we must
understand how the values held by ordinary people are
given a pre-eminent place in his framework. To do this we
must trace in detail the argument of the third chapter
of 'Social Theory and Social Policy' (Pinker, 1971).

'The main theme of this chapter is to explore the role
of value judgments today in the making of social policy
and the examination of welfare problems' (Pinker, 1971,
p. 97). Rawls's theory and theories like it are crucial
to Pinker's analysis of these issues. The theme domi-
nates four sections. In the first, Pinker distinguishes
the notions of 'normative' and 'ideological' theory. The
second contains a paradigm of the use of this distinction
in clarifying the debate between relative and absolute
conceptions of poverty. The third analyses and dis-
misses frameworks employed by the 'new Left'. The fourth
is concerned with the relation between democracy and the
social sciences. There are two minor themes: the use of
values in normative and ideological theorizing, and the
extent to which students of social policy pay attention
to what most people actually think.

'Normative theory tells us what will happen if we do
x rather than y, but it also states explicitly or implicitly which end of action we ought to prefer when there is
a choice of ends' (Pinker, 1971, p. 127). Ideological
theory, by implication, sets values before empirical data
on the association of phenomena, and obscures the distinction between values and data. Pinker warns that: 'the
danger in all forms of theorizing and model-building in
social policy is that sociologists may confuse their own
constructs with the subjective reality of ordinary users'
of the social services (1971, p. 98). Titmuss is praised
both because he makes his value position explicit, and
because 'more than any other theoretician in this field,
Titmuss is able to evoke the subjective realities of
everyday life for the poor' (Pinker, 1971, p. 101). It
would seem however that values are central to both normative and ideological theory, if preferred ends are under
discussion. Can the distinction be maintained?

Pinker gives a paradigm of normative theory: 'Bowlby's
theory of maternal care and deprivation is a good example

of the way in which scientific enquiry in the social
sciences is inspired rather than bedevilled by value-
factors' (p. 127). However, Mead (World Health Organization, 1962, p. 58) points out that:
     the effects [of Bowlby's original monograph] have been
     partially nullified, by the reification into a set of
     universals of a set of ethnocentric observations on our
     own society, combined with assumptions of biological
     requirements which are incompatible with homo sapiens,
     although possibly compatible with an earlier stage when
     a two-year-old could fend for himself and the family
     did not exist.
Wootton (1959 - see also World Health Organization, 1962,
pp. 63-73) has produced a substantial critique of cultural
bias of Bowlby's work and of its tendentious influence on
social work theory. The extent to which we regard value
factors as inspiration or bedevilment in such theorizing,
particularly when applied to practical social policy-
making, would seem to depend very much on our own preferences and attitudes. How is the normative evaluation of
empirical phenomena to be rescued from a critique that
demolishes ideological evaluation? Pinker's approach to
this problem is demonstrated in his discussion of the 'new
Left' theory in the third section.
     Marcusan critical theory contrasts the 'false' needs
of individuals created by 'particular social interests in
their repression', with their 'true' needs that lie in
the realms of possibility. 'The world of facts is one-
dimensional' (Marcuse, 1967, p. xi). The object of
theorizing is 'to break through the concreteness of op-
pression in order to open mental space in which this
society can be seen for what it is and what it does'
(Marcuse, 1969, p. 81). The yardstick by which reality
is judged is transcendent, and grounded only in a particular theory of society. Pinker (1971) argues against the
'new Left' assertion: 'what men desire is the product of
their social situation'; that 'propositions of this
order are ... no more provable than those that underlie
the procedures of psychoanalysis, where the therapist's
diagnosis is vindicated as much by the patient's denial
as by his acceptance of its validity' (p. 119). Leaving
on one side the question of whether the most formidable
left theorists hold such a deterministic position,
Pinker's point is certainly well made. Later he claims
(1971, p. 125): 'by confusing normative theory with
ideology and rhetoric, and through the misuse of concepts
like alienation and false consciousness, a tenuous but
bogus relationship is maintained with both democracy and
scientific procedure' by 'new Left' social critics. The

real question is whether anyone else has found a solution
to the problem - whether social science can be done in a
'democratic' and 'scientific' manner without the assumption of consensus in social values and positivism in the
analysis of social phenomena.

It is not clear how policy is to be assessed, if not
through the use of the values favoured by the theoretician in question. Pinker's strategy is to rule out of
court all theorizing based on abstract constructs, by
focusing attention on what citizens actually believe. The
beliefs of members of society have a 'democratic' reality
superior to that of the beliefs of social scientists. One
such is the notion of 'felt stigma' as a 'subjective
reality', as against the social process of stigmatization. There is a clear and obvious sense in which the
experience of the former is an immediate and inescapable
element in the consciousness of the stigmatized individual.
Apprehension of the 'social fact' of the latter may be
confined to the social scientist. It is by appeal to the
consciousness of 'the man in the Rover 2000 and the old
age pensioner in the Clapham omnibus' (Pinker, 1971, p.
169) that stigma as interpreted by Pinker becomes the 'central issue' in social policy analysis.

Leaving aside the arguments of those who question whether we can have access to the subjective reality of various social groups, and whether there is sufficient coherence for our purpose in such perceptions, there are
further problems with Pinker's approach. The point is
well put by Stedman Jones (1967): 'Those who tried to
create theory out of facts never understood that it was
only theory that could constitute them as facts in the
first place' (p. 42). Pinker is compelled to find an
independent argument to buttress his appeal to the views
of ordinary people; the mere description of these views
does not constitute substantive social theory. Pinker
quotes Stedman-Jones, and continued (1971, p. 120):

It does remain open to other theorists to question the
way in which a given body of facts is selected and
interpreted. It is incumbent on social theorists,
who place so great a reliance upon unsubstantiated inferences about human psychology, either to provide
better causal explanations about the nature of human
personality and motivations, or to recognize the hypothetical nature of their claims.

However, if the claims of marxists are to be seen as
conditional on unsubstantiated premises, the same would
seem to apply to other writers. Pinker is as vulnerable
as anyone else to phenomenological reduction.

It is not clear how ideological value-bases that direct
and mould analysis of social reality can be distinguished
from normative value-bases in such a way that the former
are demonstrated to be inadequate and the latter adequate.
A solution to this problem is implicit in the discussion
of relative and absolute notions of social need in the
second section of the chapter. Pinker argues: 'the
relative definition of social needs can be seen as an
ideological attempt to provide the kind of empirical
evidence that will justify radical social reform' (p.
110). Why is a relative approach grounded in any more
ideological assumptions than an absolute one? Because
it does not take account of the subjective reality of
ordinary people. Therefore 'we need better maps of the
current levels of satisfaction and discontent, and more
convincing explanations of why people hold the range of
attitudes and expectations they do' (p. 133). Pinker
describes Runciman's attempt to chart inequality and
grievance with approval, and concludes (1974, p. 115):

> It is these brute facts of relative social contentment
> or indifference to even modestly bourgeois criteria of
> social justice that deprive the concept of relative
> deprivation of its radical significance. None the
> less, normative social theory may yet effect the neces-
> sary conversion or re-interpretation of the evidence.

In the preceding section, we showed how Runciman relied
on Rawls's theory of justice to transform his discussion
from one of inequality and the perception of inequality to
one of grievance and how far it is justified. Pinker
discounts relative models of poverty, because the perceptions of disadvantaged groups (as mapped out by Runciman)
do not measure up to the criteria of 'modestly drawn
standards of social justice'. Thus, Rawls's theory is
central to this example of how the analysis of social
welfare should be carried out. Justice as fairness is the
most powerful contemporary exemplar of the type of theorizing that must be accepted for Pinker's project to succeed. If the argument that underlies Rawls's theory is
inadequate to generate the particular model of justice
used (or, indeed, any particular model of justice) and
simply expresses a particular set of values, the enterprise fails. Pinker becomes vulnerable to a species of
intellectual totalitarianism. For there is no secure
criterion left whereby to assess the consciousness of
ordinary people, so that we can discriminate between perceptions when discussing policy. The question is not
whether perceptions measure up to a particular model of
social justice, but simply what perceptions exist - and
if ordinary people do not happen to adopt a consensus,

the outcome is chaotic. The study of social policy reduces to the descriptivism of questionnaire survey. No
place for the theorist, since all theory can be refuted
by reference to what people happen to think.

The discussion of democracy and social justice contains
an implicit attempt to resolve this difficulty. Pinker
writes (pp. 130-1):

the first function of any kind of scientific theory is
not to criticize what exists, nor to 'transcend' what
exists, but to help us to distinguish correct from
incorrect knowledge....

There is no reason why sociologists should impose
a self-denying ordinance on themselves, any more than
doctors should desist from warning the public of the
dangers of smoking.... Democracy is nothing if not an
educative process, and education is nothing if it lacks
a moral purpose.

This is what the debate is about. There is general
agreement that on certain assumptions probabilistic evidence in medical science relates health problems to
smoking. If there isn't, we at least know how to check
the assertion. We don't know how to convince people of
the truth of a particular analysis of social policy.
Harvey, Merritt and Nevitt differ on the key issues relating to housing, and in fact what on the major problems
are. Atkinson, Gough and George give different accounts
of postwar income-maintenance policy. Halmos, Leonard
and Lees disagree on the significance of the statutory
social work explosion in our society. There is a problem
about reconciling those who look at things differently.
Where is the correct knowledge - the basis of moral
education?

The distinction between ideological and normative
theory cannot be maintained. The position reduces to
relativism. The suffrage of 'subjective reality' may
support the view that stigma is the central issue in
social policy. On the other hand, those who base theory
in a democracy of perceptions have no way of contesting
the views of those who happen to differ from themselves,
and no way of protecting their analysis from shifts in
public opinion.

The use of Rawls's theory by George and Wilding is especially interesting. 'We adopt a conflict approach, for
both social problems and social policies reflect events
and processes in society, and we see society as essentially conflict-ridden' (George and Wilding, 1976, p. 1).
How can such a conflict model accommodate a theory that
has been used to establish and defend one value-system
against all comers?

GEORGE AND WILDING

The thesis of 'Ideology and Social Welfare' (George and
Wilding, 1976) is that 'it is impossible adequately to
understand the views of those who write about social welfare policy, without taking account also of their social
values and social and political ideas' (p. vii). Four
value-systems are delineated, each coupled with the corresponding analysis of state welfare. The final chapter
of the work is relevant to our theme. The authors
demonstrate, with little difficulty, that social policy
has failed to achieve the avowed ends of reformers in a
number of fields. The point is hardly controversial. What
is significant is the way in which the argument transforms
an account of the relationship between values and the understanding of the views of those who write on social policy,
to an explanation of the failure of reform that is couched
in terms of values. The problem is stated on p. 129: 'we
see the conflict between the values of capitalism and the
ethic of welfare as the underlying reason for the failure
of social policy to achieve agreed aims.' On the next page
a remedy is suggested:

> While inequality has been legitimated by the values of
> individualism and equality of opportunity, equality on
> the other hand has lacked a justifying value framework
> that would appeal to the public. Recent work on the
> nature of social justice has, we believe, provided a
> possible basis for a new and more vigorous egali-
> tarianism.

If justice is 'the first virtue of institutions', can a
new notion of justice help us to change institutions?
     The view that concepts are motors of policy, or of
events at all, is trenchantly criticized in an anecdote
of Marx (Marx and Engels, 1974, p. 37):

> Once upon a time a valiant fellow had the idea that
> men were drowned in water only because they were
> possessed with the idea of gravity. If they were to
> knock this out of their heads ... they would be sub-
> limely proof against all danger from water. His
> whole life long he fought against the illusion of
> gravity, of whose harmful results all statistic
> brought him new and manifold evidence....

In the world of natural science, events are normally
understood as following certain laws, independent of our
conceptualization of those laws. Assimilation of society
to that world transports a similar determinism into
natural science. Rawls, and all ideology, is then irrelevant to social change. The alternative view argues
that human consciousness (to some degree and under certain

circumstances) affects human affairs. There are two
possible roles for the theory of justice as fairness
within the broad scope of such an approach. If Rawls's
theory is held to be compelling, if he has in fact discovered behind the veil of ignorance a standpoint that is
'objective and expresses our autonomy ... to see our place
from the perspective of this position is to see it *sub
specie aeternitas*: it is to regard the human situation
not only from all social but from all temporal points
of view' (Rawls, 1972, p. 587), the significance of the
theory is clear. Their common rationality will enable
radicals to press just ways of ordering the distribution
of rewards on power-holders. Even vested interests might
be reluctant to act in ways that they had been convinced
were morally indefensible.

If however Rawls has failed to establish an 'Archimedean point' (and it is worth noting that the unique
foundation of the theory has been appealed to in support
of a range of positions, including the mild Fabianism of
Crosland (1974, pp. 1-2) as well as the avowedly radical
marxism of George and Wilding) this goal is not achieved.
Nevertheless, Rawls expresses a particular value-position
with force and elegance. 'A Theory of Justice' may be
seen as ideology - ideas used to buttress and justify a
way of looking at the world.

We have argued that the use of the theory as a way of
resolving conflicts between different viewpoints each
expressing a different underlying value-system is blind
justice without the sword. It is vitiated by its two
basic assumptions: that it is possible to conceive a
consensus on the 'laws' of social and behavioural science,
and that it is possible to devise a compelling and
rational theory of the human evaluation of life chances.
The questions of social science do not have right answers.
The value-judgments of human subjects do not follow universal rules. It remains for us to consider why, if
flawed, Rawls's approach has appealed to students of
social policy, and what job the theory has done in en-
abling them to interpret and evaluate state welfare. In
discussion of the ideological role of the theory, it is
impossible to set out a cogent argument. The following
sections suggest a line of thought that at least seems
to provide an elegant explanation.

RAWLS'S APPEAL

George and Wilding (1972) have argued that 'functionalist
and order theories of society have dominated discussion of

142   Chapter 6

the development of social policy in this country' (p.
236). The influence of consensus and humanism 'has been
greatly exaggerated in the literature of social administration, while the influence of class conflict has been
almost completely ignored' (p. 236). There are perhaps
three reasons for this eclipse. First, the origins of
the subject and its historic connection with social work
have made the reform of the social services its dominant
concern. Second, a pragmatic rather than utopian approach
has meant that social administrators will win glamorous,
lucrative and possibly influential positions as government advisers. Third, writers have tended to adopt a
consensus model of society working in a tradition traced
from Durkheim to Talcott Parsons. We may add two further
factors. The expansion of state welfare, and indeed
intervention in virtually all areas of social organization,
has resulted in an ever-growing need for an army of social
administrators, planners, organizers and other profession-
als who require training and the provision of information
and relevant theory. In the UK, the study of social policy
has become a prime location in the process whereby 'the
social sciences become a well-financed technological basis
for the welfare state's effort to solve the problems of
industrial society' (Gouldner, 1972, p. 345). In addition,
it is perhaps possible to explain why an approach that
George and Wilding associate with Parsonian functionalism
has tended consciously or unconsciously to be adopted by
academic social administrators, by examining the role that
its tradition, opportunities and aspirations have described
for their subject.

A brief review of some attempts to define the subject
will indicate the contradictory demands that have moulded
social administration theory. Heisler writes in the preface to a recently published introductory text (1977,
p. xi):

    Social administration has emerged as an empirical study
    whose outlook has been fashioned by social philosophy
    more than social science theory. There is a large
    chink in the armour of social administration as a result
    interposed between social philosophy and the assumed
    understanding of actual conditions.
Titmuss, in his inaugural lecture delivered some twenty-
seven years earlier, pointed to a similar disjunction
(1958, pp. 14-15):

    Social administration may broadly be defined as the
    study of the social services whose object is ... the
    improvement of the conditions of life of the indi-
    vidual in the setting of family and group relations.
    It is concerned with the historical development of

those services ... with the moral values ... with the
role and functions of the services, with their economic aspects, with the part they play in meeting
certain needs in the social process. On the one
hand ... we are interested in the machinery of administration ... on the other, in the lives, needs and the
mutual relations of those members of the community for
whom the services are provided.

By 1967 he had grown more cautious. In the keynote lecture
to the inaugural meeting of the Social Administration
Association, he stated (1968, p. 20):

I refuse to offer a definitive explanation of the subject.... Basically we are concerned with the study of
a range of social needs and the functioning in conditions of scarcity of human organizations traditionally
called social services ... to meet those needs.

These characterizations of the subject share one feature in common - the contrast between the analysis of the
needs of political/economic organizational structures
called welfare states, and of how social policy satisfies
these, and the discussion of individual human need, and
how it is to be met by social services. The problems
associated with defining human needs are problems of
social philosophy. The functioning of welfare states
would traditionally fall within the domain of political
theory and social science. Social administration is
forced to confront in a peculiarly direct manner the
unsolved problem of how one links the two. This issue -
the relation of value and fact/theory - is of course a
central problem for all social thought. The point is well
brought out in an essay of Carrier and Kendall, who summarize definitions of the subject used by Marshall, Briggs,
Wedderburn and Titmuss. The common feature is a notion of
the study of those social activities whose 'manifest
purpose is to influence differential "command over resources" according to some criteria of need' (Heisler,
1977, p. 27). How do we graft the 'study of social activities' on to the specification of 'criteria of need'?

If it is to avoid the dead ends of historicism or
descriptivism, social administration requires a theoretical
basis that deals clearly and adequately with the identification of individual human needs and at the same time with
the working of a social system that may or may not meet
those needs. An approach derived from Parsonian functionalism is uniquely fitted to do the job.

'The Structure of Social Action' (Parsons, 1949) can be
viewed as a solution to the Hobbesian 'problem of order' -
the problem of how separate individuals with different
interests which must inevitably come into conflict can

come together to form a coherent, stable and enduring
society. To simplify, the solution views the social system
as consisting of identifiable elements in functional relationship, and attributes social stability to the capacity
of the system to socialize individuals into the value-
systems that co-ordinate human action. The problem of
relating individual and society dissolves. Gouldner
(1972, p. 218) puts it as follows:

> When the Parsonian conception of a system is brought
> to bear on the relation between individuals and the
> group as a whole, what is emphasized is the indi-
> vidual's plastic potential for conformity. Emphasis
> is placed on the conformity of individuals with the
> social position in which they find themselves or with
> the needs of the group: thus tensions between the
> individual and the group are seen as fortuitous...,
> not as universal, but as situational.

The outcome, for social policy theorists, is that the gulf
between the social philosophy and the social policy
aspects of their discipline disappears. Individual needs
can be conceived as moulded largely by socialization, by
the imposition of social system. Giddens (1976) claims
that the result is a misleading over-simplification: 'it
is impossible to make satisfactory conceptual recognition
of the diversification of interests in society, which
intervene between the actions of its members and the overall structure of the global community' (p. 98). To use
the common biological analogue of functionalism, if
society is conceived as an organization of interlocking
parts, understood solely in terms of the services they
perform for each other, the needs of the individual and
of a social system consisting simply of a patterned relation of individuals coincide. Society constructs human
needs, as well as meeting them. There can be no separate
(philosophical) problem of identifying human needs and
then relating them to the social system. The question is
whether such an approach represents the elegance of Occam's
Razor or the sterility of conceptual blinkers.

   Functionalism has influenced writers on social policy
not only because the approach synthesizes disparate elements in the subject. The view of social systems as
integrated and organized has an inherent conservative
bias attractive to the governments who fund study of the
welfare state. The consequences of interpreting social
problems in relation to a central value-system rather than
a class or power system is less likely to threaten established, dominant interests. Moreover, the approach can
confuse the issue by masquerading as value-free, and even
radical, as Gouldner (1972, p. 334) points out in his

critique of Merton's essay on manifest and latent functions. However, certain problems have led some writers to revise their approach.   Giddens (1976, p. 21) summarizes four difficulties:

> The reduction of human agency to the 'internalization' of values ... the concomitant failure to treat social life as *actively constituted* through the doings of its members ... the treatment of power as a *secondary* phenomenon with norm of 'value' residing in solitary state as the most basic feature in social activity ... the failure to make conceptually clear the *negotiated* character of norms, as open to conflicting 'interpretations' in relation to divergent and conflicting *interests* in society.

The first three features limit the usefulness of the approach for the study of social policy - the study of how social problems are identified and how society 'produces' solutions to them.   The fourth vitiates functionalism as a resolution to the problem of identifying human needs in relation to social administration.   The resulting vacuum in theory has led to a number of attempts to establish a value-basis for the study of welfare.

Some writers, notably Webb (Hall *et al*., 1975) and Heisler (1977), have attempted to reconstruct functionalism. In arguing for the 'merit of starting with a systems approach', Webb writes (Hall *et al*., 1975): 'students of social policy ... are frequently charting unmet needs.... A systems viewpoint forces us to look at the same problem in terms of the 'needs' of the system...' (p. 24).   Later, this leads to an eclecticism in the characterization of the system: 'there does seem to be a good argument for producing a synthesis of the pluralist and class models as a basis for understanding changes in social policy' (pp. 150-1).   There is a marked similarity between an approach that interprets policy in terms of the needs of a political system that operates within a pluralist perspective on the analysis of 'the making of day-to-day policy on social issues', but within limits set by 'elites which for many purposes are indistinguishable from ... a ruling class' and functionalism.   This solution may be termed 'functionalism with class-conflict icing', since the study of social policy is carried out in a language of pluralism, accounting for micro-level developments in terms of systemic need, in an arena bounded by the domain of conflict theory.   It is not itself contaminated by conflict since it takes good care not to go too near it. However, the net result seems to restrict the range of the subject, since it becomes impossible to move beyond the study of social service organizations to discuss

questions such as why advanced industrial societies have
constructed broadly similar welfare states without entering the arena of conflict. Macro-level social policy, in
one sense, consists of a sum of micro-level developments,
even if the former is not to be explained as the latter.
How do we draw the demarcation line then between conflict
and consensus theory?

Heisler (1977) plumps rather more firmly for functionalism, through the assertion that the business of social
administration is societal integration: 'social administration is the body of intelligence which contributes
to the making of policies and the distribution of sanctions to eradicate social disorganization' (p. 21). It
is hard to see how either of these solutions can avoid the
problems of functionalism without becoming incoherent, *if*
they are to range over the whole of the field of interest
identified for the subject in Titmuss's original statements. It is clear how they succeed in the specification
of 'criteria of need', through the needs of social systems,
or through the underlying hypothesis of a basic need of
society for stability.

Rawls's theory operates as a convenient support for
those who wish to go one step further in rejecting the
sterility of functionalism on the one hand, while
locating themselves firmly in the tradition of social
administration by retaining a central place for the consideration of value in their analysis. George and Wilding,
self-confessed conflict theorists, castigate traditional
social administration on the grounds that (1972) 'very
few of the discussions of social values, however, extend
beyond a kind of ritual mention. There is virtually no
analysis of what is meant by social values....' (p. 236).
In the introduction to 'Ideology and Social Welfare'
(George and Wilding, 1976, pp. 16-17), the functionalist
perspective is vigorously refuted. Yet ideology remains
central. The motor of social change is not seen as the
historical development of any element of society, not even
as conscious, undetermined class struggle. Instead, the
recipe for structural revolution is in the intellectual
analysis available to 'radicals'. Rawls fills the bill,
in providing a coherent, persuasive, sympathetic and reformist ideology.

Pinker wishes to demolish ideology, yet to construct a
model of policy that allows room both for the uncorrected
perceptions of citizens and for the normative theory of
academics. Rawls's theory is the basis for an illustra-
tion of how to choose between ideology and normative theory
which at the same time provides the intellectual with a
yardstick for assessing the views of the man in the street.

We can respectably retain some values, dismiss other judgments, and interpret the outcome as educated democracy.

Runciman uses the theory in a similar way to orientate his map of the ideology of his respondents in relation to the transcendent loadstone of social justice.

Thus Rawls provides an admirable instrument for writers who wish to abandon a functionalist approach, yet to retain an engine for the justification of a particular set of values. This is one element in an account of its relevance to social administration. However, the academic study of social policy does not float free from its social environment. This prompts us to ask what features of the modern welfare state make a theory like Rawls's peculiarly appropriate to their analysis - or, to reverse the question, how well does the theory of justice fit out the modern state system with a made-to-measure ideology?

RAWLS AND THE RATIONALITY OF INTERVENTIONISM

It is easy to point to trends in the recent development of capitalist society that can be legitimated only by preconceptions similar to those that underlie the theory. A tradition of writers stretching back to Weber have emphasized the tendency I shall characterize as rationalization in our societal organization. Roszak expands the analysis to define the totalitarian spectre of the 'technocracy' (1971, pp. 5-6):

> That social form in which an industrial society reaches the peak of its organizational integration.... The meticulous systematization Adam Smith once celebrated in his well-known pin factory now extends to all areas of life, giving us human organization that matches the precision of our mechanistic organization.

The importance and convergence of planning by the state and the business corporation has been widely recognised. To emphasize planning and intervention in free markets on the economic plane is not to be forced to the dismal conclusions of Hayek (1944) or Polanyi (1957, see especially chapters 17, 18 and 20). To point out that the trend appears more or less acceptable to all effective political groupings does not entail acceptance of Bell's thesis (1960) that ideological conflict is outdated. The road to welfare is not necessarily the road to serfdom or to political torpor. However, what Gough (1975) terms 'the huge political economic weight of the modern state' (p. 53) is a factor with which the study of social policy must clearly come to terms, and a phenomenon that requires

evaluative analysis. The approach that underlies Rawls's
theory is in harmony with the value-system required to
legitimate this development. I hope to indicate its
ideological implications by bringing out the values that
underlie massive interventionism encapsulated in Pahl and
Winkler's persuasive analysis (1974) of the extreme form -
corporatism. The corporatist thesis highlights key features of the growth of social planning. First let us consider the explosion of interventionism.

   Perhaps the clearest brief analysis is in Myrdal's
'Beyond the Welfare State' (1960). Myrdal argues that
'in the western countries one of the least informed and
intelligent controversies of our time has concerned the
question of whether we should have a planned or a free
economy' (p. 1). Despite the empty clangour of ideological conflict, 'the irony is ... that ... our national
economies have become increasingly regulated, organized
and co-ordinated ... this has all happened in a piecemeal
and almost offhand way' (pp. 6-7). Myrdal traces the
influence of international crises, the changing structure
and role of the market, democratic pressures for equality
and participation, state commitments to full employment
and fiscal budgeting, the organization of the working
class, world war, cold war and a multitude of other factors on 'the unplanned development of planning'. He
stresses the consequences of state planning in the developed world for less developed countries - the essentially
nationalistic, rather than global, perspective of the
welfare state. What system of values is appropriate
to the legitimation of such a state-planned social system?

   The term 'corporatism' has been used to characterize
the political order wherein group conflicts are subordi-
nated to social goals - the integrated, organized, essentially planner - (or rather plan-) dominated society.
Pahl and Winkler (1974, p. 72) summarize the essential
values of a corporatist system under four heads. The
trend to planning in the welfare state can be seen as a
social development that would express its legitimation in
values such as these. The values are order, unity,
nationalism and success. The values of unity ('the substitution of co-operation for competition'), nationalism
('the elevation of general welfare to complete priority
over self-interest or sectional advantage') and success
('the attainment of national objectives established by
the state') presuppose scientific social planning. If
sectional interest is to be suppressed in favour of
nationally defined welfare goals, we need to have a good -
and universally accepted - idea of what welfare is, and of
what steps to take to achieve it. In short, we need a

social science that is both normative and universal, and
can thus eliminate any necessity for political contests
between different viewpoints. Otherwise, social engineer-
ing is susceptible to the kind of disputes and communication problems that dogged the Tower of Babel project.

Order ('the elimination of the anarchy of the market in
all its forms'), nationalism and success require a rational
science of judgments. The substitution of planning for
market allocation presupposes that we can predict what
people need. The elevation of national welfare and national goals as positive values assumes that the needs of
the community (and the goals that enshrine them) can be
uniquely specified - that it is possible for planners to
predict how citizens will weight alternative goods, and
combinations of goods.

A theory of justice that interprets the term as predi-
cated on a social science in which no important areas are
essentially contested implies that there exists such a
universal social science. Moreover, only a society so
ordered that the state could put into practice the fruits
of such an unassailable normative theory (or, more simply,
truth about human affairs) could reasonably claim to be
just. Similarly, if human preferences in choosing between
different advantages and dis-welfares are rationally predictable, then only a society that in fact sets up the
apparatus of rational planning to make the predictions and
order citizens' life-chances accordingly can maximize
fairness. Moreover, were the predictability hypothesis
capable of demonstration, societies that did not realize
the opportunity for just social organization that it offers
would be turning their back on social justice.

The analogy between the knowledge, motives and procedures
of such a planning apparatus and the account of Rawls's original position is clear. Rawls's theory of justice is not
in itself an ideology for corporatism. The principles that
Rawls derives from the impartial, rational deliberations
of primitive negotiators behind the veil of ignorance are
the complete opposite, the most humane and wholehearted
liberalism. However, the preconceptions of the theory bear
a close resemblance to elements in the value-position that
buttresses important trends in modern social and economic
policy. For this reason among others, the approach is
relevant, fruitful, compelling. Unarticulated, such values
are implicit in some aspects of the contemporary social
order.

It would certainly be misleading to overstress the
hegemony of corporatism. To assign a dominant role to
the value-system sketched out above would be to reproduce
the weaknesses of the functional analysis or social order.

Similarly, to account for the rise of Rawls in armchair
social administration solely in terms of an ideological job
that some features of the theory seem equipped to do in relation to contemporary welfare statism, would render futile
analysis of its unparallelled intellectual achievement, in
relation to modern moral philosophy. However, just as the
theory generates a suitable output to solve conceptual problems that face students of social administration, the
structure of the argument neatly harmonizes with the ideological preconceptions of any attempt to legitimate the
untrammelled interventionism of our society. Are the
problems at the former level the theoretical reflections
of the crisis of material reality associated with this
development?

CONCLUSION

Rawls's account of the concept of justice seems to offer
a ready-made framework for the analysis of social policy
equipped with that peculiar persuasiveness that derives
from a foundation in rational premises. We have argued
that the theory can't do this job satisfactorily. It
involves assumptions about the status of social science
and about the principles that would guide the decisions
of persons freed from the constraints of vested interests
that are unprovable. Nevertheless, it remains a powerful
contribution to debate in this area, not least because it
is an accurate and convincing summary of a dominant contemporary value-position.

If Rawls's argument is inadequate, discussions of
social policy based on the theory are vitiated. Where
does this leave Runciman, Pinker and George and Wilding?
Runciman's analysis of inequality and of how various
groups in society perceive social difference escapes
unscathed. The status of the fourth section of 'Relative
Deprivation and Social Justice' - the critique of the justification of grievance at inequality - becomes simply an
analysis from a particular viewpoint. The epigraph to the
work, Weber's comment that 'any meaningful assessment of
someone else's aspirations can only be a criticism of them
in the light of one's personal view of the world, a struggle
against alien ideals from the standpoint of one's own', becomes doubly apposite.

The limitations of Pinker's approach become obvious.
Any attempt to pin policy evaluation on the values of a
group in society is trapped in circularity. Why choose
one set of values rather than another? George and Wilding's attempt to base a radical critique in a theory of

justice is undermined. The struggle to change policy
reduces to the struggle between incompatible value-
positions to which Weber refers. In this sense, Rawls's
theory is simply ideology. It is an ideology that is
peculiarly fitted to meet the needs of the academic study
of social policy.

The ideology that results from such applications of
Rawls's theory is important at a material level because
the interpretation of the rules of social justice as the
outcome of an impartial rational negotiation in an abstract original position relates to elements in the ideology that would justify a significant trend to a planned,
rationalized capitalism in our society. Since this trend
denies the significance of citizen participation, it is
one of which students of social policy should be particularly cautious. The conclusion that such a perspective
on the basis of Rawls's theory inevitably leads us to is
that we can know what kinds of consensus rational people
would arrive at when laying down 'the foundation charter
of their society', if only they would shelve their vested
interests. Who needs citizens, when the social planner
can construct the just world by thought-experiment, without bothering to consult their views?

7   True and false needs

An assumption running through these essays is that 'need' is a justifying expression in arguments about social policy, so that if we can establish that something is a need it will follow that it ought to be provided, if possible by society or by some individual or group on whom falls the duty of satisfying the need. If this is so, it is obviously important to establish what needs people have. This in turn raises two problems. One, discussed in an earlier chapter, is the problem of finding anything that one can legitimately call a need without making moral assumptions. The other, to be discussed here, is the question of whether what people seriously believe that they need corresponds to what they 'really' need. Some aspects of this have been discussed in the previous chapter; in the present context we shall take up the most radical answer to the problem, the idea that people may be systematically mistaken about their needs, because the standards that define need in a society are themselves false standards. Can false consciousness about need be so pervasive?

The problem cannot be avoided, as some people have thought, by refusing to talk about needs, and using only wants and desires to justify policies. It is more obvious that people do not always know what they 'really' need than that they do not always know what they 'really' want, but both occur. People always know what they want in the sense that they know what desire they are currently feeling. But desire in this sense cannot justify social policies.

To see this, consider someone (A) who has placed himself under an obligation to carry out someone else's (B's) wishes. Suppose that, as in Mill's famous example, B wishes to cross a river via a bridge that A knows to be unsafe but B does not. Suppose that A also knows, or

strongly suspects, that B would not want to step on to the
bridge if he knew it was unsafe. It seems clear that A's
obligation is to follow what B would want if he had the
relevant information, i.e. to restrain him from stepping
on to the bridge, and that B would have the right to com-
plain if he did not. This is often expressed, as Mill
puts it himself, by saying that B 'does not want to step
on to the bridge' ('Liberty', chapter 5) or 'does not
really want to'. Objections have been raised to this
locution, and to the implication that a person can 'really'
want what he does not want, and 'not really' want what he
does.

But even if one does not put it this way, there are
circumstances under which the appeal to wants and desires
that justify policies will have to be not to actual felt
desires but to what people would desire if they had proper
knowledge. So, whether or not the actual expressions are
used, the distinction will have to be made between 'true'
and 'false' desires, i.e. desires, actual or hypothetical,
that justify policies and desires that do not.

In this respect needs parallel desires. But with
needs the terms 'true' and 'false', or 'real' and 'not
real', seem quite proper. We have defined 'need', in the
morally justifying sense, as what is necessary for a good
or desirable end. From this it follows that there are
two ways in which people can believe they need what they
do not, or can fail to recognize what they do need: they
can be wrong about the desirability of the end, or they
can be wrong about the necessity of the means.

The second mistake is usually factual. Either someone
does not know that something is essential for what he wants
or ought to do, or for life itself, as when a diabetic does
not know that he needs insulin; or he believes that something is essential when it is in fact dispensable (as when
Victorian Englishmen in India believed that they had to
wear solar topees in order to escape sunstroke) or positively harmful. An interesting example of this is the
situation in which someone who desires something very
much - the possible objects are many and various - tries
to legitimize his desire by pretending to himself that
he needs it, i.e. that he cannot live his life, cannot
function properly, without it. Occasionally, this may be
true - but usually there is self-deception involved, and
the supposed 'need' is merely a desire.

'Mistakes' about the desirability of an end, and hence
about whether the means to that end is really a need, are
of two kinds. They may be relative to a person's own
values, so that he does not realize that something is
desirable or undesirable by his own standards of desirability.

The difference between this and a mistake about means is often purely verbal: when, for example, nineteenth-century Benthamites supported *laissez-faire* economic policies in the belief that they increased human happiness, an opponent of this belief could describe it either as a mistake about what means led to human happiness, or as a mistake about the moral characteristics of the policy itself.

On the other hand, it may be that one person, in judging the attitude of another, sees him as making a moral mistake and as pursuing the wrong standards and having the wrong notion of what is desirable. This can occur only when two people or societies differ radically about morality, and at a basic level. This is probably fairly rare: often there is agreement about basic values, such as the desirability of human happiness; and the disagreement is over how to achieve this in practice. But if and when it does occur, each party, if its view of ethics is an objectivist one, can regard the other as being mistaken about ends, and not merely means. What action on the basis of such a belief might be justified - if any - is something to be considered later.

MARCUSE ON REPRESSION AND FALSE NEEDS

To call needs 'true' or 'false' in any of these senses is fairly straightforward, though the moral problem of when one may use coercion to force a person to satisfy 'true' needs or to refrain from satisfying 'false' ones is certainly difficult and complex. But there are two other more complex uses of these expressions, both of which are important for social and political theory. On one view, true needs are those that arise naturally and spontaneously, or would arise under natural conditions, such as the basic biological needs. To these most writers would add specifically human needs, in particular the need to do something significant and worthwhile; Freudians such as Marcuse, although not Freud himself, would add a need for 'liberated' sexuality, as opposed to the 're-pressive', monogamous, genital-centred sexuality imposed by 'bourgeois' civilization. In contrast, needs such as that for the latest model in some line of consumer durables are 'false' in that they are induced by deliberate propaganda, or by the influence of social attitudes, and do not arise from a person's own nature.

But while it is possible to distinguish needs according to how they arise, it does not seem useful to do so unless this coincides with the distinction already made

between needs that are felt but rest on a mistake and
needs that rest on a correct understanding of one's
situation. Otherwise there is no reason why we should
regard needs that arise naturally as of any more importance than those that are felt only as the result of
persuasion. There is clearly no logical connection between the spontaneity of a need and its genuineness in
the sense of being really required for something worthwhile,
or for worthwhile action in general. There is often an
empirical connection; when a healthy person spontaneously
feels a physical or psychological need, this may well be
a sign of a real need. But this is not always the case:
diabetics spontaneously desire, and perhaps feel they
need, sugar; but they really need insulin. Similarly
with psychological needs: even if spontaneously arising
sexuality would be as some Freudians suppose, it is dubious
that 'polymorphous-perverse' promiscuity would actually
make anyone happer.

However, Marcuse, who is the main contemporary writer
to distinguish true and false needs, does not stigmatize
felt needs as false only or primarily on this ground.
Marcuse (1964, p. 5) says:

'False' [needs] are those which are superimposed upon
the individual by particular social interests in his
repression: the needs which perpetuate toil, aggres-
siveness, misery and injustice. Their satisfaction
might be most gratifying to the individual, but this
happiness is not a condition which has to be maintained
and protected if it serves to arrest the development of
the ability (his own and others) to recognize the disease of the whole and grasp the chance of curing the
disease.

By 'particular social interests' Marcuse means the groups
dominating society, especially business and military groups.
These groups, according to Marcuse, maintain domination,
in an advanced capitalist system, not in the main by force,
but by making it in the interests of most sections of
society to support the system - they do not quite succeed
in making it in the interests of all. This is achieved
largely by making people not merely desire but actually
need - i.e. be unable to do without - things that only
the system can supply, notably more and more consumer
goods. These needs are created, maintained and increased by propaganda in the mass media, which can work
either directly, through advertising, or indirectly, by
continually reinforcing belief in the merits of a 'con-
sumerist' way of life.

Marcuse says that in one sense these needs are perfectly genuine: people find it essential to satisfy them

if they are to operate within the existing system. They
are false, first, because, as we said above, they are not
natural spontaneous needs: they do not arise through biological necessity, like the needs for food and clothing,
or from the specifically human desire for self-expression
and self-improvement, which they work against, but from
manipulation and indoctrination. Second, though their
gratification produces genuine satisfaction, it is a much
lower level of satisfaction than could be obtained if the
present social system, with its competitiveness and insistence on increased production, were overthrown and an
attempt made to set up a society with more leisure, human
contact and satisfying work. The price of gratifying
these needs is thus the giving up of any search for the
conditions of really deep and long-lasting satisfaction,
the strengthening of a system that works against any
such satisfaction, and acceptance in place of real happiness of what Marcuse calls 'euphoria in unhappiness'.

Any critical discussion of Marcuse has to consider
two points - the justice of his criticism of our social
system (although he is talking primarily about America,
what he says is intended to apply to all advanced industrial societies), and the legitimacy of his concept of
'false needs'. To evaluate the first would be impossible
without sifting an enormous amount of evidence - indeed,
much more than Marcuse himself has probably looked at.
Until then, one can only rely on pre-scientific common
sense impressions. These suggest that, although Marcuse
grossly exaggerates the extent and endemic nature of these
evils, he has put his finger on something that is seriously wrong with our society. We are all under pressure -
and many of us succumb - to think we need, or even actually
to need, things we would be better without; and a prime
cause of this today is commercialism.

But Marcuse, as well as exaggerating this, over-simpli-
fies the way it comes about. In an unpublished article
called Wants and Needs, I. Gough, of Manchester University
Department of Social Administration, in the course of a
criticism of J.K. Galbraith and E.J. Mishan which can also
be applied to Marcuse, points out a number of ways in
which an economic system can produce and stimulate needs
without any conscious effort or intention on anyone's
part; and he suggests that these may have much more
effect than advertising and marketing. They include the
'emulation-effect', i.e. the effect of observing consumption by others, and, more importantly, needs created by
the necessity to escape from the disadvantages created by
the system of production and consumption:

dirt, noise and ugliness, for instance, may be avoided
by purchasing a suburban house ... if the very process
of satisfying these wants creates further disamenities
... (necessitating, for example, a further move out
into the country, as more people flock to the suburbs),
a self-renewing dynamic enters into the creation of
such wants.

Lastly, citing Dobb (1970), Gough mentions 'demand clusters',
i.e. the way in which the use of a particular item leads
both to the creation of new needs whose satisfaction is
necessary in order to continue using it, and also to the
development of a new life-style, which in its turn can
be maintained only if a new set of necessary conditions
are met. Thus the expanded use of the motorcar requires
'simultaneous investment on a large scale in roads, road
lighting, road service-stations, roadhouses, motels and
the like' (Dobb, 1970, p. 219) and creates 'new wants for
weekend travel, for a home further from work, etc' (Gough,
unpublished paper).

To all this one should add Marx's observation that a
social system can reduce needs as well as create them: it
can make it possible to live and work while doing without
what would be essential under natural conditions. Indeed,
Marx saw capitalism as both converting 'whims and caprices'
into needs, and making natural needs dispensable: 'even
the need for fresh air ceases for the worker. Man returns
to a cave dwelling ... the simplest animal cleanliness
ceases to be a need for man'. While everything is done to
stimulate the needs of consumers, the worker's need is
reduced to 'the barest and most miserable level of physical subsistence' (Marx, 1975, p. 359).

By and large, in modern capitalist systems this reduction of biological needs takes place less and less. But
Marcuse himself and others have pointed out the way in
which the other, specifically human, needs for self-
expression and worthwhile activity are restricted. An
obvious example is the way in which it is often not
thought necessary that paid work should be fulfilling, so
that many people accept without question that their true
lives begin when they leave work. Another example, discussed by Marcuse (1964, chapter 3) is the way in which
certain social forces stimulate the need for physical sex
while at the same time discouraging the need for love: the
first need is one with which the system can cope; the
second always carries with it the threat of disruption by
the substitution of personal for market morality.

Finally, in contrast to the various writers mentioned,
it is important to stress the contribution of the individual to the changes in what he feels to be a need, and

the extent to which he may be a willing victim of propaganda or of these social forces, or to which the forces
may do no more than encourage the work of personal fantasy, or self-deception or obsession. These personal
fantasies and obsessions may lead to needs similar or
different to those generated by the social system; but
in either case the general situation is similar, and one
can contrast what is needed if a person is to operate
within the system he has constructed for himself with his
'real' need to escape from that system.

One obvious example of this is physical addiction:
there is a sense in which an addict genuinely needs, and
no longer merely desires, his drug; and yet what he needs
for a really satisfying life is to break free of the addiction. But people can be 'addicted' (if the metaphor
is not too forced) to situations as well as to drugs - to
conceptions of their place in the world that bolster
their self-esteem and render what they are doing important;
or to a round of activity that is in fact useless but
gives the illusion of significance; or to systematic
fantasizing, whether pornographic, romantic or whatever.
Here again, they may genuinely need to keep the illusion
going in order to continue functioning, and yet 'really'
need to break the illusion. We should note, though,
that this sometimes may be so only in principle, and not
in practice, because there is at the time no way of breaking the illusion that will not do more harm than good. We
still have Ibsen's 'Wild Duck', and many real-life examples,
as awful warnings of the dangers of forcing reality on
someone in the wrong way and at the wrong time.

Sometimes personal fantasy and social forces combine to
produce a real institution with elements of collective
game-playing. Berdyaev (1960) draws attention to the
unreal quality of the world of high finance, and its
resemblance to the world of sexual fantast (part 2, chapter
4, section 4):

The ... love of money for its own sake creates one of
the most fantastic worlds ... of capitalism, of banks,
stock-exchanges, paper money, cheques, I.O.U.s, adver-
tisements ... a terrible phantasmagoria, utterly remote
from the world created by God (or even that created by
man, one might add), and adding nothing to its fullness,
richness or perfection.

The same could be said of some aspects of legal argument
and intrigue - see 'Bleak House' - or bureaucracy or aca-
damic research, in which the same element of collective
fantasy appears. (This does not detract from the value of
real production, administration, justice or learning.)

Finally, there is the situation in which previously
existing needs of a general kind, whether biological or
specifically human, are so shaped by social forces and
the social system that they come to exist in a 'perverted' form, i.e. a form in which when they are met the
satisfaction to the individual is very low, although
enough for him to continue to function, and in which considerable harm may be done to others in the process.
Marx, in the 1844 manuscript already quoted, mentions how
in Ireland the need for food had become a need for potatoes,
and the worst kind of potatoes at that.

A more complex example is developed by Erich Fromm
(1973). Fromm distinguishes between 'benign' aggression,
which mainly takes place in self-defence, and malignant
aggression, as the urge to be cruel, to exercise power over
others, or simply to destroy. This arises, according to
Fromm, when a person finds it impossible to satisfy his
'existential' needs, i.e., roughly, his need to do something significant, in a way that is creative and construc-
tive; and so tries to fulfil himself by destroying rather
than creating. This may come about because of a person's
own character, or family relationships; but it may also
be caused or encouraged by social conditions. '[T]here are
specific environmental conditions conducive to ... the
development of the life-furthering syndrome ... to the
extent these conditions are lacking, he will become ...
characterized by the presence of the life-thwarting syndrome' (Fromm, 1973, chapter 10, section 4, part 2).

These conditions are named as 'freedom, activating
stimuli, the absence of exploitative control, and the
presence of "man-centred" modes of production' (Fromm,
1973, chapter 10, section 4, part 2). 'Activating stimuli',
according to Fromm, such as 'a novel, a poem, an idea, a
landscape, music, a loved person', invite a response of
active interest and mental or physical activity, and do
not produce satiation or boredom when repeated. Passive
stimuli produce an immediate thrill, followed by release
of tension, followed by boredom and the need for a new
stimulus of a different kind, since there is no novelty
created by the response. Hence in a society in which
passive rather than active stimuli are the most easily
available, there will be a growing tendency to gain easy
excitement by arousing malice and destructiveness: 'it
is much easier to get excited by anger, rage, cruelty or
the passion to destroy than by love and productive and
active interest' (Fromm, 1973, chapter 10, section 3,
part 4). This is not determined inevitably by social
circumstances, but is heavily influenced by them: 'man
is never so determined that a basic change ... is not

possible ... environment inclines, but does not determine' (Fromm, 1973, chapter 10, section 4, part 5).

One may agree or disagree with all or any of these
writers to a varying degree. But one thing that emerges
from the work of all of them is that only the most general
needs are independent of social conditions. Indeed, some
writers have followed Marx in regarding the effect of conditions as so fundamental that to all intents and purposes
it creates the need. Gough quotes from Marx's 'Grundrisse' (1973, pp. 35-6; cf. chapter 6):

> Hunger is hunger; but the hunger that is satisfied
> with cooked meat eaten with fork and knife is a dif-
> ferent kind of hunger from the one that devours raw
> meat ... production produces consumption; first, by
> furnishing the latter with material; second by
> determining the manner of consumption; third, by
> creating in consumers a want for its products as
> objects of consumption.

But this is too sweeping a conclusion. It remains true
and important that everyone has a need for food, however
different the forms that this need takes. It also remains
important that the evidence suggests that everyone has
a need to do something significant, even though this is
even more vague and more dependent on social conditions
for its precise form, whether those conditions provide a
choice of ways of satisfying it, channel it into one path,
so that it becomes a specific need, or block some forms of
satisfaction, so that others appear. It is still the
same general principle at work; and the way it varies
under different conditions can be studied. Incidentally,
if Fromm's interpretation of Marx is correct, Marx himself recognized that there were needs independent of social conditions: in a footnote in the section already
cited (Fromm, 1973, chapter 10, section 4, part 2), he
quotes Marx, as opposed to vulgar marxism, as proposing in
'Capital' a concept of 'human nature in general' as distinct from 'human nature as modified in each historical
epoch'.

Nevertheless, the distinction that emerges is very much
a distinction between general and specific, rather than
spontaneous and induced, needs. Even though a need may be
rooted in human nature, the precise form it takes will
always be determined in part by social conditions. Hence
one cannot contrast needs that arise spontaneously and
needs that are produced by society: actual needs are too
often spontaneous inasmuch as they are bound to arise in
some form, and conditioned in so far as they have this
form. Nor can one contrast present needs with the supposedly spontaneous needs that would arise after a revolution,

as Marcuse does: the post-revolutionary needs, like the
pre-revolutionary ones, will still be socially conditioned.

But Marcuse has still given us an important distinction
between what is needed 'within the system' and what would
really satisfy. 'Within the system' can have one of two
implications: it can refer to what is needed in order to
function as a member of a particular social system (which
may not be needed in another system), or to the way in
which a universal need, such as the basic biological ones,
has to be satisfied within a given system. In a sense, the
second implication is included in the first, since functioning is not possible unless these needs are met in
some form. If in some other system these needs would be
more adequately met, and/or the system as a whole would
better meet people's needs, in the sense of better providing the necessary conditions for doing what they want,
or think they ought, to do, then one may say that the
'real' need is for a change of system. It follows that
people may or may not be aware of their real needs, so
that real and felt needs will by no means always coincide.
Indeed, since to be aware of one's real needs in such a
situation will require being able to see the possibility
that the *status quo* might be altered, it is inevitable
that many people will be unaware of them simply for this
reason.

But Marcuse's theory as a whole requires two important
qualifications. First, as we have seen, his account of
how false needs arise is too simple: it gives too much
weight to propaganda and manipulation, and too little to
the working of the system itself, on the one hand, and to
individual emotions and fantasies, on the other. We have
to recognize that in addition to social systems there are
individual 'systems' - i.e. ways of life coupled with
views of what the world is like. The two interact in all
kinds of complex ways, and the contrast between true and
false needs has to be made on both levels.

Second, Marcuse's criticism of modern capitalism is, as
I have already suggested, far too sweeping. He draws
attention to genuine and all too frequent evils. But he
fails to prove, or give much evidence for, his implicit
assertions (a) that these evils are endemic and a fundamental part of the capitalist system, (b) that they are
ineradicable within the system, (c) that the need to
eradicate them makes revolution a moral necessity, and (d)
that the post-revolutionary society would be an improvement on the present one.

CAPITALISM AND HUMAN NEEDS

Criticisms of modern capitalism, with regard to whether
or not it satisfies human needs, focus on what it produces, what it encourages people to want, the ethic it
encourages, and the type of work involved in maintaining
it. A fundamental criticism from Marx, Marcuse and
others is that it is geared as a system to satisfying
desires rather than needs. This is true, but it does not
follow that it does not satisfy needs via desires: this
depends on whether people by and large know what they need
and so desire it. Often, they do not; but they may be
right more often than a group of bureaucrats making the
decision on their behalf would be. It remains to be shown
that the concentration on satisfying desires leads, as a
system, to any less satisfaction of need than any other:
even though this is not an aim of the system, it may still
be achieved by it.
     But this can be possible only if too large disparities
of income are avoided: otherwise, the whims of the rich
will, via the working of the system, take precedence over
the necessities of the poor; and, as in present-day New
York, the same city can contain both a shop stocking 102
kinds of eye-shadow and children suffering from malnutri-
tion. A pure *laissez-faire* system cannot meet needs; but
a relatively free market together with redistribution of
income probably can. The practical problem involves the
question of what sort of redistribution to use: one can
simply redistribute money, e.g. by a 'negative income
tax', and hope people will use it to meet their needs and
the needs of their families; or one can use money from
taxation to set up institutions that ensure needs are met.
The first has the merit of preserving more freedom; the
second guarantees a higher level of need satisfaction.
     Second, it has been pointed out that a capitalist
system is geared, both regarding what it produces and to
what people are encouraged to want, to concentrating on
what can be marketed. This means, first, that, as we have
seen, the system does not have overall the merit alleged
for it of giving people what they spontaneously want,
since many of their wants are produced or modified by it
in the first place. It also means that the need and
desire to consume are well catered for, but the 'existential' needs are neglected: people are condemned to
boring and unsatisfying jobs and are encouraged to seek
'passive' rather than 'activating' stimuli (in Fromm's
sense) and to find satisfaction in using and possessing,
rather than in doing and creating. Moreover, not only is
the stimulation of needs one-sided, but also, because the

system is geared to growth, wants and needs have to be
stimulated faster than output, in order to maintain demand, so that people have to be kept in a condition of
permanent dissatisfaction. This is an unconscious process, but essential to the system: '[Capitalism] differs
from other economic systems in that the continual growth
of the sphere of consumption is an imperative for the survival of the system itself' (Gough, unpublished paper).

Can these evils, which clearly exist (though to what
degree is arguable), be modified within the present system? The concentration on material needs seems to be something for individuals and educators to resolve. It is
natural that, in a society that pays great attention to
commerce, attitudes appropriate to marketing will spread
to other spheres where they are utterly inappropriate,
so that, for example, people try to buy enjoyment or treat
sex as a competition. But though natural, it is not inevitable; and it does not seem to be confined as a phenomenon to one economic system, since a socialist system
can equally concentrate on the material at the expense of
the personal: 'Both capitalism and socialism adopt the
economic point of view, i.e. distort the hierarchy of
values, putting the lower and subordinate values above
the higher' (Berdyaev, 1960, part II, chapter 4, section
vii).

Apart from the fact that this particular problem requires a change of heart rather than a change of system,
the system itself generates more than one moral attitude.
Macpherson (1973) sees in the type of liberalism closely
associated with capitalism both a view of man as consumer
of utilities, and a view of man as doer and producer. The
second view, like the first, can be perverted, and can
produce an insistence on competitiveness and success
where this is inappropriate. The truth may be that both
doing and consuming can take healthy or unhealthy forms;
but while the range of choice is in both cases largely
determined by the system, the wholesomeness or otherwise
of the way things are done depends less on its particular
nature than on the attitudes of those operating it.

On the other hand, the problem of unsatisfying work
seems to require much more public intervention and modification of existing arrangements. The problem is one
of creating what Fromm, in the passage already cited,
calls 'man-centred' modes of production, which meet the
needs of the worker. In theory, a free market should
meet equally the needs of workers and consumers, this
being enforced by the dissatisfied consumer withdrawing
his custom and the dissatisfied worker withdrawing his
labour and moving to another employer. This may be true

under conditions of perfect competition; but it is not true in the real world, unless the system is modified. Even the consumer who knows his needs has to take what he is given, unless he has sufficient money; the worker's practical choice is still more limited by the fact that he is effectively forced by his training to choose one sort of work and by his family ties to stay in one place.

What is involved in a 'man-centred' mode of production? One element may be some kind of involvement of everyone in decision-making. This can be done by workers' participation; but is also possible in a hierarchic system, if there is in practice informal consultation. The only problem here is that sooner or later the 'virtuous paternalists' who run the hierarchy will probably be replaced by men who are either corrupt or inefficient or both. Hence in practice this need of the worker to be involved in decision-making can in the long run probably be met only by formal participation, democratic or semi-democratic.

Another element in the need for satisfying work is the need to produce something useful or valuable, whether in the form of goods or services. This seems to be sometimes a matter for the individual, who can change his work if he finds it unsatisfying; but as we have seen this is often not possible in practice, or is possible only at great cost. On the other hand, for the same reason that a fully state-run economy is unlikely to fulfil the needs of consumers better than a free market – namely, that in practice this hands over the decisions to a bureaucratic minority – it is unlikely to fulfil the needs of workers. The two problems are really one: it is the same goods that satisfy consumer needs (as opposed to 'whims' or 'caprices') and that are worthwhile to produce.

Appropriate public intervention, though, could alleviate the problem. There is much worthwhile work, ranging from cleaning up and improving the environment, especially the urban environment, to looking after the old, young, ill or disabled, which the free market by and large does not tackle. There are many people able to work whom the free market does not employ, either because they are physically or mentally handicapped or because they are numerically superfluous: for many years the second problem was purely short-term, but we may well be moving into a condition of chronic unemployment. Much might be done by public schemes of 'alternative' work – just as it is increasingly accepted that a society, even if it operates a free market, should ensure a minimum level of subsistence for all, so we should turn our attention to ensuring the opportunity for worthwhile (if inevitably not always well-paid) work for all.

The third feature of 'man-centred' production is that
everyone should be able to relate his particular task to
the whole, even where labour is highly divided and specialized: the alienation produced by having to do one
repetitive and dull job not obviously connected with other
people's work is by now well-known. This problem is connected with the problem of participation, with the consequences of excessively large units of production, and with
methods of organization. It is probably a problem that
only those engaged in industry can solve; and while outsiders, such as academics, can legitimately point out its
existence, it is presumptuous and dangerous to offer advice on how to solve it. Once again, it seems to be a
problem caused by a particular stage of technology, and
not confined to any one economic system.

In general, then, the creation of man-centred production
seems to require an extensive modification of the system
rather than its overthrow: the problem is not peculiar to
one sort of economic institution, or fundamental to it.
Similarly, it is not clear that continual growth is necessary for capitalism. It is true that an individual firm
cannot really stand still, and that if business does not
expand it will contract. But even an individual firm could
exist indefinitely by expanding at some periods and contracting at others, and an economy all the more. It is
also true that the urge towards growth is an important
force behind capitalism, but it is not its only psychological basis. *Homo economicus*, who is governed above all
by the wish to maximize profit at all costs, does not
actually exist: and if he were really necessary to the
working of the system - as its extreme defenders and
extreme opponents agree in supposing - it would have
collapsed long ago.

Two other reasons for growth are more clearly the product of particular circumstances. One is the need to
raise the living standards of the less well-off; but
this could also be done by redistribution of wealth, and
the cake need not be made larger indefinitely. The other
is the need to maintain exports in the face of international competition, 'to run very fast in order to stay
in the same place'. This problem faces any country taking
part in international trade, whatever its internal arrangements; and may again depend on a particular situation,
rather than a particular system.

Finally, we come to criticisms of the capitalist ethic.
We have touched on some of these already, in particular
the insistence on success as a goal, coupled with the
interpretation of success as necessarily competitive, i.e.
involving someone else's failure, and as involving gaining

possession, rather than worthwhile activity. But the
fundamental moral criticism is usually levelled against
the notion of an unlimited right of property - unlimited
both as to how much a person may rightly acquire, and as
to what he may legitimately do with what he owns. 'No
one can be an absolute unlimited owner - not the individual, not the community, not the state.... Both the
individual and the state abuse their absolute right of
property and the power which it gives them, and become
tyrants and exploiters' (Berdyaev, 1960, part II, chapter 4, section vii).

Two criticisms, of logically different types, are
contained here. One is that the notion of unlimited
property rights is in itself morally indefensible. It
can be shown that it is one for which no rational justification can be given, since any justification of property
rights as such - for example, that they reduce conflict,
or that they are necessary for individual freedom and
self-development - will also justify their limitation when
they do not achieve the appropriate purpose. But if a
person insists, as for example, Nozick seems to do, that
the 'sanctity' of property is an ultimate principle, it is
hard to refute him. One can, though, point out the im-
plausibility of this position, since if there are rights
at all there must presumably be a right to life, which
ought to take precedence over the right to property, since
property is of little use to the dead!

The second criticism is an empirical one: if a society
accords unlimited property rights, in practice they will
inevitably be used to do harm. Property rights, if effective, necessarily give power to the owner. If one
person, or one group, owns a great deal of property, with
no restriction on what may be done with it, they may
control both jobs and the supply of commodities, and may
control much more, through their influence on people who
want one or the other: Tawney (1967, p. 77) claims that

> In America there are cities where the company owns not
> only the works, but halls and meeting-places, streets
> and pavements, where the town council and police are
> its nominees, and the pulpit and press its mouthpieces,
> where no meeting can be held to which it objects and no
> citizen can dwell of whom it disapproves.

Given human nature, it becomes inevitable that sooner or
later - probably sooner - this power will be misused.

It should be noted that this can come about either
through the concentration of property in a few hands or
through the absence of any acknowledged obligation to use
one's property to benefit others. It applies to the
state as much as to private owners; as Berdyaev rightly

points out, where state officials control jobs they appear
to misuse their power more than do monopoly capitalists,
if only because their power is that much greater. In
theory, what is publicly owned is owned by everyone and
controlled by no one; in practice, it is controlled
at best by the majority, and usually by a relatively
small group of administrators.

The moral criticism of absolute ownership, capitalist
or socialist, seems fully justified. But absolute ownership is not a necessary condition of a system of private
property. Opponents and defenders of capitalism unite in
supposing that it is, on the ground that ownership must be
either absolute or non-existent, so that if there are
limits on what a person can do with a piece of property
it is not his. However, one can break down property
rights into a large number of rights to use something in
various ways. It is perfectly possible for someone to
have the right to use property in one way but not in
another - for example, to be denied the right to destroy
it, or to do harm, however defined, with it, or to sell it
in perpetuity. This happens often legally, and can be
maintained even more easily in the moral sphere: 'I have
no absolute right of property even over the pen with which
I am writing this book; I may not do anything I like
with it and break it to pieces for no reason at all'
(Berdyaev, 1960, part II, chapter 4, section vii).

So there is no conceptual or practical difficulty with
limited ownership. It simply means that one has a right
to use something in certain ways, whether few or many,
and may not be interfered with when using the object in
question in any of these ways. But this is consistent
with being prohibited from using it in other ways, or
being limited as to the extent of the property rights
one is entitled, legally or morally, to acquire. If one
conceives of property rights in this way, as rights to
use, or as limited, rather than absolute, titles, a legal
system of such rights is in principle morally unobjectionable, though one might well take exception to the provisions of particular systems. Indeed, such a system is not
merely unobjectionable, but is actually necessary for the
satisfaction of human needs. In an earlier chapter, we
argued that there was a need for freedom from arbitrary
interference, and that this involved the existence of a
system of rules, formal or informal. These rules must
include rules about property rights, in the sense that
they must define who is entitled to use what and in what
way: a certain amount of vagueness is possible, but only
a certain amount, if the conditions for purposive action
are to be maintained. Moreover, the system itself must

prohibit excessive inequality in the distribution of property rights: otherwise the resultant inequality of power
will make arbitrary interference possible *de facto*, though
not *de iure*.

Together with the preceding points, this all shows that
the present economic system, even though it is by no
means a pure capitalist system, requires considerable
modification, if it is to meet needs successfully.   It
also shows that the particular virtue claimed for the
system, of giving people what they want, is something of
a myth, since the wants are themselves often generated or
modified by it.   Finally, it shows that Marcuse is in
principle right to point out that what people need in
order to function within the system does not coincide with
what they 'really' need, i.e. what would create adequate
conditions for purposive and worthwhile activity.

But none of this warrants a radical alteration of the
system, least of all a violent one.   First, every system
generates desires and needs: the free market is no better
in principle than any other in this respect, but it is
also no worse.   Second, as we have seen, the obstacles to
need satisfaction which the present system generates -
inequality of power, materialism, tedious and pointless
work, unnecessary stimulation of wants, the competitive
spirit, the non-moral attitude to property - are not
fundamental to the system: they cannot be dealt with in
a pure *laissez-faire* system, but they can be greatly
alleviated, if the will is there, in a mixed one.   Third,
the main practical alternative, that of state capitalism,
seems to have in practice all these drawbacks to an even
greater extent, perhaps because it is that much more mono-
polistic, and that much less in touch with human needs.

Other systems, such as the ownership of the means of
production by workers, as opposed to the state - what
some people would call 'real' socialism! - may one day
prove more satisfactory than either of these.   At the
moment those who think this would be desirable should
probably adopt a piecemeal method of working for it, partly because little is known about its practical merits and
demerits, and partly because an attempt at rapid change in
this direction might produce state capitalism - socialism
as popularly understood - instead of workers' ownership.
What seems to be particularly needed is a change of attitude towards property, work and the market - an acceptance
that these institutions ought to satisfy needs as well as
desires, and that it is legitimate - and indeed the duty
of society - to interfere with their 'free' operation
when they do not.

REAL NEEDS AND COERCION

This raises a final problem. We have rejected Marcuse's
argument for revolution in favour of arguments for reform,
but have accepted his point that what people feel they
need, and even genuinely need as long as the system is
unaltered, differs from their 'real' needs, which can be
met only if we adapt the system. The problem is whether
and when it could be legitimate to do this against the
wishes of the people affected. One has an obvious duty
to try to persuade people to see their real needs - or
what one believes to be their real needs - but if persuasion fails, or is impracticable, does one ever have
the right to use coercion?
    It seems that in principle one does have such a right,
simply because under such circumstances one would still be
carrying out the real desires of the people in question,
and doing what they would want if they had sufficient
knowledge. Morally speaking, this is only a more complex
version of the situation of the man who wants to step on
to an unsafe bridge, and who both needs and 'really'
wants to be restrained. The proper basis for policy
surely has to be what people would want or need if they
had adequate information, rather than what they feel they
need in a condition of ignorance of their situation and
the possibilities of changing it.
    However, coercion is clearly justified only if one can
be really certain that people's real needs are not their
felt needs, and that persuasion will not work. To be
sure of this, one needs to be sure that what one wishes to
provide is needed by the standards of the people affected,
i.e. that it is a necessary condition for ends that they
themselves do have, rather than ends that one believes
they ought to have but do not. This is not a problem if
the need in question is a 'human need', and a necessary
condition of any end; but otherwise it is an important
restriction on any right to coerce in the name of need;
it is one thing to coerce in order to satisfy a need
that would be recognized if people knew enough, or to
prevent people from harming each other, and another to
impose our own values on those who do not share them.
    In addition to being sure that the end is one that the
people involved would accept, one would also have to be
sure that the means really are necessary for it, and that
what one wishes to do will in fact create these conditions.
It is this last that makes coercion so rarely justifiable
in practice. For it is not too hard to know some of a
person's needs, even if one does not know what ends he has
set himself, since, as we have seen, there are needs that

people have whatever they want, or consider they ought, to
do. But to know that any particular social change will
result in better satisfaction of these needs than the
present situation, even though those affected oppose the
change, or to know that a coercive institution will succeed better than a voluntary one, is very difficult. (The
reasons for this uncertainty are well set out by Popper
(1962, vol. 1, chapter 9).

Indeed, one might ask whether it is possible for there
to be sufficient certainty on these points ever to justify
coercion in the name of 'real needs' in practice. It is
obviously justifiable when dealing with children or
people who are temporarily or permanently mentally dis-
turbed or deficient, and also under many circumstances on
the individual level when one knows with whom one is dealing and can reasonably predict the result of one's actions.
But to justify it on the political level one must look more
closely at the kinds of ignorance that arise and the kinds
of coercion that are possible.

Ignorance can be simple ignorance of fact, as when a
diabetic does not know that he needs insulin rather than
sugar. It can, as we have seen, also be ignorance of
what is possible: a person may know his needs given the
range of options available to him, but may not realize
that the system could be altered in such a way as to meet
his needs rather better. It is also possible for a person
to know in a vague sense what he needs but refuse to concentrate his mind on this point, so that he avoids becoming fully aware of uncomfortable facts, as when an
addict knows in some sense that he needs to be cured of
his addiction, but will not let himself face the fact. So
coercion will be justified if one's knowledge of what
people in general need, plus one's special knowledge of
the desires and moral principles of the relevant individual or group, plus any relevant specialized knowledge,
such as medical knowledge, makes it reasonably certain
that what the people in question would feel they needed
if they knew the relevant facts, considered the relevant
possibilities and honestly faced their position is different from their current felt needs, but there is no
time or opportunity to persuade them of this.

The clearest instances of this involve preventing
people from doing themselves harm, in the sense of doing
what is almost certain to interfere with their future
ends - examples are suicide, self-mutilation and addiction
to substances that are known to do great, if not fatal,
harm, such as heroin. As one moves away from cases of
clear and appreciable physical harm things become more
problematic, because the required certainty is less easily

obtained. Can one, for example, be justified in preventing
people from doing themselves moral or psychological harm,
or are these notions too tied to particular moral codes,
which those involved may not accept? May one force people
positively to help themselves, as Mill thought was justified in economically very backward communities? These
are very interesting questions; but they belong to law
rather than to social policy.

Indeed, the coercion involved in social policy is
rather different from that imposed by law, except in so
far as legal backing is needed in order to implement a
policy. It is not a matter of making people behave in
certain ways by imposing penalties if they do not, but
of changing their physical and social environment willy-
nilly. May this be done in a way that is coercive and
that overrides the felt needs of those affected in favour
of their 'real' needs?

These questions are in fact different. There can be
policies that everyone, or the majority, wish to see implemented, but that still cannot be implemented voluntarily,
because people are willing to do their share only if other
people do theirs. For example, every manufacturer of a
particular product may wish to reduce the pollution caused
by his factory, but may be unable to stand the expense
and remain in business unless all his competitors do the
same. The only solution is to enforce the taking of the
necessary steps. The same might apply to making work
conditions safer, or to preventing natural resources from
being exhausted.

So one can be justified in using coercion to bring about
a situation that most people want. But what about a situation in which what the experts say is needed differs
from what the people affected feel they need? Here one
needs to be sure that the expertise is real and to be
trusted, and also that all factors have been considered,
and not only those on which the expert is competent to
pronounce. There was not long ago a case of the sterilization of a West Indian girl, which was needed or advis-
able, if one considered only medical issues, but which
had the result, because of the premium on fertility in
West Indian culture, of making her almost unmarriageable
('Journal of Medical Ethics', vol. I, no. 1). To trust
the expert, rather than conveying his opinion to those
concerned, is all too often to concentrate on certain
aspects of a situation at the expense of others that may
be equally important, but may outride his competence. It
seems that there should be a presumption in favour of providing the relevant information, rather than imposing a

policy in the name of 'real' needs. There are cases
involving individuals where the issue is sufficiently
clear-cut for one to trust the expert. But this is rare
on the social level except when the question of what
social policy is needed can be solved by the application
of *one* sort of expertise. If two or more are required,
and the evidence from each points in a different direction, so that one policy will satisfy one set of needs
and another a different set, the experts are no better
placed to weigh one against the other than is anyone
else.

In principle, then, coercion in the name of 'real'
needs is justified. But in practice the situations in
which one can be sure of knowing someone else's needs
better than he does are exceptional, though not uncommon.
Examples are situations where people, if left free, will
do themselves clear and considerable harm, where coercion
is needed to implement what they want but cannot or will
not carry out voluntarily, and where the factual question
of what is needed can be settled by an appeal to the expert. Beyond this, coercion, especially on the large
scale, is unlikely to be justified. Nevertheless, the
distinction between true and false needs is a valid and
important one; and Marcuse is right to draw attention to
the ways in which the present social system satisfies
false needs at the expense of true ones. But the task of
anyone who agrees with this view, or an analogous one,
is not to compel his fellow citizens to follow what he
conceives to be their true needs, but to try and persuade
them of the nature of these needs and how economic and
other conditions might be improved in order to do justice to them.

8   Markets, needs and welfare

This chapter is concerned with the question of how the
resources of society ought to be distributed. The provision of social services outside the market system by
the welfare state has been commended and attacked on many
grounds. Some writers argue that social welfare is
necessary to counteract the inherent tendency of the
capitalist economic order to disequilibrium, whether as
a result of competition between the classes it creates,
or as a result of the tendency to disastrous depletion
of over-exploited human resources. Others claim that
welfare plays a positive role in training and socializing
citizens to fulfil the demands the system makes on them.
Yet others attempt a synthesis of these viewpoints.

On the other hand, it is maintained that the provision
of welfare is wasteful and unnecessary. It leads to
unsatisfactory, undesirable and unintended consequences,
and interferes with the successful operation of free markets.

We are not here concerned with argument on this practical level, important and fascinating though it is. This
chapter discusses the moral debate over the principles
underlying allocation - particularly the question of
whether society should try to share out scarce resources
according to some conception of human needs, or by the
criterion of people's wants. Welfare states have traditionally been described in terms of distribution according to need, however defined. Carrier and Kendal summarize definitions of the 'welfare activities of states'
proposed by Briggs, Marshall, Wedderburn and Titmuss by
arguing that: 'their distinctive feature is that their
manifest purpose is to influence differential "command
over resources" according to some criteria of need'
(Heisler, 1977, p. 27). This has been attacked as a
deleterious and unwarranted intrusion in a market system

173

that is well adapted to meet expressed wants. Acton
writes (1971, p. 100):

> the form of collectivism most favoured in Britain is
> to get basic welfare ... distributed in accordance with
> need rather than by purchase in competitive markets ...
> the complex bureaucracies necessary to carry this out
> ... would make independent discussion of the social
> and moral implications increasingly unlikely and prac-
> tically ineffective ... as many people as possible
> should have the opportunity of personal choice in these
> items of welfare as well as in food, apparel and
> amusement.

Argument at this level may describe the world rather
than change it. However, positions taken in political
debate do relate in a way that social science has not yet
succeeded in specifying to material interests in society.
To understand major contemporary ideologies is one step
towards understanding modern society. The question of
market versus welfare is sharpened by the present conflict on social service cuts. If the state distributes
less according to need, market allocation will presumably
assume a greater role.

This chapter seeks to trace certain features of the
struggle between the criterion of want and the principle
of need as standards to assess allocation in that curious
borderland between welfare economics, moral philosophy
and practical social policy wherein the more theoretical
concerns of social administration maintain an uneasy
truce with the major social science disciplines. It is
often argued that 'want' has the logical advantage over
'need' in that it is a more precise and less value-loaded
concept. Williams writes (Culyer, 1974a, p. 67):

> the word 'need' ought to be banished from discussion
> of public policy, partly because of its ambiguity, but
> also because ... the word is frequently used in ...
> 'arbitrary' senses ... in many public discussions it
> is difficult to tell, when someone says 'society needs'
> ... whether he means he needs it, whether he means
> society ought to get it, in his opinion, whether a
> majority of the members of society want it, or all of
> them want it.

Is the concept of 'want' any better off (as Williams
implies)?

The distinction between the two classes of principle is
examined in more detail below. The chapter goes on to
explore how far it is reasonable to maintain that a
principle of want escapes the normative preconceptions of
a principle of need. Difficulties in the ideological
defence of the free market system are pointed out. First
let us consider that defence in more detail.

THREE ARGUMENTS FOR MARKETS

The writings of the school of welfare economists well
represented in the UK through the Institute of Economic
Affairs (IEA) have been associated with the championing
of 'consumer sovereignty' and its expression in free markets as the effective operation of a principle of distribution according to want. 'Consumer sovereignty ... sig-
nifies that it is the preference of consumers as shown by
the ways in which they spend their money that determines
what merchandise is purchased and which services supplied....
In this way ... production is controlled by demand' (Fulop,
1967, p. 11).

    In his introduction to a commentary on the IEA's influ-
ential Hobart Paper series, the general editor, T.W.
Hutchinson, writes (1970, p. 10):

    as is well known, a distinguishing characteristic of the
    series and the main thrust of the Hobart attack consists
    in advocating and advancing the use of price and market
    mechanisms and competitive forces, based on an under-
    lying philosophy which starts from a strong preference
    for the decentralisation of initiative, and for the
    revival or extension of freedom of choice for indivi-
    duals as buyers and sellers or consumers and producers.

Why is a free market based on wants desirable? Three
separate strands can be detected in answers to this
question. The first is implicit in the unquestioned
premises of much IEA work and is clearly expressed by
Hutchinson in the passage quoted above. Wants are desirable
simply because they are wants. This 'underlying philosophy'
takes want as its irreducible starting-point and therefore
regards the satisfaction of want as the only satisfactory
criterion for the appraisal of social policy.

    The second justification is trenchantly stated in the
work of Friedman (1962). Here the ultimate, primitive, and
hence unjustifiable, value is freedom (p. 12):

    As liberals we take the freedom of the individual, or
    perhaps the family, as our ultimate goal in judging
    social arrangements. Freedom as a value in this sense
    has to do with the interrelations among people....
    There are two sets of values that a liberal will em-
    phasize: the values that are relevant to relations
    among people, which is the context in which he assigns
    first priority to freedom; and the values that are
    relevant to the individual in the exercise of his free-
    dom, which is the realm of individual ethics and
    philosophy.

Social welfare is justifiable as an intrusion only on the
rights of those who lack the capacity to exercise freedom.

Friedman later writes (1962):   'freedom is a tenable objective only for responsible individuals. We do not believe
in freedom for madmen or children.... Paternalism is inescapable for those we designate not responsible' (p. 33).
Similarly, Acton (1971) concludes 'The Morals of Markets':
'a centrally-planned economy is bound to monopolize ideas
and even to ration them, whereas in a society where competitive markets prevail, it is not only trade but also
thoughts and men that are free' (p. 101).

The third justification is contained in the work of
Hayek. In their critique of anti-collectivist thinkers,
George and Wilding regard liberty as the fundamental value
of the school. However, unlike Friedman, who is debarred
from doing so by his ultimate concern for freedom, Hayek
is as concerned as the collectivists that social organization should meet human needs. He disagrees with proponents of state welfare on how this is to be done. His
individualism is defined as 'the endeavour to make man by
the pursuit of his interest to contribute as much as possible to the needs of other men' (Hayek, 1949, p. 20;
cf. pp. 12-13). The goal of the utopian 'Great Society'
is that government action will secure 'conditions in
which individuals and small groups will have favourable
opportunities of mutually providing for their respective
needs' (Hayek, 1976, p. 2).

Hayek's major contribution has been in the subtle and
impressive elaboration of a particular theory of society.
The basis is (1949, p. 14):

the indisputable intellectual fact ... that man cannot
know more than a tiny part of the whole of society,
and that therefore all that can enter into his motives
are the immediate effects which his actions will have
in the sphere he knows, ... that ... the human needs
for which he can effectively care are an almost negli-
gible fraction of the needs of all members of society.

The theory of the essential unknowability of society underlies a powerful critique of state intervention (Hayek,
1973, p. 2):

The preservation of a society of free men depends on
three fundamental insights: ... that a self-generating
spontaneous order and an organisation are distinct and
that their distinctiveness is related to the two different kinds of rules or laws which prevail in them.
The second is that what today is regarded as 'social'
or 'distributive' justice has meaning only within the
second of these two kinds of order, the organization;
but that it is meaningless in and wholly incompatible
with that spontaneous order which Adam Smith called
the 'Great Society' and Sir Karl Popper called the

'Open Society'. The third is that the predominant
model of liberal democratic institutions in which the
same representative body lays down the rules of just
conduct necessarily leads to the gradual transformation of the spontaneous order of a free society into
a totalitarian order....
Market systems are legitimated thus: 'only because the
market induces every individual to use his unique knowledge
of particular opportunities and possibilities for his purpose can an overall order be achieved that uses in its
totality the dispersed knowledge which is not available
as a whole to anybody' (Hayek, 1968, p. 30).

The standpoints of Hutchinson and Friedman rest on the
conception of wants as values in themselves, or as expressing an underlying value of freedom: they share the
weakness of any purely normative approach. Hayek provides a far more formidable approach to the justification
of the market as the institutionalization of human freedom
in the notion that the social order is fundamentally unknowable. Any perspective that postulates distribution
according to some value - that tries to construct a yardstick of some socially just distribution whereby to assess
society's achievement - is barking up the wrong gum tree.
A socially just order cannot in principle be conceived,
because society itself cannot be known. Man is a frail
creature in a mysterious world. His inadequate understanding prevents him from consciously organizing a
social system to confront and regulate that world.

The dialectic strength of the position is that it
opposes 'justice' to 'freedom': 'Social justice can be
given a meaning only in a directed or "command" economy
(such as the army) in which the individuals are ordered
what to do, and any particular conception of social justice could be realized only in such a centrally directed
system' (Hayek, 1976, p. 69). Unless all relevant factors
can be known and controlled, Hayek argues (1976) that: 'the
concept of social justice is strictly empty and meaningless' (p. 68).

The accusation that the humanitarian opponent of the
anarchy of the market is in fact a totalitarian in dis-
guise with jack-boots under his trouser turn-ups is
calculated to make the welfare statist uneasy. However,
the position, as Schumpeter points out (1943, p. 185), is
not immediately compelling. It seems plausible that government intervention in the provision of social security,
environmental and medical health services, subsidized
housing and so on has had considerable success in better-
ing the condition of the masses since, say, mid-Victorian
times. To a superficial observer, planning has achieved

a somewhat fairer society. Where are the disastrous
'unintended consequences of social policy'?

The persuasiveness of the argument rests on a theory of
explanation in social science that imposes very strict
limitations on what can count as understanding. This
theory, methodological individualism, will be considered
in detail below. Before we review the relevance of this
approach, and the power of the arguments that rest on it,
one obstacle must be cleared. Some writers have argued
that the satisfaction of wants is scarcely admissible as
a principle of distributive justice on the same level as
the fulfilment of needs. Thus Miller (1976): 'if the
proportionate satisfaction of wants is a principle of
justice, it is much less compelling than the principle
of need' (p. 148; cf. also p. 19). If accepted, this
position would radically undermine the point of this
chapter. Are wants a plausible alternative to needs?

Miller distinguishes essential and non-essential wants,
the former class overlapping with needs. His argument is
based on the example of a society that uses a lottery to
share out resources left over after needs have been
satisfied. Such a system we could plausibly describe as
fair, provided the rules of the lottery were fair, although it would not satisfy wants. The passage continues:
'contrast the situation where everything goes into the
lottery, so that many people are left with their needs
unsatisfied. This is unquestionably unjust.' Against
this, we may argue that to show that a system that satisfies needs but not wants is more just than a system that
satisfies neither needs nor wants is not to show that it
is necessarily more just than a system that satisfies
wants and not needs. Serious philosophers, notably
utilitarians, have maintained such a position. It is
noteworthy that Rawls considers utilitarianism as one of
the two serious rivals to his own position in the early
sections of 'A Theory of Justice'. For our purposes it
is important to take account of its application to social
service provision. As Ewing (1962) points out, 'it is
of interest that utilitarianism made its mark in the field
of ... large scale social reform. In these matters ...
it comes very much nearer to providing a satisfactory
criterion than in the sphere of individual ethics' (p. 48).

In his introduction to a collection of essays on
Hayek's 'Constitution of Liberty', Seldon writes (1961,
pp. xi-xii):

In Britain good sense and common humanity are at last
enforcing a reconsideration of the nature, extent and
role of the social services; some that are only 50
years old have already outlived their day; opinion

is beginning to move and it may not be long before it
becomes possible to reorientate the weight of social
expenditure on the dwindling [sic] proportion of old
people and others in need, and to redirect social
activity to newer services that cannot be supplied
easily through the market.
  Those who urge the claims of the free market as the
centrepiece of the free society have too rarely faced
the need to ensure that it is understood and accepted
if it is to work effectively and without social disturbance.... The risks and sanctions of the market
process must receive the moral allegiance of the
people. The market must be seen not only as efficient
but as good, and as satisfying whatever canons of
justice are regarded as proper.
  It is in opposition to claims such as this that it is
necessary to consider the basis of market ideology. In
the next section we move on to consider the problems
involved in distinguishing wants from needs as criteria
for the allocation of social resources.

THE DISTINCTION BETWEEN WANTS AND NEEDS

Wants and needs are conceptually distinct. Miller makes
the point well (1976, p. 127):
  We often say of people that they want things that they
  do not need; for instance a child who demands a
  lollipop ... certainly wants a lollipop, but we are
  most unlikely to acknowledge that he needs one. We
  (rather less often) say of people that they need
  things which they do not want. We might say of the
  same child that he needs to eat more healthy food,
  though he gives us every evidence that he wants to
  do no such thing. ·
What is the precise nature of the distinction? The concepts have been discussed in chapters 2 and 3. Here, we
wish to emphasize three points relating to the criteria
of ascription of the terms, to their range of reference
and to their 'logical grammar'.

The irreducibility of want

First, as Miller goes on to say (p. 129):
  wanting is a psychological state which is ascribed on
  the basis of a person's avowals and his behaviour ...
  needing on the other hand, is *not* a psychological
  state, but rather a condition which is ascribed
  objectively to the person who is its subject.

In chapter 2 the notions of 'desirability characterizations', and of a normative concept of harm have been
deployed to show that this distinction between an objective and a subjective frame of reference is simplistic.
However, within a given social context, the statement 'he
says so' makes a perfectly satisfactory answer to the
question 'how do you know he wants x?', whereas it emphatically does not in the case of the question 'how do
you know he needs x?' It is this difference that we focus
on when we distinguish the pursuit of wants through the
market system from the pursuit of wants through social
policy; for free markets take wants as given, whereas
social policy must attempt to characterize the needs it
is designed to meet.

The 'objectivity' of a criterion of wants from the
market viewpoint is not in question: we can find out
what people want simply by asking them, and this remains
true whether or not we go on to characterize the wants
people experience under some circumstances as false wants.
To argue that some wants are imposed on people by the
social order in which they are an element is not to
argue that these wants are no longer wants in the sense
that the market school maintains: it is rather to question the legitimacy of appeal to such wants as a basis
for just distribution. The argument is considered in
relation to the philosophy of Marcuse in an earlier
chapter, and in relation to the theme of this chapter,
below.

It is not immediately obvious, however, whether it is
possible to construct a satisfactory and persuasive normative criterion of need. An appeal to the common
humanity of mankind lacks conviction among the contemporary social science community. Can an ideal of compelling rational force be produced? In recent years,
intellectual rigour has been leant to the relativist position by the growth and sophistication of the phenomenological school, well represented in social administration
by Carrier and Kendal. After presenting a powerful
critique of the positivistic bases they detect in traditional writing of social policy, they argue: 'thus to
refer to objective social conditions may be inherently
misleading. Many of the needs that welfare activities
attempt to meet or ameliorate may be most appropriately
regarded as socially defined' (Carrier and Kendal, 1973,
p. 220). Hayek's point, that 'In a market economy in
which no single person or group determines who gets what,
and the shares of individuals always depend on circumstances which no one could have foreseen, the whole
concept of social or distributive justice is empty and

meaningless' (Hayek, 1973, p. 13;   cf. 1960, p. 440), is
closely related. 'Since he maintains that advanced industrial society is in principle too complex to admit of
the effective distribution of resources in accordance
with any ideal, the impossibility of the operation of a
positive critique of social justice in practice is the
evaluative correlative of the impossibility of positive
explanation in analysis.

The scope of needs

The second major distinction between needs and wants
lies in the range of application of the concepts. Unless
we resort to the most simplistic behaviourism (which
would in itself deny the relevance of the kind of discussion to which this chapter is attempting to contribute),
we are prepared to attribute wants only to beings with consciousness - to people. Needs, however, can be ascribed
on the objective criteria. Thus, Anscombe (1958) can
write with perfect felicity of the needs of plants. Needs
can be ascribed to inanimate objects: 'This car needs an
entire new brake system' (p. 7).
    Leaving aside an animism that would extend the range of
wants to those sedimented in language in the elective
affinities of chemicals, or a behaviourism that would
simply dissolve the distinction between the two concepts,
the range of wants is narrower than that of needs. However, it is not clear that this fact has any bearing on a
discussion of needs and wants as alternative social bases
for distribution. The needs of inhuman nature do not
arise in this context. Distribution is conceived of
either as between individuals, in which case want and need
criteria are *prima facie* equally applicable, or as between social groups viewed as entities *sui generis*, not
wholly reducible to the individuals that constitute them.
Social groups, as distinct from their members, can have
needs but not wants attributed to them. The difference
in range here is subsumed under the different collective
and individual 'logical grammar' of the concepts, which
constitutes the third major difference.

Logical grammar

To ascribe a collective want to a social group is to
ascribe the same want to each member of that group (or,
since the infection of the ideology of majority voting
as interpreting choice, to each of a majority of members

of that group). Thus, 'Stockport ratepayers want to pay
lower rates' implies (at least) that a large number of
individuals who are Stockport ratepayers want to pay
lower rates. The truth of the statement is checked by
the process of asking a representative sample of ratepayers, as the present councillors will (in effect) do at
the next local election.

The case of needs statements is different. To ascribe
a need to a group does not necessarily involve the ascription of needs to each (or indeed to any) members of that
group. Thus, to say 'Stockport ratepayers need to pay
higher rates', either for some end, such as the institution of a humane level of local services, or for the
avoidance of some kind of harm, such as the harm that
will undoubtedly afflict (if we are to believe Bowlby
and Rutter) those families where young children are
separated from their mothers because of a lack of home-
less families accommodation does not necessarily imply
that any individual ratepayer in the metropolitan dis-
trict need pay higher rates. It is perfectly sensible
to imagine the statement being applied to Stockport ratepayers as a body in relation to some standard of community
welfare or collective justice, 'so that Stockport may be
a better place to live in', or 'so that the deprived in
Stockport may be better cared for', and at the same time
to imagine quite different standards being ascribed to
define the needs of individual citizens. The individuals
may need lower rates in relation to some individual end or
standard such as the maintenance of a high level of consumption, or the release of as much personal income as
possible for private charity (and we may argue that such
charity fosters the individual's true moral development
as a caring person). Indeed, unless all or a substantial
number of ratepayers were to fork out higher rates the
collective goals could not be reached. These by their
very nature can be attained only by joint action. If a
group wants, each wants, whereas if a group needs, it does
not necessarily follow that each needs. Groups may have
other goals than those of their members.

The distinction becomes even clearer if we move on to
consider collectivities at the widest social level. J.S.
Mill (1962, pp. 292-3) could perfectly correctly move from
a criterion of what each individual desired to a statement about what all individuals desired. Problems arise
(as has often been pointed out, notably in G.E. Moore's
discussion of the Naturalistic Fallacy) in moving from the
empirical to the normative - from statements about what all
desire to what is desirable for all. This 'your country
wants you [to fight in the First World War]', if it is to

have meaning, must mean that a sizeable number of your
countrymen want you to fight. Roman senators probably
took some such message to Cincinnatus at his ploughing.
'Your country needs you' makes a much better recruiting
slogan precisely because of the normative overtones involved, because it is not based on an empirical statement
about popular opinion. Yet it is only possible to move
from such a statement to statements about the needs of
individual members of the population (for you to fight)
on certain normative interpretations of the needs of
various groups and how those needs can be served by the
continuance of the British state in its present form.
Imperialism certainly needs cannon fodder. Individuals
may well need to be soldiers like they need a hole in the
head. They may need others to be soldiers like they need
imperialism - to take one contested view.

This contrast between a collective and individual
grammar of the concepts relates closely to questions
raised in the 'methodological individualism' debate about
the correct mode of explanation in social science. Individualism in explanation has a respectable ancestry leading back at least to Hobbes (according to Lukes) and possibly to William of Occam (according to Popper). In
recent times, the polemics of Hayek and Popper have stimulated response and support (see Jarvie, 1972, pp. 171-8,
and Lukes, 1973, pp. 110-24, for useful summaries). The
set-piece debate is about the correct way of explaining
social phenomena. Our concern is with two different ways
of assessing the distribution of goods in society. To
discuss the relevance of methodological individualism we
must explore the relation of explanation to evaluation.

EXPLANATION AND EVALUATION

Downie's argument, that explanation and evaluation are
closely linked because both involve the situation of
phenomena in a framework of commonly understood and eval-
uated statements, has been discussed in an earlier chapter.
Two other factors need to be taken into account. First,
there is an empirical association. Many of the major
writers who have attempted comphrehensive explanations of
social phenomena have also constructed normative theories,
and the two are often interlinked. Thus Marcuse's use of
alienation, Durkheim's notion of anomie and Reich's concept of repression serve both to describe and to condemn
certain states of affairs.

The second strand to the argument involves necessary
relations. To evaluate a phenomenon is to pass a judg-

ment on it. This implies relating it to some standard.
Explanation provides an answer to the question 'why?'.
The answer must be satisfactory in that it somehow re-
moves the need to ask the question, but not every way of
putting an end to questioning fulfils this standard.
The point may be illustrated with reference to Bernstein's
conception of restricted and elaborated language codes
(Bernstein, 1971, pp. 170-89). An example is the case of
the small child who persists in asking 'why?' of every
succeeding justification for some course of action that
his mother is recommending to him. The middle-class
elaborated code-user continues to supply explanations in
justification: 'you must hold tight in case the bus stops
suddenly. If it stops with a jerk you'll fall over. If
you fall over you'll hurt yourself', and so on. The
rough working-class restricted code-user simply stops all
further argument by 'If you don't shut up you'll get a
thick ear!' or 'Because I say so!' and socializes her
child into a framework of justification that does not
depend primarily on explanation, thus impoverishing his
conceptual development.

There are in practice a number of ways of explaining
things. One way is to attempt to formulate more or less
universal laws under which the instances in question may
fall. 'Why did the apple fall?' 'Because of the law of
gravity.' 'Why is ... evil?' 'Power corrupts; absolute
power corrupts absolutely; all great men are evil.'

Another method is to identify the instance in question
so that it is related to other unquestioned phenomena.
'Why is that Kwakiutul Indian throwing his cooking pots
in the sea?' 'He's taking part in a potlach ceremony.'
'Why is that meteorite so bright?' 'It's undergoing
frictional heating.' Such explanations presuppose unquestioned phenomena - social institutions, roles and so
forth. 'Why is that man lying under my car?' 'He's
checking the brakes for the MoT test', 'He's hiding from
the police', 'He's trying to read the inscription on a
manhole cover'. For any of these statements to work as an
appropriate explanation, they must bring about an end to
questioning at that level. This can come about only in
relation to some accepted context - not only do we need to
know what brakes, MoT tests, the police, reading and manhole covers are, we also need to understand why people
should wish to pass MoT tests, that it should be appropriate in some contexts to hide from the police, that
people can (apparently) sensibly want to read manhole
covers and so on, for these explanations to do the job. It
is this kind of explanation that is typically involved in
the interpretation of social phenomena as social problems.

The point has been elaborated in chapter 2. Explanation
by the location of phenomena within a framework of statements that serve to identify them as problematic can link
suggested solutions to basic evaluative statements. Let
us examine the topical example of the 'urban problem'.

The facts of the urban crisis - high unemployment
rates, crime rates and other indicators of social distress,
bad housing, poverty, and inadequate social services in
major cities and an ever-sharpening geographical division
between deprived inner-city ghettos and affluent suburbs -
are not in dispute. The Secretary of State for the Environment, Peter Shore, warned in a speech given in Bristol in
September 1976: 'if cities fail, so to a large extent
does our society. That is the urgency of tackling the
problem, and why it has to be of concern to everyone in
this land.' Thus, the flood of reports of inner-city
problems that has appeared since the mid-1960s and projects designed to cope with them - Educational Priority
Areas (EPAs), Urban Aid, Community Development Project
(CDP), Inner Area studies, and so on. There is a wide-
ranging debate about how to solve these problems, and
solution is linked to explanation. Broadly speaking,
three different kinds of explanation can be distinguished,
characterized not by disagreement on the data, or on the
phenomena that require remedy, but by dispute over the
appropriate level of analysis.

First, there is a focus on the level of the individual
or the immediate family group which emphasizes social
incompetence (whether due to individual inadequacy, or
transmitted through a cultural 'cycle of deprivation')
as the reason for the problem. People in inner-city
areas do not tend to succeed in grasping the opportunities
offered by our society so well as others because of their
socialization, their local culture or their personality
structure.

Second, institutional explanation blames the failure of
the governmental system to plan, provide and publicize
adequate levels of service. Administration is ineffective, and the way services are organized tends to place
obstacles in the way of effective utilization, especially
among the politically weak and the poor. The problem is
with our institutions, and these institutions must be
reformed.

Third, a structural level of explanation argues that
the nature of our society makes it inevitable that some
areas will decline and others develop at their expense.
This class of explanations can be underpinned by appeal to
Trotsky's law of combined and uneven development, or
through the Weberian tradition with its emphasis on strati-
fication and the unequal distribution of power.

The distinction between these three approaches has
become a commonplace in writing on social policy - see
Parker (1975, pp. 4-15); Coventry Community Development
Project (1973, vol. 1, p. 10); Forder (1974, pp. 58-60),
and so on. Each explains the same 'facts' in a different
way, and suggests a different solution - individual and
family casework, reformism and structural social change.
The point is that values are built into them not at the
level of argument (for the arguments do not dispute the
empirical evidence, only its interpretation), but at the
level of the unexamined premises which direct explanation. From one standpoint the accounts can indeed be
reconciled. Individual incompetence and institutional
malfunction can be seen as mechanisms whereby structural
inequalities are transmitted, sustained, justified. It
is rather at the level of where argument begins and what
mode of analysis theoreticians see as appropriate that
differences arise. Ultimately the question of level of
analysis cannot itself be a matter for explanation - if
this were the case explanation could go on for ever.
Level of analysis involves value-judgments about the important features of society. The decision to operate on
an individual, institutional or structural level of analysis is a matter of value, but it profoundly affects the
outcome explanation in the area in which we are interested -
how social resources should be distributed. Evaluation,
explanation and policy are intimately linked in political
debate. We move on to consider the relevance of individualism in explanation to our argument.

METHODOLOGICAL INDIVIDUALISM

The notion of methodological individualism is central to
the work of Hayek. The restriction of acceptable explanation to explanation in individualist terms substantiates
the position that society is essentially unknowable. For,
as I shall try to show, adequate explanation of social
phenomena requires the transcendence of the individualist
perspective, and reference to collectivities. Individualism is the denial of social analysis in principle, and
thus the foundation of the standpoint that rational
social planning to meet human need is impossible. It is
because this theory operates in his work to underpin the
justification of freedom as articulated in free markets
by the removal of a contentious alternative approach to
the satisfactory distribution of social resources, that
Hayek presents a much more convincing challenge to the
ideological proponents of collectivism. Friedman simply

nails his colours to the mast of value. Thus, Hayek
provides the ultimate theoretical foundation appealed to
by the writers of the IEA.

His position differs from the atomistic, asocial view
of man that many critics of individualism in classical
economic theory have been concerned to attack. Lukes
(1973, pp. 139-40) quotes Veblen's satirical characterization of the concept of man as:

   A lightning calculator of pleasures and pains who
   oscillates like a homogeneous globule of desire of
   happiness under the impulse of stimuli ... self-
   imposed in elemental space, he spins symmetrically
   about his own spiritual axis until the parallelogram
   of forces bears down upon him, whereupon he follows
   the line of the resultant....

Hayek writes (1949, p. 6):

   Individualism is primarily a theory of society, an
   attempt to understand the forces that determine the
   social life of man.... It does not postulate the existence of isolated or self-contained individuals instead of starting from men whose whole nature and
   character is determined by their existence in society.
   If that were true it would have nothing to contribute to our understanding of society. Our basic contention is quite a different one. It is that there is
   no other way towards an understanding of social phenomena but through our understanding of individual
   actions directed towards other people and guided by
   their expected behaviour.

It is on these grounds, he argues, that 'it is a mistake
to which careless expressions by social scientists often
give countenance to believe that their task is to explain
conscious action. This, if it can be done at all is the
task of psychology....' (1952, p. 39).

It is clear that such a position if accepted destroys
any possibility of explanation in social science. All
that there is to explain is individual action, and all
that can impinge on individuals is the result (often unintended) of the actions of other men. Similarly, any
distinction between the logical grammar of collectivist
and individualist needs and wants evaporates. Individual
needs and wants are perfectly straightforward. Collective
needs (or wants) as properties of social entities *sui
generis* that do not directly reduce to individual needs
and wants are simply nonsense. Such an approach lends
force to the analysis of distribution on a criterion of
wants, since the utility of needs in introducing collectivities into the sphere of discussion disappears. If the
normative nature of needs is not seen as infecting wants,

the balance of argument in favour of the market is over-
powering. How satisfactory is the position?

The debate is far too complex for this chapter to do
it justice. However it is possible to raise some relevant points. It is important to be clear what the individualistic position is stating. To say that social
phenomena are to be explained only in terms of statements about individual motivation which fall within the
realm of psychology as Hayek appears to, or to adopt
Watkins modified position (1959a) that 'we shall not have
arrived at rock-bottom explanations of such large-scale
phenomena until we have deduced an account of them from
statements about the dispositions, beliefs, resources
and interrelations of individuals' (p. 515) is not necessarily to assert that the former phenomena are reducible
to the latter. Jarvie writes (1972, p. 157) 'methodological individualism is not a reductionism that will
eliminate all but individuals from sociological explanation. That this is a gross misinterpretation has already
been asserted by Watkins.' He is however prepared to
argue the reductionist thesis in some cases at any rate.
Lukes (1973) quotes his 'Reply to Taylor', in which he
maintains that '"army" is merely a plural of "soldiers",
and all statements about the army can be reduced to
statements about the particular soldiers comprising the
army' (p. 116).

It seems hard to imagine what controversial position
individualism is maintaining, if it is not taking up a
reductionist stance. If society consists of individuals
and possibly of other, less transparent phenomena, called
'collectivities' as well, explanation of social phenomena
must be in terms of one, the other, both, or the relation
between them. If methodological individualism is not
reductionism and is not a trivial restatement of explanation in terms of collectivities, it appears to state
that social explanation is impossible, since all four
possibilities are ruled out. Hayek's arguments about the
complexity and incomprehensibility of large-scale economic systems sometimes seem to approach this position.
However, if this is to be the case, life becomes hard for
the social scientist; for the psychologist can do the
job of explanation for him only if the reductionist position is maintained. If social phenomena are in principle
inexplicable, rational discussion of distribution in terms
of either wants or needs is at an end. Explanation and
evaluation alike involve the location of social phenomena
in frameworks that at the least describe in an intelligible way. Anti-reductionist individualism simply denies
the possibility of any such framework.

Similarly, the reductionist position seems to involve placing limits on explanation that are not immediately obvious and require justification. Lukes points out that it is not incontestable that the processes of a trial in a court of law are any less accessible or comprehensible than the motives of a criminal. Why stick at the individual level?

It may be objected at this stage that Popper, while endorsing an individualistic method of explanation, succeeds in rejecting psychologistic reductionism. Thus in his critique of historicism, he writes (Popper, 1957, pp. 157-8):

the doctrine which teaches the reduction of social theories to psychology ... is ... based on a misunderstanding. It arises from the false belief that methodological psychologism is a necessary corollary of a methodological individualism - the quite unassailable doctrine that we must try to understand all collective phenomena as due to the actions, interactions, aims, hopes and thoughts of individual men, and as due to traditions created and preserved by individual men.

In the 'Open Society and its Enemies' (Popper, 1962, the critique is repeated, although (vol. 2, p. 91):

we must not overlook the great merits of psychologism in propounding a methodological individualism and opposing a methodological collectivism; for it lends support to the important doctrine that all social phenomena, and especially the functioning of social institutions, should always be understood as resulting from the decisions, actions, attitudes, etc., of human individuals, and that we should never be satisfied by an explanation in terms of so-called 'collectives' (states, nations, races, etc.).

It is this position, whether interpreted in terms of a psychologistic reduction or as a reduction within the framework of Popper's 'situational logic', with which we are concerned. Can the social phenomena that are relevant to the analysis of social policy be understood without reference to 'collectivities'? Is there a place for a separate understanding of the needs of such entities in our analysis?

Perhaps the strongest argument in favour of the individualist position bases itself on the nominalist thesis that only individuals are real. Why should we bother our heads by multiplying troublesome metaphysical (or as Watkins calls them 'superhuman') entities to bolster up our sociological explanation? The question now resolves itself into one of how useful the entities in question are. After all, particular concepts are man-made tools developed

to do certain jobs, and if they create more problems
than they resolve, perhaps we should discard them. Does
this argument apply to the 'collectivity'?

For present purposes we may distinguish two varieties
of methodological individualism - a strong and a weak form.
The strong form insists on explanation in terms of the dispositions, intentions, attitudes and actions of the
existing social actors who happen to be involved in the
social phenomenon in question. This seems to be the view
of Hayek and Popper. Anything that cannot be explained
in these terms cannot be accounted for at all, and is best
forgotten. The weak form is content with individualist
explanation at the most abstract level. Watkins (1959b)
is content to argue: 'the individuals may remain anonymous and only typical dispositions etcetera may be attributed to them' (p. 505).

The strong form seems incapable of doing the job we
want done. Any translation of the (exceedingly vague but
none the less useful) statement, 'the working class is by
and large now prepared to accept a fall in take-home pay,
in view of the official interpretation of the roots of
the economic crisis' into statements about the past,
present and likely future actions and conscious motives
for action in the minds of the populace is inadequate.
Motives and the whole apparatus of psychological conceptualization certainly explain individual action (though
not in an undisputed way!), but they do not explain anything more. The result of this approach is to rule out
any notion of state, crisis, class and so on. Yet these
elements certainly figure in the explanations of people's
actions. The fact that very many people are accepting a
considerable cut in living standards for the first time
in a generation requires explanation, and it is difficult to see how an explanation of this acceptance in the
case of any one individual can avoid mentioning that individual's perceptions of the actions and likely actions
of other groups of individuals conceived as social forces
shaping the social environment in which he formulates
intentional action. To reduce such explanatory statements again to statements about the actions of Tom, Dick
and Harry is to fall into the trap of circularity. To
figure collectivities *sui generis* among the elements of
psychological explanation is not to dissolve them.

A similar objection applies to the weak form. Here,
however, collectivities can be directly incorporated into
the individuals. If we are to talk, for instance, of
'typical members of the working class', with typical
structures of incentives, attitudes and so on (empirically
investigated by those intrepid members of the social science

profession who have emerged unscathed from the lower
depths, from Booth and Rowntree through to Silburn and
Westergaard), we gain nothing. The individual simply
stands for the collectivity. Even if typicality is
simply interpreted as 'being average', the question of
individualism is begged. To assume that averages can
stand for individuals in explanation is to assume that
individuals have something in common that can sensibly
be averaged out. Yet to argue in terms of something
common to individuals is to construct explanation founded
on non-individualistic social entities. This approach is
harmless, but pointless. We might as well talk in terms
of collectivity. Examination of an important study which
attempts to use individualist techniques will make the
limitations of the method clear. Let us look at Eysenck's
'The Psychology of Politics' (1954).

AN INDIVIDUALISTIC ACCOUNT OF POLITICAL BEHAVIOUR

Eysenck introduces the work (1954, p.
    I have tried to write a book about modern developments
    in attitude theory.... Science now has something to say
    about such questions as anti-semitism, the origin and
    growth of fascist and communist ideologies, the causal
    determinants of voting behaviour, and the relation be-
    tween politics and personality.
He continues, 'my purpose has been to understand and
explain' (p. 2). How? The answer is given in a nutshell
on pp. 9-10:
    It is the less spectacular but more systematic type of
    psychology with which we shall here be concerned; it
    is here and here alone that the hope of a truly scien-
    tific understanding of political problems lies. Psycho-
    logy so conceived has one advantage over other disci-
    plines that makes it of particular interest and impor-
    tance. Political actions are actions of human beings;
    the study of the direct causes of these actions is the
    field of study of psychology. All other social sciences
    deal with variables which affect political action in-
    directly. Economics ... does not deal with human
    behaviour ... directly, but ... uses a psychology of
    its own as an intermediary between economic fact and
    social behaviour. The psychologist has no need of such
    intermediaries; he is in direct contact with the cen-
    tral link in the chain of causation between antecedent
    condition and resultant action.
Lukes (1972) quotes part of the above passage and continues: 'Eysenck sets out to classify attitudes ...

then ... his aim is to explain them ... and his interest
here is centred upon modifications of the central nervous
system' (p. 83). This seems an oversimplification. If
Eysenck were able to produce satisfactory explanations of
political behaviour in neurobiological terms (remember
here that 'satisfactory' refers to 'that which makes the
unintelligible intelligible'; we are not concerned to
deny that there are neurobiological correlates of political
behaviour) and only neurobiological terms, he could certainly claim to have produced an individualist explanation
that 'worked': to have vindicated his claim for the pre-
eminence of psychology in the explanation of social behaviour; to have shown that the individual is the central
causal link. In fact, the individualist position that he
finally takes up is rather more sophisticated than the
one Lukes gives him credit for. The major conclusions of
the work is the 'hypothesis' that 'if ... socialization may
largely be equated with tender-mindedness then we should
expect extraverts to be tough-minded, introverts to be
tender-minded' (Eysenck, 1954, pp. 262-3). Extraversion,
tender-mindedness and their opposites are attitudes defined, broadly speaking, in terms of the clustering of
individual responses to questionnaires. (Perhaps it should
be pointed out that some of the questions - e.g. 'The
government must first balance the budget'; 'Labour unions
are alright, but we can't have strikes' require the res-
pondent to react to collective notions. The criticism of
Eysenck's method may be turned if the phrases are interpreted simply as stimuli, rather than as statements that
require understanding to generate response.) The important
point is: how does Eysenck explain the link between attitudes that he posits - for explanation of such an apparently
arbitrary association does seem essential to render the
unintelligible intelligible? And what does he mean by an
attitude, anyway?
    The link between tough/tender-mindedness and intro-
version/extraversion is provided by the notion of socialization. Eysenck (1954) equates the social process of
socialization with the psychological process of conditioning (p. 259). He is then in a position to account
for the association between tender-mindedness and intro-
version by pointing to empirical evidence that 'introverts form quick and stable conditioned responses, while
extraverts condition slowly' (p. 262). Conditioning
simply is tender-mindedness. However, in his account of
conditioning he writes of 'the amount of conditioning
which society ... inflicts on the individual' (p. 259).
He seems unable to escape using the collective notion of
a social whole within which the individual is situated,

and which contributes to the formation of attitudes that
themselves persist as enduring recognition of the social
whole in the mind of the individual.

In the same way, Eysenck endorses Allport's definition
of an attitude: 'an attitude is a mental or neural state
of readiness organized through experience, exerting a
directive or dynamic influence upon the individual's
response to all objects and situations with which it is
related' (Eysenck, 1954, p. 13).   What experience, and
what objects?   The concept is immediately used to discuss
the relation of class, status and voting behaviour.   Class
is 'something entirely subjective;   the belief which the
individual holds concerning his own position in the social
class system'.   Status is 'something entirely objective,
namely his relative position in the social class system
as determined by certain external criteria'.   It is hard
to see how these concepts can be used without taking for
granted the collective notion of 'a social class system'.
Eysenck does not define this, but quotes with approval
Center's discussion, which relates class to class consciousness, and status to 'the economic processes of
society' imposing on a person 'certain attitudes, values
and interests relating to his role and status in the economic sphere'.

Later, he comes to the conclusion that 'in dealing with
behaviour a knowledge of attitude is not sufficient'
(p. 239) and introduces the concept of stereotypy.   He
endorses Lippman's famous comment: 'in the great bloom-
ing, buzzing confusion of the outer world, we pick out
what our culture has already defined for us, and we tend
to perceive that which we have picked out in the form
stereotyped by our culture' (p. 240).   Culture may be
transmitted through individuals but it is hard to see how
an account of socialization can be given totally in terms
of the way individuals happen to act.

In the opening chapter, Eysenck argues (1954, p. 8):
It is fully realized that most of the problems discussed must ultimately be seen in their historical,
economic, sociological, and perhaps even anthropological context, but ... the scientist always begins by
simplifying his problem;   having thus acquired some
knowledge of the laws which describe the phenomenon
with which he is dealing, he is then ready to study
them in a more complex setting.
This is to promise more than can be done.   The social
scientific setting is irreducibly there, already built
into the concepts of socialization, attitude, class,
status, society, culture and social system that Eysenck
is forced to employ to situate his correlations of ques-

tionnaire responses in the endeavour to make them into a
satisfactory explanation of political behaviour. To re-
tort that these notions reduce to individual action and
intention is to miss the point. They may well be totally
embodied in human consciousness and interaction (in
fact, they must be), but to explain them thus is to fall
into infinite regress. The action of the explicans becomes itself explicandum. As Berger and Luckman (1967)
point out, 'society is a human product; man is a social
product; any attempt to ignore either of these two
moments is to distort social reality' (p. 79). In one
sense social phenomena can be explained by reduction to
individual human action, but only at the cost of ignoring
the social entities built into the individuals that constitute social wholes.

If Hayek's argument that society is in principal unknowable is to be founded on the problems of a rigorous
individualist reduction, it seems implausible. Thus this
attempt to rule out of order any possibility of social
distribution in accordance with needs fails. Similarly,
it does not seem satisfactory to argue that statements
about the needs of collectivities must reduce to statements about individual needs or be declared meaningless.
There seems to be no satisfactory argument for such an
abstemious position, particularly since it seems difficult
to generate adequate explanation in it. Methodological
individualism offers us a pair of blinkers that simply
reduces our capacity to achieve any understanding of the
social world.

If we reject the individualist critique of collective
need, there remain two important distinctions between
wants and needs for the purpose of programmes of social
allocation: needs involve normative standards, in a
different way to wants; the relation of collective and
individual needs differs from that of collective and
individual wants. In the next section we return to the
question of how far the values associated with wants can
effectively justify free market systems.

NEEDS, WANTS AND FREE MARKETS

After analysing the nature of the distinction between
needs and wants as foundations of social allocation, it
is possible to consider again the arguments for and
against the market. Let us assume that market systems
effectively distribute resources in accordance with
people's preferences, as their defenders claim. Is this
a reason for preferring them to allocation systems that

take some notion of need into account? The normative
nature of the concept of need has been discussed earlier
in this volume. It seems that, to function as a preferable
basis for allocation, some means of justifying the principle of want will have to be found. If Hutchinson's
appeal to want as an ultimate value is used, the most
powerful argument against the criterion of need - that
the characterization of need involves values - cannot be
employed. It is only by assenting to the primacy of a
normative principle of choice as the unjustified basis
for justification that want can gain a foothold. This
simply leads to a fruitless anarchy of naked and unsup-
ported values. Let us follow Friedman's appeal to the
value of liberty and Hayek's justification of that value
through his attempt to demonstrate that no other value can
be put into practice in a world where actions have unintended consequences (Friedman, 1962, pp. 22-3):

> A common objection to totalitarian societies is that
> they regard the end as justifying the means. This is
> clearly illogical. If the end does not justify the
> means, what does? But to deny that the end justifies
> the means is indirectly to assert that the end in
> question is not the ultimate end. That the ultimate
> end is the use of proper means.... To the liberal, the
> appropriate means are free discussion and the use of
> voluntary co-operation.... This is another way of
> expressing the goal of freedom.

Unlike Hayek, Friedman constructs no supporting argument
for his ultimate value. Instead he simply offers a powerful empirical critique of the effects of government interference in free markets, ranging from import control to
social security, and from oil price regulation to housing
subsidy. The primacy of liberty is regarded as non-
problematic.

Freedom is a useful 'hurrah'-word, as Roosevelt noted.
However, is it possible to argue that, because free markets enable people to pursue the satisfaction of their
wants, they make people more free? Barry is concerned
to criticize the equation of freedom with want-satisfaction.
He argues (1965, p. 137):

> there are two snags with this definition. The first is
> that it does not correspond with usage: to enslave
> someone is not normally said to increase the slave-
> owner's freedom, though it certainly decreases the
> slaves.... The serious objection underlying the point
> is that the definition does not then allow one to make
> the distinctions within wants for which 'freedom' is
> normally used.

These arguments do not seem totally satisfactory. It
is perfectly sensible to describe slave ownership as
enhancing the master's freedom so long as it enables him
to do things that he wants to do. The reason why we
don't ordinarily equate the power to direct others to fulfil our ends with freedom is that slave-owning doesn't
necessarily increase the ratio of satisfactions to frustrations for the slave master. If I want to live in an
ideal home and I engage servants to do the domestic
labour, I can describe myself as freed from domestic
drudgery, though I may not be freed from the curse of
having nothing to do with my time except give orders. It
only makes sense to say that my positive freedom is en-
hanced in the boring case that the major desire in my
life is the fear of household entropy. Barry goes on to
distinguish frustrations of wants that are felt as legitimate grievances within a particular social context from
those that are arbitrary, or the result of acts of God.
He uses freedom in such a way that the first class of
obstacles can be said to restrict freedom, whereas the
second cannot. This distinction is certainly useful in
his discussion. However, it seems that the convenience
of this definition in this context cannot be used as an
argument against those who find a more extensive range of
the concept, over all the wants that the free market can
be held to enable people to satisfy, desirable. Can markets then be said to enhance freedom by the criterion of
want satisfaction?

THE RELATIVITY OF WANTS

To assess this argument it is necessary to consider the
relation of man and markets further. The classical economists regarded the wants of the great mass of mankind as
determined by prevailing social conditions. These writers
often use 'want' and 'need' interchangeably. It is clear
in the following passages that the irreducible psychological notion of want as consumer demand, rather than any
externally ascribed notion of need as means to end, is
under consideration. Adam Smith, in discussing the wants
that people will try to satisfy through the market, writes:
'by necessaries, I understand not only the commodities
which are indispensably necessary for the support of life -
but whatever the custom of the country renders it indecent
for creditably people, even of the lowest order, to be
without' (1904, vol. 2, p. 354). A similar notion of average socially determined wants is built into Ricardo's
theory of the natural price of labour (1971, p. 115; cf.
p. 118) as:

> that price which is necessary to enable labourers to
> subsist and perpetuate their race without either in-
> crease or diminution.... It is not to be understood
> that the natural price of labour estimated even in
> food and necessaries (i.e. rather than in money wages)
> is aboslutely fixed and constant. It varies at dif-
> ferent times in the same country and very materially
> differs in different countries.

One is reminded of Townsend's paradox (1970, p. 1) of the
relativity of poverty lines in different societies. Rowntree in his monumental investigation into poverty in York
at the turn of the century found it necessary to construct,
in addition to a 'primary' poverty line (the income at
which a family could maintain 'mere physical efficiency'),
a 'secondary poverty line', which took into account the way
households chose to spend their income (Rowntree, 1902,
pp. 86-7).

Galbraith, in his critique of the conventional wisdom
associated with the 'market revival', expands the point
(1962, pp. 138-9).

> The theory of consumer demand ... is based on two
> broad propositions ... the first is that the urgency
> of wants does not diminish appreciably as more of them
> are satisfied.... When man has satisfied his physical
> needs, then psychologically-grounded desires take
> over.... The second proposition is that wants origi-
> nate in the personality of the consumer or in any case
> that they are given data for the economist.

Later (pp. 146-7) he argues:

> There is a flaw in the case. If the individual's
> wants are to be urgent they must be original with
> himself. They cannot be urgent if they must be con-
> trived for him.
>
>   And above all they must not be contrived by the
> process of production by which they are satisfied. For
> this means that the whole case for the urgency of
> production based on the urgency of wants falls to the
> ground. One cannot defend production as satisfying
> wants, if that production creates the want.

However, it has been argued that Galbraith's case
against market capitalism is a little like stalking a
pantomime horse. Many economists have pointed out that
production creates wants, and one wonders how important
Galbraith's rhetoric has been in convincing us that the
opposite was 'conventional wisdom' in the first place.
Thus Knight wrote in 1933 (pp. 318-19):

> it is common to think of the economic process as the
> production of goods for the satisfaction of wants.
> This view is deficient in two respects. In the first

place, the economic process produces wants as well as
goods to satisfy existing wants, and the amount of
social energy directed to the former activity is
large and constantly growing.

Compare Schumpeter: 'innovations in the economic system
do not as a rule take place in such a way that first new
wants arise spontaneously in consumers and then the productive apparatus swings round.... Consumers ... are, as
it were, taught to want new things' (1934, p. 65). Even
Sir Keith Joseph writes: 'our experience of markets
society shows that needs expand *pari passu* with possibilities, if not faster' (1975, p. 15).

These writers not only focus on the mechanisms of
demand stimulation, such as advertising, and the manipulation of markets (shortage scares, loss-leading, loading
profit on to items such as spares for which effective
demand is generated by selling the original at a discount
and so on); they also emphasize the point that, until
production has developed technically to the stage where
it can satisfy a given want, it makes little sense to
say that such a want exists. There is certainly something
bizarre about wanting potato-chips, or a hot-air balloon,
in the Europe of 1302, although people may have desired
a tasty snack or the ability to fly (Marx, 1973, pp. 35-6):

Hunger is hunger but the hunger that is satisfied with
cooked meat eaten with a fork and knife is a different
kind of hunger from the one that devours raw meat with
the aid of hands, nails, teeth.... Production not only
supplies the want with material, but supplies the
material with a want.... When consumption emerges from
its first stage of natural crudeness and directness ...
it is itself as a desire mediated by its object.

Miller writes: 'in technologically advanced societies it
has been accepted as a matter of course that levels of
production will rise, and as a result that people's wants
will change and increase' (1976, p. 137). He points to
some intriguing social research to support the thesis.

The work of Halbwachs, for example, shows how the increased affluence of American workers in the 1920s meant
that they were able to possess a wide range of consumer
durables. 'These new goods quickly became part of the
standard of living accepted by the class as a whole....'
Halbwachs backed up this claim by showing that when wages
sumpled the workers did not give up the new goods, but
saved on the basic items, food and clothing. A similar
process has been detected through the analysis of expenditure data in relation to the cuts in real incomes of the
mid-1970s. ('New Society', 1976, p. 620.) Of course, the
interaction between the production and the desirability of

the product is complex. Consider motor transport. People
certainly want cars, and, measured by effective demand,
the desire to own one's own car has expanded enormously
since the early years of the century. However, competition
from motor transport has systematically destroyed alternative means of travel. For many people the car is essential for work, shopping and the satisfaction of other
needs in a way in which it was not in 1902. Were it not
for the fact that at least one-quarter of the population
does not have access to one, it would be sensible to argue
that the very pervasiveness and competitiveness of motor
transport has transformed the car from a luxury into a
necessity. But where exactly does want end and need start?

   Marx has developed the point particularly in the
'Grundrisse' to argue that the relationship between the
development of wants and the development of productive
capabilities is a necessary one. Under capitalism, 'the
production of relative surplus-value based on the growth
of productive forces requires the creation of new consumption; at the heart of the sphere of circulation, the
sphere of consumption must grow in line with the sphere
of production' (Marx, 1973, p. 312). This viewpoint
generates a deterministic conception of wants in this particular form of society (1973, p. 36):

   Production thus produces consumption; first by furnish-
   ing the latter with material; secondly by determining
   the manner of consumption; thirdly by creating in consumers a want for its products as objects of consumption.
   It thus produces the object, the manner and the desire
   of consumption. In the same manner, consumption creates
   the disposition of the producer by setting him up as an
   aim and by stimulating wants.

   There is a relation between society and human wants. No
more than needs are wants independent of standards imposed by man's social location. The rhetoric of liberty
and of existing wants as immutable features of the essential human condition can no longer be maintained. Does
the fact that wants are socially generated in itself resolve the conflict between wants and needs?

   A materialist approach that accepts the relativity of
wants yet points out that a particular conception is
grounded in a particular form of society still seems feasible. The relation between the expansion of wants and
the development of productive forces is (we have argued)
systematic, in a way that does not necessarily seem to be
mirrored by the relation between normative notions of need
and society. Wants may change through history. All this
implies is that a particular conception of wants does not
furnish a universal yardstick. It is difficult to see how

one can criticize the use of a yardstick of the wants
appropriate to a particular form of society as a criterion
of social justice. One is reminded of the relativist definition of justice given by Marx in an aside in Book
Three of 'Capital' (1959, pp. 339-40):

> the justice of the transactions between agents of pro-
> duction rests on the fact that these arise ... out of
> production relations ... this content is just whenever
> it corresponds, is appropriate to the mode of production.
> It is unjust whenever it contradicts that mode.

However, we cannot accept the thesis that wants are
socially produced and defend the notion that want satisfaction equals freedom.

The slave master may be freer if he can satisfy his
wants. Yet it seems hard to maintain this position while
accepting that his wants are derived from the institution
of slavery. We might as well regard the convict in the
treadmill as free, because he satisfies the want to step
on to the next rung that the system offers. All act under
coercion; there is no role analogous to that of the slave
master in a free market system. The link between markets
and the value of freedom cannot be maintained.

What of the third justification for the free market -
that human society is intrinsically unknowable? If social
action can have unintended results, how can we plan to
meet need intelligently?

We have seen that the argument that society is unintelligible rests heavily on a restriction of explanation
to methodological individualism. Such an approach however seems incapable of providing a satisfactory account
of social phenomena. At the same time there seems no
compelling reason why we should adopt it. The collectivist alternative seems equally plausible. Are there any
advantages to an approach that enables us to differentiate
between collectivities and individuals in our analysis of
social phenomena?

The advantage is simply that this perspective provides
us with a wider range of ways of analysing the social
world. To take a simple example, Pat Thane (1974) analyses social policy developments over the last century
in terms of social control. George and Wilding (1972) relate social policy to a particular conception of the social
class system. Wilensky and Lebeaux (1965) interpret welfare as the response to the logic of industrial development. There are only three among many accounts of social
welfare. It is difficult to see how any of these perspectives could be formulated from the standpoint of a
thoroughgoing individualism. To say this is not to argue
that any (or all) of them are correct in any sense, simply

that they provide us with different ways of explaining,
of 'making intelligible', the phenomena in question.
Individualism would deny us this scope. So why choose it?
If this is the case, Hayek's ideological arguments for
the free market lose force.

  These considerations are not in themselves justifications of state intervention in the market to meet social
need. They are merely intended to show that the position
that opposes wants to needs and defends the free market
as the institutionalization of distribution according to
want is as much a statement of particular values as the
claims of social welfare. To attempt to move from this
to take sides in the contemporary political debate would
be to move from an 'is' to an 'ought'. These issues,
however, are of particular concern at a time when state
welfare provision is being cut back for economic, ideological and political reasons. As to which approach is
right, 'you pays your money and you takes your choice'!

Part Three

Community, welfare and social policy

The most obvious thing a doctrine of community tries
to do is to determine what sympathetic social relations
would look like and thus to describe the political
equivalent of love.

Roberto Unger

The general obligation to help and sustain one another
which Max Gluckman describes as characteristic of the
tribal society and especially the kinship group, and
for the lack of which the Great Society is generally
blamed, is incompatible with it.

Friedrich von Hayek

9   Community and the legitimation of social policy

Earlier, in chapter 4, we encountered the concept of
community as an important concept in social policy.
Sometimes, as we saw, the values of community and fraternity are counterposed to a picture of society based upon
recognition of rights and duties and to what might be
thought of as procedural relationships between people.
Titmuss particularly seemed to operate with this kind of
distinction. In the present chapter it will be argued
that the concept of community is far too protean and unclear to play a straightforward role in either understanding or legitimating social policy. In the following
chapter Titmuss's views will be examined in more detail.
   Of all the concepts in terms of which we characterize,
organize and constitute our social and political experience, the concept of community seems to be the one most
neglected by social and political philosophers. Other
concepts, such as rights, power, authority, freedom,
democracy and justice, have all been subjects of pene-
trating and sustained analyses. In contrast, the concept
of community is strangely neglected. Such a neglect
greatly hinders any understanding of social and political
life and, more importantly, is an abrogation of responsibility. The notion of community is central to discussions
of social policy and is widely used to characterize and
legitimate almost any valued social achievement. 'Community action', 'community development', 'community work',
'community organization', 'community politics','community
care', 'community medicine', 'community power', 'community
school' are all part of the available stock of descriptions for defining and evaluating the social world. However, while the concept of community may be central to us,
its very vagueness has become an embarrassment. In an
important article on the appeal to community as a legitimating device in social policy, A.H. Halsey (1974) has

argued that it has 'so many meanings as to be meaningless',
a complaint echoed by Michael J. Hill and Ruth Issacharof
in 'Community Action and Race Relations' (1971) and by
Robert Morris and Martin Rein in 'Social Work Practice'
(1962). The latter describe how this vagueness can be
used in working out social policy (p. 183):
> An integral part of the search for shared goals and
> the use of democratic procedures is legitimation by
> the community.... Thus the goals emanate from a now
> legitimate source - the community itself, further
> buttressed by the use of democratic procedures so
> important in our culture. Characteristic of this
> strategy is the indefiniteness with which the term
> 'community' is used. The term is meant to cover all
> persons and interests, but it is not defined. Nor
> are mechanisms available which permit us to reach
> such an ideal community, so that it remains vague
> and indefinite.
Indeed, in a celebrated article in 1955 in which he sur-
veyed definitions of 'community', George A. Hillery came
up with ninety-four definitions and claimed that the
only feature they had in common was that they all dealt
with people! (Hillery, 1955). Many theorists have gone
so far as to recommend that it should be dismissed
entirely as a category in social and political description. Margaret Stacey, for example, has argued that it is
a 'non concept' (1969), and R.E. Pahl has stated that the
word 'serves more to confuse than to illuminate the situation in Britain today' (1970, p. 102). One of the few
recently published books on the nature of community quite
aptly captures the current state of confusion in its
title: 'Contemporary Community - Sociological Illusion
or Reality?' (Scherer, 1972).

In this chapter it is hoped to promote a better understanding of the concept of community. The analysis
offered will not dissipate the ambiguity at the very
heart of the concept, but hopefully it will show that
there is something explicable and indeed predictable
about this ambiguity. Equally, the analysis is intended
to be critical of the uninterpreted use of 'community' as
a legitimating notion within the field of social policy.
It will be pointed out that beneath this are important
ideological undertones of one sort or another and that
the term is thus used to give an air of consensus to
social policy, a spurious consensus that evaporates once
the inherently normative structure of the concept is
realized.

COMMUNITY AS A NORMATIVE CONCEPT

One way of trying to account for the vagueness of the
concept of community is to concentrate on it as an evaluative concept that plays a major legitimating role in
our talk about institutions. The word is one of those
descriptive/evaluative terms that have been the subject
of a good deal of attention in recent moral philosophy.
(Searle, 1962.) When the term is used in ordinary discourse, it is used not only to describe or to refer to a
range of features in social life but also to put into a
favourable perspective those features. Community is a
valued and valuable achievement or social state. This
point has been clearly taken up in two recent treatments
of the concept (Greer and Minar, 1969, p. 9, and Bell and
Newby, 1972, p. 21):

> Community is both empirically descriptive of the social
> structure and normatively toned. It refers to a unit
> of society as it is and to aspects of that society that
> are valued if they exist and are desired in their
> absence.

> Sociologists no more than other individuals have not
> been immune to the emotive overtones the word commu-
> nity constantly carries with it. Everyone - including
> sociologists - has wanted to live in a community;
> feelings have been much more equivocal concerning life
> in collectivities, networks and societies.

Just as the pejorative force of the term 'fascist' can
best be understood by looking at the history of Europe
over the past fifty years, the commendatory force of the
term 'community' can best be understood by looking at the
last two hundred years. In this time the notion of community has been used almost universally by social and
political philosophers to point up some of the drawbacks
and baneful characteristics of urban industrial society and
to point the way towards new and more humane forms of
social relations. Indeed, Wolin has argued that this view
of community characterizes modern political thought (1960,
p. 363):

> The political thought of the 19th and 20th centuries
> has largely centred on an attempt to restate the value
> of community, that is the need of human beings to dwell
> in more intimate relationships with each other, to enjoy
> more effective ties, to experience some closer solidar-
> ity than the nature of urban industrial society seemed
> willing to grant.

This view of the role of community has also been a major
feature of Nisbet's (1970a and 1970b) various interpretative

essays on this theme. Thus an understanding of the history of the concept of community is necessary for a full grasp of the high degree of consensus that exists across the political spectrum about the positive evaluative meaning of the term.

However, it might be argued that such a consensus does not help us in any way to understand the concept's current ambiguity, especially since it seems to imply there *is* no ambiguity. The critic might also point to a descriptive/evaluative term such as 'industrious', which is not notably ambiguous in its meaning. The word is clearly commendatory, and there would be wide agreement about the type of behaviour commended. In this case, the fact that the word is both evaluative and descriptive does not make it ambiguous, so why should it in the case of 'community'? The answer lies in the complex relationship between the evaluative and descriptive meanings of the word. The high degree of agreement about the commendatory force of 'community' is lacking in the case of its descriptive meaning. 'Community' has a complex range of descriptive, often incompatible, meanings. Conventionally the term is used to refer to locality; interest group; a system of solidarity; a group with a sense of mutual significance; a group characterized by moral agreement, shared beliefs, shared authority, or ethnic integrity; a group marked by historical continuity and shared traditions; a group in which members meet in some kind of total fashion as opposed to meeting as members of certain roles, functions or occupational groups; and, finally, occupational, functional or partial communities. Clearly, not all of these meanings are compatible, but each has its defenders. What makes 'community' particularly ambiguous is the relationship between this descriptive complexity and incompatibility and the evaluative meaning of the term. While there is formal consensus that to talk about 'community' is to talk in a commendatory way, there is no such consensus about what precisely is being commended in terms of empirically detectable features of social life. The positive evaluation of 'community' takes place within different ideological/normative groupings, and what is being commended often differs between these groupings. Raymond Williams has drawn attention to this point (1976, p. 6):

> Community can be the warmly persuasive word to describe an existing set of relationships, or the warmly persuasive word to describe an alternative set of relationships. What is most important, perhaps, is that unlike all other terms of social organisation (state, nation, society etc.) it seems never to be used

unfavourably, and never to be given any opposing or
distinguishing terms.
It has often been remarked that both conservatives and
socialists value 'community' very highly (Halsey, 1974;
Wolff, 1968), but what they understand by the social
relationships that would embody a sense of community differs very widely.

COMMUNITY AS AN ESSENTIALLY CONTESTED CONCEPT

In this way the concept of 'community' might be thought
to be much more indeterminate than democracy, for example.
Quentin Skinner has argued that there is a consensus over
the evaluative meaning of democracy and a similar consensus
about the formal specification of its descriptive meaning,
namely 'rule by the people' (1973). Of course, there
will be difficulties about the interpretation of the notion
of rule by the people, and these disputes will be very
severe. However, they do seem to occur within the limits
set by the formal specification of the descriptive meaning
of the concept. Given the list of possible meanings for
'community' cited earlier, which is by no means exhaustive,
and the evident incompatibilities among them, it might be
thought that disputes about descriptive features are so
severe as to rule out any agreement over even the formal
specification of the descriptive meaning of 'community'.
If this is granted, then 'community' would become an
'essentially contested' concept in Bryce Gallie's sense of
the term. As we saw in chapter 1, Gallie has listed
various criteria that mark out a concept as essentially
contested, and these criteria seem to apply very clearly
in the case of community (Gallie, 1955-6):

1   An essentially contested concept must be appraisive;
    it must be concerned with some kind of valued
    achievement. As we have seen, this is characteristic
    of community.
2   This achievement must be of an internally complex
    nature. Again, we have seen that community has many
    incompatible meanings.
3   In explaining the worth of a concept, a person must
    be able to make reference to its constituent parts,
    rival claimants putting these in different orders
    of priority. This is a clear feature of debates
    about community. The traditional conservative, for
    example, may put great emphasis on locality and
    attachment to place, whereas the liberal may be much
    more inclined to think of community in terms of in-
    terest or occupational groups and assign very little

if any importance to locality.

4   The accredited achievement must allow considerable modification in the light of changed circumstances. It is precisely the applicability of the concept of community to changed circumstances to, for example, functional or occupational groups that is disputed between the conservative, the liberal and the marxist.

5   The users of an essentially contested concept must be aware of rival interpretations and maintain their particular one. In debates about community different users of the concept seem to be aware of the disputed nature of the concept.

6   The concept must be derived from an original exemplar. If this condition is not satisfied then those arguing about the concept might be thought to be arguing about different things under the same name. There must be some paradigm case, perhaps drawn from the remote past, that all parties using the concept in their different ways are willing to regard as falling under the concept. In the case of community there do seem to be clear attempts to secure paradigm cases.   The Greek city state was widely propounded by German philosophers and literary figures such as Hegel, Schiller and Hölderlin to be a prime example of community; the feudal village has been seen in much the same way, particularly by William Morris, some of the Guild Socialists and, in a quite different way, by Peter Laslett (1965). Others have turned to works of fiction as portraying incontestable paradigms of community. W.J.M. Mackenzie, for example, cites 'Mrs Gaskell's "Cranford", Trollope's "Barchester", Winifred Holtby's "South Riding", Faulkner's "Yoknapatawpha"' (Mackenzie, 1967).

7   There must be the probability that the continued competition between users enables the original exemplar's achievement to be sustained. This again is a necessary condition for the debate about community not to be a debate about different things under the same name.

Thus it can be argued that community fits quite neatly into this analytical schema and this approach to the explication of social and political concepts has indeed recently been revived and defended by Alasdair MacIntyre in his influential paper, On the Essential Contestability of Some Social Concepts (1973), and in a more extended way by William Connolly in his 'The Terms of Political Discourse' (1974).

It could also be argued, however, that Gallie's sixth criterion concerning an original exemplar might be much too

strong so far as community is concerned. The heterogeneity
of the examples mentioned above might lead one to question
whether there is in fact an agreed exemplar here. As
William Connolly has said, 'sometimes contestants argue
not just over the weighting and specifying ingredients in
an agreed and original exemplar, but over which experience
or construct counts as the best exemplar': the Greek
polis, a medieval manorial estate, a nineteenth-century
Cheshire village or a working-class neighbourhood in a
large British town between the wars. It does seem that
there can be disagreement over the original exemplar, and
if so, it follows that this exemplar is not like some
golden thread running through all the different debates
about community and, as it were, making them debates about
community. This feature of community would make it perhaps more radically contestable than any other central
social and political concept.

However, there are those who would argue that this
approach to community, or for that matter to any other
concept central to social and political life, commits us
to an extreme form of Protagorean relativism and the aban-
donment of any claim on the part of the social sciences
to be free from ideological taint. If the concept of
community is radically contestable in the way indicated,
and if it can be given a fixed definition against a particular ideological or normative background, then any
theory developed within the social sciences that makes
use of such a concept is going to embody ideological/
normative assumptions. This is certainly a difficulty
that worries many social scientists, and in order to
avoid it many have claimed that it must be possible to
produce a straightforward descriptive definition of those
concepts that are central to the social sciences. In
support of just this kind of conclusion Felix E Oppenheim
has recently argued (1973, p. 56):

> For the purposes of a scientific study of politics,
> we must attempt to provide basic political concepts
> with explications acceptable to anyone regardless of
> his normative and ideological commitments so that the
> truth or falsity of statements in which these concepts
> thus defined occur will depend exclusively on inter-
> subjectively ascertainable evidence.

This requirement is put starkly so far as community is
concerned by Hillery (1968) in 'Communal Organisations'
(p. 4):

> The moral to be drawn is a scientific one: our defi-
> nitions must be wedded to facts - those things which
> we perceive through the senses. The error which is
> often made in the definition of concepts of community

is what may be referred to as the sin of pronouncement. Students have pronounced upon the traits which they felt should be contained in community and then have proceeded to look at the facts.

One can certainly sympathize with this. If the basic concepts of the social sciences are ineradicably normative/ ideological, then this will have very severe consequences at least so far as social scientists wish to be allied with the natural sciences as the positivist programme would require them to be. However, in the light of what has already been said, the question to be asked is whether an agreed core of descriptive meaning to social and political concepts, and *ipso facto* to community, is feasible? Our answer to this will be a very qualified yes, but we shall also argue that such an agreed descriptive meaning is so formal that it will be of no use in social and political analysis, and that once a move is made beyond this formal agreement then we are back with contestability and ideology once again.

So far as community is concerned, an important attempt has been made to produce a consensus descriptive meaning for the concept by a theorist who is quite well aware of the way in which normative or ideological factors can enter into the definition of social and political terms. In his article The Concept of Community: A Re-examination, David B. Clark (1973) argues that a core descriptive meaning of community must be established if the concept is to be of any use in social and political science (pp. 403-4):

a good deal more confusion seems to have arisen as a result of researchers concentrating all their attention on the social expression of community without having first clearly defined what is its essential nature. The two fundamental communal elements of any social system are a sense of solidarity and a sense of significance.

In this passage Clark sees himself as having set out the necessary and sufficient conditions for the use of the term 'community' and he feels that this definition, if it could be sustained, would meet Oppenheim's requirement that a term in social and political science must have a clearly defined non-ideological meaning. Behind the surface play of difference, interpretation and ideology there is an essential core meaning to the term, namely solidarity and significance. This core meaning is, to use Lukes's terminology, the underlying concept of community, that which all views or expressions of community have in common.

Lukes, in his 'Power: A Radical View' (1974), links
his account of the relationship between the underlying or
primitive concept and the various views yielded by that
concept with Rawls's distinction between concept and conception, a distinction that was fully adumbrated in his
'A Theory of Justice'. According to Rawls, 'it seems
natural to think of justice as distinct from various conceptions of justice and as being specified by the role
which these different principles have in common' (1972,
pp. 5-6). A concept of X, where X is a concept characteristic of social and political life, is defined as what
all conceptions, views or expressions of X have in common.
In the case of justice there are many divergent and incompatible conceptions of justice - deserts, merit, need,
moral worth, historical entitlement - but what they have
in common as conceptions of justice is, in Rawls's view,
the idea that there are 'no arbitrary divisions between
persons in assigning the basic rights and duties of
social life'. All conceptions of justice have this feature in common, and this common core constitutes the essential nature of the concept in question. Thus, according to Clark, divergent uses, conceptions, views or, to
use Clark's term, many expressions of community such as
locality, interest group, ethnic integrity, shared traditions, total interaction and shared authority does not
mean that community is an essentially contested concept
incapable of other than ideological definition. Rather,
all these conceptions presuppose a core descriptive meaning 'a social structure is a community if and only if it
embodies a sense of solidarity and significance'. On
this account we have cut through contested ideological
accounts by distilling what all these conceptions have in
common and arrived at a purely descriptive account that
would, on the face of it, satisfy Oppenheim's criterion
of applying to 'intersubjectively ascertainable empirical
evidence'.
    However, the extent to which this is a gain is not at
all clear. Leaving aside the question of whether Clark's
list of descriptive features is exhaustive (one might,
for example, want to say something about size; with the
proposed definition a family would be a community, and yet
it would seem better to keep them apart), it does not seem
that the advantage gained by specifying this supposedly
incontestable core to the concept is very great. The
whole point of this kind of exercise is to rescue concepts
such as 'community' from ideological and normative taint
in order to make them useful once again for social and
political analysis. As they stand, the features constituting Clark's necessary and sufficient conditions for the

use of community are entirely formal and abstract: there are no definite requirements expressed or implied for the institutional structure of a community so defined. Before the concept of community can be used in social and political analysis, these necessary and sufficient conditions have to be interpreted and provided with some 'cash value'. The same is true of similar specifications of the concept of justice by Rawls and of democracy by Skinner. The underlying idea of justice may be that there be no arbitrary divisions between persons in the assignments of basic rights and duties, and that of democracy may be rule by the people, but until these underlying ideas are further specified and operationalized they are useless for social and political explanation. However, once these underlying concepts, whether of community, justice or democracy, *are* operationalized, we seem to end up again with a contestable view, conception or expression of the concept in question. Formal and consensus concepts have to be transformed into debatable and contestable conceptions before they can be used in social science, but once this transformation occurs it is difficult to see how ideology, in the sense of a basic set of normative preferences, can be avoided. Rawls put this point very clearly in regard to the transformation of the concept of justice into the various substantive conceptions of justice: 'The various conceptions of justice are the outgrowth of different notions of society against the background of opposing views of the natural necessities and opportunities of human life' (1972, pp. 9-10).

The same is true *mutatis mutandis* of community. The rigor and precision of the concept of community established by Clark is bought at the cost of empirical vacuity; the terms of the definition themselves have to be further specified, and once this occurs we are back in the thick of ideological assumptions. Our ideas about the kind of institutional structures that are going to embody a sense of solidarity and significance are going to involve our deepest assumptions about the basis of human nature, its capacities and powers, and about the possibilities inherent in human life.

Whether an institution or social network embodies a sense of solidarity and significance cannot be a straightforwardly empirical question, not only because there are problems as to what exactly these words might mean, but also because it is important not to beg questions about false consciousness. It may be that members of a collectivity subjectively have a sense of solidarity and significance, but to the political analyst such a sense of community may obscure other features of the relationships

within the group that might count against this perceived
sense of fraternity. For example, some business corpora-
tions may embody a sense of solidarity and significance
as subjectively experienced by the workers, but a marxist
might deny that such an institution could be a community
because the sense of community is too engineered and
sectional and disguises the fact of exploitation, which,
once subjectively realized, would destroy the sense of
community.

Of course, we do not wish to deny that subjective experience is of vital importance to a sense of community;
indeed, in the next chapter we shall argue against Rawls's
claim in 'A Theory of Justice' that the difference principle embodies a sense of community. Clearly, before we
can speak of community or of solidarity, significance,
fraternity and so on there has to be an intention among
the members of a group to act in certain ways towards one
another, to respond to each other in particular ways, and
to value each person as a member of the group. However,
although this is central and important, the question as
to whether these features are present in a particular
relationship does not depend entirely on the avowals of
those belonging to the group. For example, the marxist
may point out that, although the workers within a business
enterprise may avow a sense of identity with others working
for the company, there may well be grave difficulties
within the corporation involved in acting in accordance
with these sentiments, just because of competition for
rewards within the company, the promotional structure, the
salary scales and so on. This is clearly not the place to
probe arguments about false consciousness, but the important point to note in the present context is that the
question whether X is a community is not directly an empirical one to be settled by ascertaining the perceptions
and sentiments of those who belong to X. Although this
evidence is important, it is not finally decisive.

We have seen that the concept of community as an essentially contested concept is not entirely correct. The
relativism implied by the essential contestability thesis
can be overdone. It is impossible, on one hand, to
establish a definition for the concept of community of
which different conceptions are contestable and politically committed interpretations. To this extent theorists such as Oppenheim are correct in thinking that it is
possible to give a core definition of a social concept that
will be acceptable to all parties across the ideological
spectrum, and that this core definition will be descriptive and free from ideological and normative taint. On the
other hand, this approach, while it may help in terms of

clarity about the structure of a concept, is going to be useless so far as social science explanations are concerned. These core descriptive definitions are too formal to be used as tools in substantive analyses of social structures and processes, but once the terms in the formal definition are interpreted or give a 'cash value', then we are back with normative and ideological assumptions once again. What is needed in this kind of context is some recognition of the ways in which social and political concepts are like Hegel's concrete universals, embodying universal, formal, definitional elements that at the same time have to be interpreted and specified further, a process that will be conducted against a background of assumptions about human nature, moral values and the nature of social life. A full grasp of the concept of community requires that we should hold together these aspects; as Hegel argues, 'the shapes which the concept assumes in the course of its actualisation are indispensable to the knowledge of the concept itself' (1952, p. 14). In what follows I shall try to show very schematically how all of this works in practice by looking at the shapes that community has assumed both in history and in the present time. Taking Clark's definition of the concept of community, I shall try to show how, when interpreted, it yields various irreconcilable views of community and how these have been both embodied in different forms of social life and are closely related t- some of the varieties of political thought - conservative, marxist, liberal and social democratic.

MARXISM: CLASS, COMMUNITY AND THE FUTURE

Clearly the marxist will want to cast his conception of community into a form that will accommodate a sense of solidarity and significance, but he will differ fundamentally from both the conservative and the liberal/social democrat in his vision of what these features in fact entail in terms both of institutional and less formal relationships between persons, and of a critique of existing bourgeois institutions. Marx himself did not write extensively on the shape that community would assume within socialist society, but it is possible to piece together the general lines of his understanding of community if one looks at 'The German Ideology' and the material in 'The British Rule in India' (Marx and Engels, 1974).
    Within existing capitalist societies, Marx argues, community is illusory in that men do not meet as primary social beings whose needs demand mutual co-operation and

solidarity; rather, they meet as isolated individuals in the market, each seeking to maximize his own utilities, 'separated from the community, withdrawn into himself, wholly preoccupied with his private interest and acting in accordance with his private caprice.... The only bond between men is natural necessity, need and private interest, the preservation of their property and their egotistic persons' (Marx, 1963). Capitalism is a system of competition and mutual antagonism; any sense of solidarity can exist only on the basis of changing constellations of economic interests. In addition, because production is geared to satisfying wants rather than needs, there is a progressive division of labour and the consequent attenuation of human powers characteristic of the alienation of man in capitalist society. Within such a system of production men loses any sense of his own significance and worth: he is treated as an object in the productive process or, in the more usual imagery, as a cog in the mechanism of production.

Feudal society, in Marx's view, with all its degradation and superstition, embodied far more of a sense of community than capitalist society is able to do. Within the manorial system men were related to one another in complex ways, with mutual rights and duties attached to the various hierarchically arranged functions, and were secure in a sense of mutual relationship: 'The estate is individualised with its lord; it has his rank ... his privileges, his jurisdictions, his political position ... for those belonging to the estate it is more like their fatherland. It is a constricted sort of nationality.' These social ties, which were intimately interwoven with each person's sense of identity and significance were pared down by capitalism (1959, pp. 61-2):

> Free industry and trade abolished privileged exclusivities. In its place they set men free from privileges which isolate him from the social whole, but at the same time joins him to a narrower exclusivity. Man is no longer bound by the semblance of communities. Thus they produce the universal struggle of man against man, individual against individual.

Within capitalist society the state is often portrayed as the community, that which stands above the self-seeking of the market and the general exploitative relationships between men in the market. This was clearly the vision of Hegel and Lasalle, and Marx decisively rejects it. The state for Marx is one more illusory community within capitalist society. Far from being the universal that reconciles the fractures in civil society and the mutual antagonisms of the market, it embodies a particular sectional interest, namely that of the capitalist class.

However, it would be a great mistake to imply that
Marx's own conception of community was greatly influenced
by the feudal, pre-industrial model. Although he clearly
saw the *Gemeinschaft* pre-capitalist social order as medi-
ating important social bonds, he also saw it as hierarchical in ways that were thought to express the natural necessities of the human condition. Within the European tradition these natural necessities were linked to the purposes
of God, whereas in oriental societies they were thought to
express the ineradicable consequences of karma. Marx
particularly exphasizes this point in his account of
British rule in India (Marx and Engels, 1974):

> We must not forget that these idyllic village commu-
> nities, inoffensive as they may appear, had always
> been the solid foundation of oriental despotism, that
> they restrained the mind within the smallest compass,
> making it the unresisting tool of superstition, en-
> slaving it beneath traditional rules.... We must not
> forget that these little communities were contaminated
> by caste and slavery, that they subjugated man to ex-
> ternal circumstance instead of elevating man to be the
> sovereign of circumstance, that they changed a self-
> developing social state into a never changing destiny.

Pre-capitalist communities were, as Colletti argues, co-
hesive but confining (1973, p. 259); the growth of capitalism however brought with it mobility and human autonomy, but a corresponding loss of communal ties. A truly
human community is for the future, when both the claims of
community and autonomy will be reconciled in a socialist
society. To achieve such a society a revolution is necessary in order to break the structure of domination over
individuals and in order to change the basis of economic
activity to a much less competitive and dehumanizing form.

It is at this point that the marxist political commitments relate to current preoocupations on the Left about
the nature of community. If a truly human community can
be achieved only after the revolutionary transformation of
a society, then a necessary condition of this is the development of class consciousness on the part of the pro-
letariat; yet it is just this requirement that often
comes into conflict with the admiration many socialists
feel for traditional working-class communities, communities that are being broken up by urban renewal. Many
socialists have been in the forefront of protests about
the breakup of these neighbourhood communities; but
other marxists, perhaps being more consistent, have found
this attitude very difficult to understand. John Westergaard has pointed out very clearly the difficulties
facing the marxist in this position: on the one hand, he

admires the strong sense of community within working-
class areas; and on the other hand, he feels that the
development of class consciousness may actually be inhibited by the attachment that working people feel
towards persons from their own area and by the consequent
exclusivity involved (Westergaard, 1965, pp. 107-8):

> Not only has it become fashionable to deplore the
> dilution of traditional working class culture *per se*,
> a reaction which reflects an odd, conservative nos-
> talgia for a way of life moulded by insecurity,
> seclusion and crude deprivation both material and
> mental, but this cultural dilution has not infrequently
> come to be equated with a decline in class conscious-
> ness and its replacement by narrow preoccupations of
> status and respectability or sheer apathy. No sub-
> stantial evidence has been offered for this equation:
> it has been asserted, not proven. Underlying it there
> is commonly a premise which deserves explicit examina-
> tion. This is the assumption that the kind of working
> class unity which finds expression in industrial or
> more particularly political action draws its nourish-
> ment from the simpler and more intimate loyalties of
> neighborhood and kin. Consequently it is postulated
> that as the latter are weakened so the former declines.
> This assumption is highly questionable, for it implies
> that the solidarity of class which is social in its
> sweep and draws no nice distinctions between men of
> this place and that, this name and that, this dialect
> and that, is rooted in the kind of parochial solidarity
> which is its very antithesis.

In similar vein Frank Parkin points out that: 'a class
outlook is rooted in a perception of the social order
that stretches far beyond the frontiers of community.
It entails a macro-social view of the reward structure
and an understanding of the systematic nature of inequality' (Parkin, 1973, p. 10). Indeed, within the history
of political thought there is a good deal of negative
evidence in support of this conclusion. The British Hegelians, particularly T.H. Green, B. Bosanquet and Sir Henry
Jones, all rejected a class analysis of politics and
counterposed to this a communitarian view, claiming that
within modern society there is a common good, the existence of which can be demonstrated by philosophical argument
and which all men, whatever their social class, may aspire
to play a part in attaining (see MacIntyre, 1967). Earlier
in the nineteenth century Thomas Chalmers, in his 'The
Civic and Christian Economy of Large Towns', argued that,
if the minds of working people could be turned inward to
the problems of their own locality, this would in fact

inhibit the development of class consciousness.

This tension between the claims of class and the claims of the local community, which has its roots in the nineteenth century, is a major problem in some current areas of social policy. In Great Britain, where many radicals have taken posts as community workers and have played roles in officially sponsored community development projects, precisely the same kinds of problems have arisen. Is the concentration of attention on the problems of the local community and the competition for scarce economic resources between communities acting as a way of disguising what for the marxist must be seen as the systematic nature of inequality in modern society? (Sennett, 1976). Faced with this problem many radicals have tried to link their work in community development with the labour movement and with trade unions, but without conspicuous success. Indeed, one hard-headed radical line here has been that the decline of traditional working-class communities is not to be mourned because the ensuing increase in the privatization of life and the enchroachments of business enterprises into the centres of cities (usually areas of working-class housing) reveal to people very starkly the reality of the economic forces that have caused their plight, and will thus do more to develop among workers a sense that their interests are not best furthered within capitalism than would the preservation of the narrow perspective of existing working-class communities.

The dilemma for the marxist here depends crucially upon his conception of community and what he sees as the necessary conditions for furthering his vision of human community. On the one hand he assumes ultimately that a really humane community is of the future in a society devoid of class and exploitation, and that a condition of achieving this is the development of class consciousness; on the other hand he understands that existing working-class communities can be valuable sources of strength and support within existing capitalist society, while at the same time, because of their local strength, these neighbourhood communities may well hinder the development of class consciousness and thus of the ultimate form of human community. The tensions involved in this position are tied up with assumptions made by marxists, both about the possible character of human nature in different social circumstances and about the range of possibilities that can be brought about by change in human society. Eugene Kamenka has put both the goals and the problems involved in the marxist view of community in the following way (1967, p. 116).

Here lies the fundamental problem of Marxist humanism. Classical Marxism welded together in one tremendous act of fact and faith the affirmation of industrial development and the longing for the brotherhood and community of the feudal agrarian village. The machines that robbed man of his individuality had a historic mission: while they seemed to support and extend the marked divisiveness of commercial society, they would by overthrowing it and lead into the Kingdom of Ends. Whatever is left to the future in the marxist conception of community, and whatever tensions this conception produces for marxists *vis à vis* existing working-class communities, two things stand out that mark off this vision of human solidarity from both the conservative and liberal/ social democratic standpoints. The conservative vision of community as a functional hierarchical order is regarded by marxists as embodying some genuine elements of community, but at the same time these elements play an important ideological role in masking other, equally important, features of hierarchical systems: the lack of autonomy for those in a subordinate position in the hierarchy and the economic exploitation of the same by those better placed. Indeed, some commentators have seen the lack of hierarchy as the only thing that marks off the marxian view of community from the conservative approach. Kamenka, for example, says explicitly: 'The socialist vision of the non-commercial society is distinguished from the Romantic conservative view by the rejection of hierarchy and by that alone' (1967, p. 116). Within liberal capitalist society the marxist sees genuine community to be at a vanishing point. There are only transient constellations of individuals around perceived material interests; as we have seen, the sense of community that exists within the working-class is in conflict with the claims of class to the extent that these loyalties can become so exclusive as to cover up the ultimate reality of being working class.

CONSERVATISM: COMMUNITY AND TRADITION

While the Marxian view of community has been based ultimately on a Promethean view of man - a vision of man in 'community with others having the means to cultivate his talents in all directions' (Marx, 1943, p. 75) - traditional conservative thought is based on far less optimistic assumptions about man and his perfectibility. The conservative conception of community is usually backward-looking, its appeal connoting a return to a *Gemeinschaft* type of order, and thus may support attempts to resist change and to buttress the existing power and authority structure. Community then is characterized by hierarchy, place and mutual obligation between groups in different positions within the hierarchy. Its vision is one of organism and its ethic one of mutual service: the social order is an organic unity within which each individual has an allotted place and a part to play. The parts of the hierarchy are ordered functionally and are interdependent. These social arrangements are not to be regarded as constraints and inhibitions on the potentially Promethean nature of man, but rather as giving a balanced institutional structure within which men can thrive: They are not chains that bind, but are rather an inherited social framework that constrains men's propensity for brutishness and his disposition for anarchy. It is, in Burkean terms, a harmonious union that 'holds all physical and moral natures each in its appointed place'.

Usually this organically related hierarchical order has been held to be a matter of necessity expressing either the will of God, the empirically discernible order in nature, congenital and ineradicable differences between men, or some mixture of the three. A good example of this kind of thinking is found in Edmund Dudley's 'The Tree of Commonwealth': 'God hath set an order by grace between himself and Angel and between Angel and Angel; and by reason between Angel and man and between man and man and man and beast ... which order from the highest point to the lowest God willeth us to keep without any enterprise to the contrary' (Dudley, 1948, p. 86). Probably the most developed form of the argument that human society must be seen in an hierarchical way corresponding to a natural order in the cosmos as ordained by God is in Hooker's 'Of the Laws of Ecclesiastical Polity'. In this work there are of course many fine evocations of this theme but among the most direct is the following: 'God's purpose is to amiably order all things and suitably with the kinds and qualities of their nature.... The whole world consisting in parts so many, so different is by this only thing upheld; he which hath formed them in order' (1836, p. 28). This conception of human community was more than just an intellectual construction found in works of political reflection; it was a view that entered very deeply into people's lived experiences in the pre-capitalist era in Western Europe. Not only did such conceptions tie in very closely with the perceived social structure, but the social structure itself received symbolic reinforcement through religious, particularly Anglican, teachings, as both Laslett and Schochet have shown. This kind of teaching, which was very difficult to avoid, expressed in less subtle language precisely the vision of society encapsulated in works like 'Ecclesiastical Polity'. Indeed, the religious reinforcement for such a conception of community may well have lasted much longer than might have been expected.

10   Markets, community and welfare

COMMUNITY AND LIBERALISM

As we have seen, the appeal of community is extremely
strong, and since the late eighteenth century many social
and political theorists have invoked one or another conception of community to throw into relief what they have
taken to be the baleful effects of the economic market,
the growth of the commercial spirit and the atomism of
liberal capitalist society. They have sought to articulate a vision of a way of life in which individuals could
be bound by more effective ties and more intimate relationships than the predominant forms of social relationship within capitalism seemed to allow. It is widely seen
as a central failure of the liberal tradition
of social and political thought that it has failed, despite the efforts of Green and others, to provide an adequate conception of overall community. In his widely
read tract on 'The Poverty of Liberalism' (1970) Robert
Paul Wolff has argued that this failure to provide an
adequate theory of community is one of the roots of the
poverty of the liberal tradition, and one that calls into
question not just liberal social theory but also its
attenuated conception of human nature. Even as sympathetic a critic as Kenneth Arrow has pointed to this gap
in liberal theory (1972, p. 184):

> The picture of a society run exclusively on the basis
> of exchange has long haunted sensitive observers
> especially since the earliest days of capitalist
> domination. The ideas of community and cohesion are
> counterposed to a drastically reduced society in which
> individuals meet only as buyers and sellers of commo-
> dities.

In 'Lark Rise to Candleford' Flora Thompson writes about
an Anglican sermon in the village church of Candleford

in the closing years of the nineteenth century (1945, p. 201):

> Another subject was the social order as it then existed. God in his infinite wisdom had appointed a place for every man, woman and child on this earth and it was their bounden duty to remain contentedly in their niches. A gentleman might seem to some of his listeners to have a pleasant easy life compared with theirs as field labourers; but he had duties and responsibilities which would be far beyond their capabilities. He had to pay taxes, sit on the bench of magistrates, oversee his estate and keep up his position by entertaining. Could they do these things? No of course they could not; and he did not suppose that a gentleman could cut as straight a furrow or thatch a rick as expertly as they could.

The author does not indicate the kind of text on which this kind of sermon may have been preached but the parson may well have had in mind Ecclesiasticus 38:24-34, which is quoted by Burke to make much the same point (1910, p. 46).

The idea that ineradicable differences in human capacities and powers are going to be reflected in an interdependent hierarchical structure is central to the traditional conservative vision of human community. The exercise of capacities and powers, however humble they may be, is morally worthy and the accompanying ethic is one of 'my station and its duties'. Although this conception of community may now be thought to have lost its legitimating basis - the will of God, the unalterable order of the cosmos, ineradicable differences between persons' capacities and powers - empirical studies in political sociology have shown that it does retain some kind of hold in the most unlikely places, among, for example, working-class conservative voters. As described by Parkin (1972, p. 85):

> deferential interpretations of the reward and status hierarchy stem from an acceptance of the dominant value system by the members of the subordinate class. It should be emphasised here that deference as a general mode of understanding and responding to the fact of low status does not necessarily entail a sense of self abnegation. Rather it tends to be bound up with a view of the social order as an organic unity in which each individual has a proper part to play however humble. Inequality is seen as inevitable as well as just.

McKenzie and Silver (1968) make this latter point even more explicitly in their classic study of working-class Tory voters (p. 249):

English deferentials feel themselves to be the moral, if not the social, equals of the elite because they appear to hold the classic doctrine that all who properly fulfill their stations in life contribute worthily to the common good.... English working-class deferentials are provided with a sense of esteem by the very ideas which justify and explain their social and political subordination.

A conservative conception of community will then be one of a stratified but organic and interdependent social order reflecting the necessary but complementary and functional inequalities in human endowment, the whole being bound together by an ethic of mutual service between the ranks in the hierarchy. The idea that inequalities are necessary and ineradicable, either because they reflect the will of God, the natural order of the cosmos, or because they are genetically transmitted is important to the survival of such a hierarchical society. This point has been brought out particularly well by Bernard Williams: 'what keeps stable hierarchies together is the idea of necessity that it is somehow foreordained and inevitable that there should be those orders' (1962, p. 201). Trying to mirror in community the order that inheres in nature, rather than trying actively to impose order upon it, is a central hallmark of conservative social thought, and its role has to be understood in the light of Williams's remarks, which in turn are given empirical backing by the work of McKenzie, Silver and Parkin. The marxist criticism that the feudal village community constrained and inhibited human development is vitiated for the conservative by the over-optimistic assumptions made by the marxist about human nature and the natural necessities and contingencies of human life; in neither case can their conceptions of community be understood without taking into account these background assumptions.

For the marxist and the conservative, community is something of an embarrassment. The marxist sees community in capitalist society used primarily to describe specific localities marked by neighbourliness and kinship, its particularity and exclusivity standing in stark contrast with the universality of class consciousness without which there can be no transformation of society and no community of human kind. The conservative sees that the social structure and the attendant modes of consciousness and ethical conviction intrinsic to his vision of community have fallen away and that the various natural necessities that appeared to make his vision both viable and compelling are losing their force. Both however are agreed in seeing modern Western liberal/social democratic society as becoming more

and more bereft of a sense of community, and the various
forms of community work and development financed by the
welfare branches of liberal/social democratic societies
as being a somewhat frenetic and misplaced realization of
this. As Robert Paul Wolff says, 'the conservative locates
community in a cherished past and the radical in the longed
for future', (1968, p. 184).

We shall now explore some of the immense difficulties
that the liberal/social democrat faces in trying to articulate a conception of community consistent with a strong
commitment to individualism, and shall try to relate some
of the dilemmas of the liberal/social democratic tradition
to issues that specifically concern welfare and its provision.

One strategy that might be adopted in the face of the
communitarian critique would be for the liberal to admit
the charge of being indifferent to the claims of overall
community but to reject it as a criticism. He might
point out that the liberal tradition had its very origins
in a critique of communitarian institutions. Many theorists, particularly of the seventeenth and eighteenth
centuries, tried to come to terms with new social developments, such as the development of market society, increasing division of labour and urbanization, and attempted to
provide an understanding of man and society that would
help to explain and justify the loss of the old communities. This type of social theory sought to justify the
basis of human association not in tradition and habit but
in the contract and consent of naturally free and independent persons. The individual was taken to be the basic
reality, and all forms of social interaction were taken
to be constructions out of the motives and desires of these
palpable, free, self-conscious individuals who derived
their sense of freedom and conception of themselves precisely from the decline and loss of closer, more communal
forms of social relationships. Thinkers in this tradition,
particularly Hobbes, have profoundly influenced our concept of man and a *fortiori* our views about the limits
and possibilities of community. Bentham was so beset
with the decline of community that he regarded the questions 'Who are you?' and 'With whom do I deal?' as central
to modern society, but they are not questions that would
have made any sense in a small village community pervaded
by shared values, beliefs and expectations. Eric Hobsbawm
(1975) has pointed out the extent to which the whole liberal tradition is deeply ambivalent on the whole subject of
community:

> The tradition of middle class liberal political thought
> has not known quite what to do with it. The essence

of that tradition was individualist, and the shadow of individualism lies over it still. Fraternity, in this tradition, can only be the by product of individual impulses, of such qualities as Bentham's benevolence or of those social sympathies with which schools like the positivists operated.
On such a view the decline of an overall sense of community is to be seen in terms of liberation, of the emancipation of the individual from his position within a hierarchy of status to a position of a consuming, exchanging and contracting individual in the market. Any attempt to recreate an overall sense of community is likely to involve the risk of coercing individuals into substantive agreement about the ends of life and the goals that individuals ought to value and pursue. Community might be thought to be impossible without such normative agreement, and yet the achievement of such an agreement in modern society will involve the imposition of a set of standards and ends on individuals and their coercion by either law or public opinion within the community if they do not.
Against a communitarian ethic, resting as it does on substantive normative agreement, liberals might seek to counterpose the idea of an open society, a great society, or a catallaxy within which individuals will have mutual freedom to pursue their ends in their own way. Certainly liberals such as Hayek and Dahrendorf have taken this view. Dahrendorf, in 'Society and Democracy in Germany' (1968) has argued very strongly that the appeal to community is politically illiberal in the way I have described, and Hayek, in 'The Road to Serfdom' (1944), has indicated some of the grave dangers of a communitarian ethic, particularly the use of the notion of *Volksgemeinschaft* by the Nazis.

PARTIAL COMMUNITIES

Of course, the rejection of an ethic based on an overall sense of community does not mean that the liberal is indifferent to the appeal of community when it operates in a more restricted manner. While an open society may well be hostile to the idea of substantive normative agreement and seeks only a framework of law protecting mutual freedom to pursue a variety of ends, there can still be a role within such a society for voluntary community groups within which individuals who share values and interests may choose to come together and in such coming together may form a very strong sense of mutual solidarity. Older forms of partial communities were often based upon accidents of

birth, so that one's inclusion or exclusion from such
community would be something beyond the voluntary choice
of individuals; in contrast to this, the suggestion is
that such partial communities should be based upon voluntary participation and should relate to shared values and
interests that each member of the community has chosen for
himself. Society on this view would be seen as being an
aggregate of partial communities with no single individual
passing his life solely within the ambit and ethos of a
particular group unless he should choose to do so. The
emphasis upon freedom of choice here is important because
a number of sociological studies have suggested the extent
to which occupational groups may develop the features of
a community, and while in some respects the liberal may
welcome this, there is a clear danger of the development
of a sort of moral 'closed shop', with individuals who
perform their work role adequately but fail to subscribe
to the dominant ethos of the occupational community being
forced out.

This theory of partial communities is developed in some
detail by Nozick in 'Anarchy, State and Utopia' (1974),
and his argument rests in part on the recognition of the
extreme diversity of human desires, goals, purposes and
interests coupled with the ethical principle that individuals are inviolable. If individuals are inviolable then
it is morally wrong to coerce individuals into any communities that fail to express their interests or provide the
means for the realization of their desires. Human nature
is so complex that there is not one form of human community
that is likely to meet and be adequate to the complexities
of human nature (Nozick, 1974, p. 310):

> The different kinds of life are so different that there
> is not one kind of community (meeting certain constraints
> which objectively is best for everyone.... For each
> person ... there is a wide range of very different kinds
> of life that tie best; no other is objectively better
> for him than any other in this range, no one within the
> range is objectively better than any other. And there
> is not one community which objectively is the best for
> the living of each selection set from the family of
> sets of not objectively inferior lives.

Under the proposal made by Nozick each individual chooses
to live in the actual community that comes closest to
realizing what is most important to him; if there is a
diverse range of communities more persons will be able to
come closer to how they wish to live than if there is only
one kind of community. If there is a wide and diverse
range of communities that they can enter if they wish to,
shape according to their wishes, pursue experiments in

living, then inviolable individuals will be able to pursue
different styles of life and different visions of the good
can be individually or jointly pursued.

Such groups will not be so large as to preclude the
existence of those intentional attitudes towards other
members of communities that are so important to the notion
of community. One such attitude is altruism, and an
understanding of community in the sense provided by Nozick
enables altruism and fellow feeling to have an important
place. Within the liberal tradition it is frequently
assumed that altruistic resources are limited and are
usually directed towards individuals known to the giver
or to those with whom he has ties of affection. As Hume
argues, 'I may still do services to such persons as I love
and am more particularly acquainted with without any prospect of advantage'. Altruistically sustained fraternal
relationships depend upon the range and reciprocity of
affection and knowledge and must be limited in scope.
Obviously, community reduced to the smaller scale envisaged by Nozick would be consistent with the operation
of altruistic sentiments according to these constraints.
The other major constraint usually placed upon altruism
and benevolence within the liberal tradition is the importance of choice. We must, on this view, be able to
choose those towards whom we exercise benevolence and to
choose the characteristics of the recipients of our gifts.
Voluntarily entered micro-communities are most likely to
be able to maintain these characteristic features of benevolent and fraternal attitudes.

Such communities may play an important part in welfare.
Based as they are upon voluntary co-operation, and consistent as they are with the operation of benevolence and
altruism, they may well operate in such a way as to meet
the needs of their members. Though the framework within
which communities exist is libertarian and *laissez-faire*,
individual communities within the framework need not be.
Voluntary communities could involve elaborate schemes
for mutual insurance, redistribution between members and
unilateral transfers for those in need. This possibility
follows from the fact, as Nozick argues, that individuals
may contract into various restrictions that the government
may not impose on them. Although state welfare infringes
rights and does not respect the inviolability of persons,
individuals might well contract into various forms of
communitarian welfare.

However, there are those who would regard such a conception of community as far too attenuated. On such a view,
only an overall conception of community is legitimate, and
a vision of society as merely an aggregation of partial

communities held together by the minimal state is not
sufficient. There might be several reasons why this might
be thought to be so. Wolff for example argues that such
a conception will lack a theory of the common good; more
abstractly other thinkers, mainly within the liberal
Hegelian tradition, have argued that individuals have a
universal aspect to their characters and that they need
to realize this universality in a sense of solidarity with
their fellows that transcends the partial communities of
the sort advocated by Nozick and the segmented forms of
solidarity encapsulated within them. Another reason for
thinking the view insufficient would be that, while within
partial communities individual welfare might be taken care
of in the manner suggested above, there might still be
individuals who have extensive needs but do not belong to
any partial communities. This possibility is certainly
allowed by Nozick when he argues that 'someone may be
refused entry into a community he wishes to join on individual grounds or because he falls under a general restriction designed to preserve the particular character of the
community' (1974, p. 352). Of course one such ground may
be the extent of the individual's need for particular resources that the community may have at its disposal. If
this point is taken seriously then it leads easily to the
suggestion that certain kinds of goods are too important
to be distributed according to the lights of particular
voluntary communities and that the state has a duty to
provide welfare for its citizens. In addition, such state
provision of welfare might be thought to involve communitarian aspects in that it is responding to need and in
that it seeks to integrate the individual into the life
of society from which he may be excluded by his degree of
deprivation.
     If we are responsive to the criticisms of the partial
community approach, then we have to address the question
of whether there is a conception of overall community
that can be founded upon liberal assumptions. In response
to this kind of problem we can discern two sorts of strategies, each of which contains the same fatal defect.

THE PROBLEMS OF OVERALL COMMUNITY

The first strategy is fairly modest and consists of the
idea that in the economic market individuals, while pursuing their own interests and seeking to maximize their
own utilities, are thrust into relationships of mutual
interdependence, and lack a sense of overall community
only in the sense that they fail to recognize the overall

nature of this interdependence. To grasp and understand the role of the invisible hand, in which each 'man is led to promote an end which is no part of his intention', is crucial for the perception of this interdependence and thus of community. The metaphor is sometimes changed - Mirabeau thought the hidden hand to be a process of magic, steuart called it a 'tacit contract', and Hegel regarded it as the result of the 'cunning of reason' - but the point is the same: when we comprehend the network of relations in which we are enmeshed in the market, then we shall understand that the markety lays down its own forms of mutuality. Hegel is the political and social theorist who argues this case most vigorously and in whose work the fatal flaw in this approach most clearly reveals itself. He makes the point about the interdependence engendered in the market in the 'Philosophy of Right' (1952), although it is important to remember that this does not exhaust his account of community in the modern world (para. 199):

> When men are thus dependent on one another and reciprocally related to one another in their work and the satisfaction of their needs, subjective self seeking turns into a contribution to the satisfaction of the needs of everyone else. That is to say by a dialectical advance self seeking turns into the mediation of the particular through the universal, with the result that each man in earning, producing and enjoying on his own account is *eo ipso* producing and earning for the enjoyment of everyone else.

When we comprehend the fact of our mutual interdependence then we have discovered a communitarian aspect of market activity. What appears to be made over to subjective self-seeking and private maximizing is revealed to embody forms of mutuality and community. The most important aspect of this is the comprehension of the relationships, and hence social theory and philosophy has an important role to play in constituting this community because it is not a form of *sinnliche Harmonie* but rather a form of relationship that has to be grasped in thought and may in fact be understood in a different way by those involved in it. Indeed, in Hegel's view a conceptual grasp of the complexity of economic interdependence is difficult to gain, and in political economy only the first steps have been taken (1952, para. 189):

> Political economy is the science which starts from this view of needs and labour but then has the task of explaining mass relationships and mass movements in their complexity and their quantitative character.... It is to find reconciliation here, to discover in this

sphere of needs this show of rationality lying in the
thing and effective there; but if we look at it from
the opposite point of view, this is the field in which
the Understanding with its subjective aims and moral
fancies vents its discontent and moral frustration.

It seems clear that in the final sentence Hegel has in
mind various romantic critiques of commercial society, and
he suggests that, because such critics have not recognized
the deep interconnected aspects of life in civil society,
they have been unable to see modern society as a bearer of
community. However, such a form of community is not to be
understood in terms of persons having particular kinds of
intentional relationships to one another. The individual
does not have to entertain fraternal sentiments even though
his work may satisfy the life needs of others. As Hume
put the point in his discussion of how the self-interested
commerce of men begins to predominate in society, 'I learn
to do a service for another without bearing him any real
kindness.'

Herein lies the difficulty of this version of the market
theory of community. It makes the existence of community
a matter of the upshot, of the unintended consequences of
a sequence of actions undertaken for different reasons.
Community is a matter of grasping these inuntended consequences; it is not a matter of relating to persons in
terms of fraternal feeling and attitude. However, it is
difficult to see how a concept of community can operate
without making some reference to the values in terms of
which members of the community perceive themselves in relation to one another. Community is not just a matter of
particular outcomes, but of right intentional relationships,
relationships that involve benevolence, altruism, fraternity.
The obvious answer to this difficulty, and the one that
Hegel, in so far as he sees the problem, appears to give,
is that once we comprehend the facts of our interrelation-
ship this knowledge will enter into our motivations in the
market, and we shall consciously work for the satisfactions
of the needs of others (Hegel, 1910, p. 377):

The labour of the individual for his own wants is just
as much a satisfaction of those of others as of himself,
and the satisfaction of his own he attains only by the
labour of others.

As the individual in his own particular work ipso
facto accomplishes unconsciously a universal work, so
again he also performs the universal task as his *conscious* object. The whole becomes in its entirety his
work, for which he sacrifices himself and precisely by
that means he receives back his own self from it.

This is now a different claim, and one that it is difficult

to sustain. The first claim was that private maximizing activity in the market lays down forms of community and mutuality as an unintended consequence of such activity, and there is a need to grasp this in thought. The second claim is that, when this is understood, individuals will pursue such forms of *Gemeinschaftlichkeit* in a self-conscious way and will actively seek to promote the satisfaction of the needs of others. This second claim has the advantage from the point of view of community theory that it does make reference to the conscious relationships between individuals; the disadvantage, though, is that it is not at all clear how the market would operate with such changed motivations present in the previously maximizing individuals. The market that yields community in an unintended fashion will itself be modified by the realization of its community-engendering capabilities because these will be consciously fostered as a result of such realization.

The second strategy for coming to terms with the notion of overall community from the liberal point of view is to be found in the work of Rawls, which, as we shall see, produces very similar problems to that of Hegel. For Rawls a sense of community is engendered not by comprehending the facts of human interrelationships in the market, but rather by constraining the market in the interests of justice, and he suggests in 'A Theory of Justice' (1972) that there can be an interpretation of community in terms of the just distribution of resources. The connection between justice and community comes about via the operation of the difference principle, and its connection to central liberal assumptions comes via the contract and the veil of ignorance, in which rational mutually disinterested individuals choose principles of justice without knowing how those principles will affect them. The difference principle would be chosen in such circumstances and in its turn it yields an interpretation of community (Rawls, 1972, p. 105):

A further merit of the difference principle is that it provides an interpretation of the principle of fraternity. In comparison with liberty and equality, the idea of fraternity has had a lesser place in democratic theory ... the difference principle does seem to correspond to a natural meaning of fraternity: namely the idea of not wanting greater advantages unless this is to the advantage and benefit of others who are not so well off. The family in its ideal conception and often in practice is the one place where the principle of calculating the sum of advantages is rejected. Members of a family commonly do not wish to gain unless they

can do so in ways that further the interests of the
rest. Now wanting to act on the difference principle
has precisely this consequence. Those better circum-
stanced are willing to have their advantages only
under a scheme in which this works out for the benefit
of the least fortunate.

This looks to be a very important argument because it
ties together a number of important features of community:
there is the idea of a principled set of relationships, so
in this sense community is not an arbitrary and unintended
outcome of a set of activities; it seems to incorporate
some of the intentional attitudes that are important to
community, because Rawls links up the altruistic and fraternal consequences of acting on the difference principle
with wanting to act on the principle; finally, it links
community and fraternity to welfare and acting in the
interests of those in need and deprivation, which would
enable us to shed some theoretical light upon the dominant
usage of the concept in contemporary social policy.

Unfortunately, it is not at all clear whether this
powerful conception is coherent. A very great deal depends
upon what is involved in the idea of wanting to act on the
difference principle because it is through this desire that
Rawls is able to tie up communitarian outcome with communitarian sentiment. Underlying Rawls's difference principle
is his contract argument, and the principle is derived
as a result of considering the rational choices that could
be made by the contracting parties in conditions of radical
uncertainty. However, the contractual argument does not
make any strong assumptions about altruism; on the contrary, in fact: the contracting parties are supposed to
be mutually disinterested. If at any point after the
principles of justice have been agreed someone were to
ask, 'why ought we to act on the difference principle?' the
answer would be given by referring back to the contract
argument and not to considerations about altruistic motivation. Persons do not act on the difference principle
because they have fraternal and altruistic concern for all
others in society, but because this principle would have
been chosen by mutually disinterested contractors in a
situation of radical uncertainty. Again, the problem for
the understanding of community and fraternity is similar
to the one identified in the case of Hegel. It may well
be that the effect of acting on the difference principle
will be as Rawls describes, but such benefits as accrue
to deprived individuals under the operation of the principle are not part of the explicit justification for the
principle. Community again is seen in terms of particular
kinds of outcomes and not justified on the basis of

altruistic or fraternal sentiment. The tradition of
liberal political thought that has put limits on the
operation of altruism has made it impossible, granted
these constraints, to produce an overall view of community
that manages to do justice to the dimension of community
that involves institutional outcomes and the dimension
that makes communitarian attitudes to be of central importance. A considerable amount of justice can be done to
the first of these requirements, but only a partial view
of community seems compatible with liberal assumptions
under the second heading.

If we take the view that community can exist only
when individuals have particular kinds of relationships
towards one another in certain ways, then we have to reject the view that it can exist as an unintended outcome
of actions undertaken for other reasons. This clearly
presents a dilemma for any overall theory of community.
Surely the universality of such a community is going to
make it impossible for the range of communitarian attitudes - benevolence, altruism, kindliness, fraternity -
to exist between members of such an overall community.
If the liberal tradition is correct in suggesting to us
that virtues such as benevolence and altruism are necessarily limited and constrained, then we are forced to
admit that community in the modern world has to be on a
small scale and that the Nozickian theory is the only
account consistent with such principles. The consistent
liberal perhaps cannot provide an account of 'the political equivalent of love', as Unger calls that range of
attitudes that would link members of a community together.
It is just because he rejects these kinds of constraints
on the operation of communitarian sentiments that makes
Titmuss's book, 'The Gift Relationship' (1970) such an
important contribution to social philosophy. Following
Boulding's characterization of the sphere of social policy
as distinct from the market, Titmuss distinguishes the
sphere of the social from that of the market by arguing
that the former is centred on those institutions and prac-
tices that create integration and discourage alienation.
In the particular case of blood donation, which is the
major subject of study in the book, this is seen by the
fact that for Titmuss such donation is a form of altruistic
giving. Blood is a gift, and because for Titmuss motivation is a centrally important feature of community he is
able to provide an account of what appears to be lacking
in an overall conception of community compatible with
liberal assumptions. Such motives and intentions are of
a broadly altruistic sort and help to prolong the lives of
others who are in need. These forms of creative altruism

imply an allocation of resources in which 'there is no
sense of separateness between people'.

If we accept the link between altruism and community,
on right relationships and not merely just outcomes, then
we need to examine further the nature of the altruism and
benevolence in question and the way in which it may shed
light on the conception of altruism held for example by
Hume and Hayek. Following Grice in 'The Grounds of Moral
Judgement' (1967), Titmuss argues that the giving of
blood, or more generally acts of creative altruism, are
ultra obligations, and in the view of Grice and Titmuss
there are a number of features of ultra obligations.

(a)   The person who performs the ultra obligation can-
      not have a strict duty to perform it and someone
      who fails to perform it is under no moral censure
      from his 'failure'. So to use Grice's example,
      if Sir Philip Sidney, lying injured and parched
      with thirst after the battle of Sutphen, had not
      handed over his mug of water to another wounded
      soldier, we would not think that we would have the
      moral right to censure his conduct. Similarly,
      with blood donation there is 'no remorse, shame or
      guilt attached to the failure to give blood'.

(b)   Corresponding to the fact that there is no strict
      obligation to perform an ultra obligation is the
      connection between the actual performance of such
      an act and the character of the agent. The per-
      son concerned regards it as obligatory for *him* to
      give, and we cannot make the performance of an
      ultra obligation intelligible without some form of
      moral psychology. Grice brings this out very
      clearly.

(c)   If the performance of an ultra obligation is not
      a strict duty of all persons, then there can be
      no *right* on the part of those who would benefit
      from such a performance to the fulfilment of the
      obligation. If the provision of blood and welfare
      benefits generally are matters of ultra obligation,
      then there can be no moral right to them.

(d)   Such ultra obligations cannot be explained on a
      contractual basis, otherwise all the other condi-
      tions cited above would become void.

(e)   Ultra obligations depend on the recognition of
      need. Those who might be thought to be the bene-
      ficiaries of such obligations must be thought to
      suffer from some need or deprivation.

Of course, both Hayek and Hume would agree with a great
deal of this: acts of altruism are discretionary in their
performance and there can be no corresponding right in

potential beneficiaries of such acts. However, there are
some differences between Titmuss's views and the others.
Hume for example argues, as we have seen, that altruistic
giving is limited to those whom I know and with whom I have
affective ties. Titmuss clearly rejects this, and with it
the implied limitations on the extent of fraternity,
granted the necessary link between such attitudes and
community. In blood donation the donor gives to 'strangers',
to anonymous others. All that is known is that there is a
need for blood and that the universality of need is sufficient to generate the altruistic response without the ties
of affection, and this willingness to be involved in the
needs of others does not require that we know them as persons. Titmuss also rejects Hayek's view that we must be
free to choose not just whether to give or not to give,
but also to whom we shall give. Again, in this view this
is not a necessary feature of altruism in that in blood
donation the donor is not allowed to prescribe the 'characteristics of the recipients' and this does not affect the
willingness of donors to give. In so far as such attitudes are necessary for community, such communities need
not be limited by the constraints imposed by liberal
writers.

The other difference, and much the most important one,
is that it is a mistake in Titmuss's view to see altruism
as a limited resource in the sense that there are dangers
in using it up and depleting it by basing social policies
on its operation. Arrow for example clearly feels that
altruism is a scarce resource which should be husbanded:
he argues that we should not wish: 'to use up recklessly
the scarce resources of altruistically motivated behaviour'
(1972, p. 185). This of course is perhaps the central
problem for altruism and overall community: if altruism
is a scarce resource, and if it is necessarily linked with
the existence of community, then the chances of there being
a viable form of overall community would be very poor, and
certainly welfare provision would not be able to rely on
such broad communitarian sentiments. However, one response
that can be made to the point made by Arrow is to argue
that altruism breeds altruism, and the extension of both
the economic market and of state activity may both atten-
uate altruism even among those who may have had altruistic
motivations. This is a central aspect of Titmuss's own
rejection of the development of a market in blood, and
Goodin (1977, p. 499) has suggested that

there may be a form of Gresham's Law at work whereby
bad motives drive out good ones. Perhaps the offer of
material payoffs debases what would otherwise be a
noble act, causing a sort of motivational flip flop.

In that case Hume's social system designed for knaves,
far from protecting against preexistent nastiness,
turns kindly souls into knaves.
In 'Anarchy and Cooperation', Taylor (1976) produces a
similar argument about the role of the state in which he
argues that 'positive altruism and voluntary co-operative
behaviour *atrophy* in the presence of the state and *grow*
in its absence' (p. 134).

In a sense then Titmuss's argument, despite his own
socialist predilections, may well prove attractive to
libertarians. On his view there is a political equivalent
of love; this is not a scarce resource, and might be expected to grow rather than diminish the more we rely on it.
In addition, the role of the state could decline the more
we rely on altruism, partly because of the claim that
state activity leads to a decline in altruism and partly
because, as an ultra obligation, state coercion of such
acts is morally illegitimate. Such altruism will respond
to the universality of need and will not be limited to
those whom we know and love, and thus could provide a
basis for non-state forms of welfare. Finally, it will
enable us to envisage a form of overall community consistent with liberal theory because the rejection of Hayek's
and Hume's assumptions about the necessary limitations of
altruism are not central to liberal assumptions.

However, there are a number of residual questions left
from this discussion. The first consists of a doubt about
the richness of Titmuss's view of community, and perhaps
this problem has best been posed by Arrow (1972, p. 186):

Indeed there is something of a paradox in Titmuss'
philosophy. He is especially interested in the expression of impersonal altruism. It is not the richness
of family relationships or the close ties of a small
community which he wishes to promote. It is rather a
diffuse expression of confidence by individuals in the
working of society as a whole. But such an expression
of impersonal altruism is as far removed from the feelings of personal interaction as any market place.

If this is a paradox it is one that Titmuss has to embrace,
and one that any liberal theory of overall community has
to live with. If altruism and community go together,
then in a large society community has to rest on acts of
impersonal altruism, which as we saw is a central feature
of Titmuss's account as opposed to the more limited assumptions of Hume and Hayek. If we are to reserve the idea of
community to intimate, reciprocal face-to-face relationships,
then there can be no sense of overall community in modern
society; on the other hand, it seems that Titmuss has made
out a theoretical and an empirical case for the view that

there can be impersonal altruism generating a sense of
community across the board in society. If this view is
rejected then, granted the difficulties in accepting the
thesis that community can be defined in terms of outcomes
rather than in terms of relationships, the liberal will
have to jettison the idea of overall community and accept
Nozick's conception of partial, voluntary communities
within which face-to-face relationships would be possible.

ALTRUISM AND ULTRA OBLIGATIONS

It seems quite possible that Titmuss is correct in seeing
the specific case of a voluntary blood donations system
as an exercise in altruism. If the system operates
mainly on the basis of altruism, then he seems to be
clearly right in seeing blood donation as an exercise in
ultra obligation, deriving, as he argues partly following
Grice, from our character. However, it is important to
see why blood donation is an ultra obligation and *not*
necessarily the best model for understanding the more
general obligations to provide welfare. Here lies one
of the difficulties: Titmuss often refers to welfare as
a gift, and generalizing from the case of blood donation
he argues in 'The Gift Relationship' that 'much of social
policy' is concerned with these ultra obligations (1970,
p. 212), and it is not clear what areas he has in mind
and how this follows from the rather singular case of
blood donation. The reason why it is proper to see blood
donation as an ultra obligation and not as a strict duty
is that if it were a strict duty those who are in need
of blood would then have a *right* to blood, and thereby
would hold a property right in some anonymous person's
body, and the state would have a right and indeed a responsibility to see that those who needed blood were able
to exercise their right to the blood of these unspecified
people. This does appear counter-intuitive. If, as
Grice argued in a passage cited earlier, the soldier
lying next to Sir Philip Sidney has no right to the water
that Sidney offered him, it seems even plainer that no
person has the right to another person's blood, or for
that matter to his transplantable organs, at least while
he is alive. Blood is a gift, and Titmuss is clearly
correct in making this a central part of his argument
(although of course we found his case for not allowing it
to be a commodity for those who wish to regard it as such
to be unpersuasive). While blood in a donor system is a
gift and in a market system is an exchange commodity, there
seems to be no place for regarding it as something to which

others have a right. If they did have such a right then
this would involve the idea of surrendering one's ownership of one's own body. This seems to be the underlying
reason why blood has to be either freely given or, *pace*
Titmuss, freely exchanged. But most welfare goods are
not necessarily like this, or are they? Nozick, of
course, wishes to argue that they are; that the products
of one's labour belong to one as a consequence of the
inviolability thesis as much as one's blood, and that the
view that the needy have rights against those with resources gives them property rights in the better off just
as much as if we were to concede a right to the blood of
healthy persons to those who are in need of transfusions.
Indeed, Nozick goes so far as to suggest in 'Anarchy, State
and Utopia' that those who argue for some kind of right to
welfare are logically committed to granting property
rights in the persons of the better off to those in need,
and he brings this out quite sharply by suggesting that
the handicapped might be thought to have a right to some
of the body parts of the healthy (1974, p. 206):

> May all entitlements be relegated to relatively super-
> ficial levels? For example, people's entitlements to
> parts of their own bodies? An application of the
> principle of maximising the position of the worst off
> might well involve forceable redistribution of bodily
> parts ('You've been sighted for all these years - now
> one - or even both - of your eyes is to be transplanted
> to others'), or killing some people early to use their
> bodies to save the lives of those who would otherwise
> die young. To bring up such cases may sound slightly
> hysterical.

It is clear in Nozick's terms why this should be so. In
a state that pursues redistributive social policies and
employs the tax system to help the needy, the handicapped,
the deprived, etc., the state is in fact giving the disadvantaged property rights in the better off, and his
point about the forcible redistribution of body parts is
just a dramatic way of bringing out this point and its
absurdity (Nozick, 1974, p. 172):

> Seizing the results of someone's labour is equivalent
> to seizing hours from him and directing him to carry
> on various activities. If people force you to do
> certain work, or unrewarded work, for a certain period
> of time, they decide what you are to do and what pur-
> poses your work is to serve apart from your decisions.
> This process whereby they take this decision from you
> makes them a part-owner of you; it gives them a pro-
> perty right in you.... These principles involve a shift

from the classical liberal's notion of self ownership
to a notion of (partial) property rights in other
people.

It is clear on the basis of this argument that all of
welfare should be seen in terms of charity and ultra
obligation. The disadvantaged do not have a right to
welfare because this would mean having a right to the
products of the labour of others or to their time, and
this would involve giving them a right to their bodily
parts. As the latter offends against the deeply entrenched view of self-ownership that we have, so too does
the former, although in a less than obvious way. In the
following passage we can see how this follows clearly
from Nozick's highly individualistic account of the productive process (1974, p. 172):

they [redistributive principles] give each citizen an
enforceable claim to some portion of the total social
product; that is to some portion of the sum total of
individual and jointly made products. This total
product is produced by individuals labouring, using
means of production others have saved to bring into
existence, by people organising production or creating
means to produce new things in a new way. It is on
this batch of individual activities that patterned
distributional principles give each an individual an
enforceable claim. Each person has a claim to the
activities and products of other persons, independently
of whether other persons enter into particular relationships that give rise to these claims, and independently of whether they voluntarily take these
claims upon themselves, in charity or in exchange
for something.

It is not at all clear, however, that this picture of
the process of production is at all plausible, and yet it
is at the very basis of Nozick's argument here. For his
argument to work, the total social product, which the
state divides to help the needy, is seen by Nozick to be
traceable back to the particular productive actions of
individuals in such a way that individual entitlements
and property rights arising from such actions are being
infringed by the redistributive activities of the state,
and moreover giving the needy property rights in the products of the labour and thus the bodily movements of the
producers. But it is surely difficult to filter out of
the total social product individual entitlements of this
sort. Production requires such a scheme of social co-
operation that it makes it very difficult to see how
individual contributions can be disentangled from the
social product just because we lack a coherent notion of

an identifiable marginal product in a complex, non-stationary industrial economy. Not only this, but it also has to be shown that such contributions would yield entitlements *to* and property rights *in* the individually traceable fragments of the joint product. This Nozick attempts to do in his rather sketchy account of justice in acquisition in which he defends a variation of Locke's theory of property acquisition in which I come to own something with which I have mixed my labour subject to Locke's proviso that there be 'enough and as good left in common for others'. On this Lockean basis Nozick develops the view that the process giving rise to a permanent bequeathable property right in a previously unowned thing is a combination of the property-owners having mixed his labour with the thing and not worsening the position of others who are no longer at liberty to use the thing. However, the notion of property rights arising as the result of mixing one's labour with an unowned object is a very difficult one, and Nozick himself discusses many of the difficulties in the Lockean conception without in fact being able to solve them (1974, pp. 174-82). In addition to this, some sympathetic critics have pointed out that before an individual has reached a sufficient stage of maturity to mix his labour with anything the community will have an investment in him through the support of his long childhood, including the training that is prerequisite to his meaningful labour. Nozick's arguments against redistribution require two assumptions which, as Lukes has pointed out (1977, p. 194), are really pre-sociological. One is the highly abstract conception of the productive process which is seen as fundamentally uncomplicated with marginal products being capable of subtraction from the total social product; the second, which in some way parallels the first, is that individual labour creates property rights without any real investigation of the philosophical difficulties involved in explaining how this comes about and without considering the social context within which labouring appears and the social investment that labour itself may represent. At the same time, the theoretical force of the criticism of welfare right theory is only as strong as these two assumptions. Overall, as we saw in a previous chapter, Nozick claims that his theory derives from an attempt to draw out the consequences of the Kantian principle of treating persons as ends in themselves (Nozick, 1974 and Steiner, 1975). However, earlier we argued that, while this is *one* way of understanding Kant's principle, it is by no means the only one, and probably not the way in which Kant thought that it should be interpreted. There seems to be no reason therefore why we should be too impressed with Nozick's anti-welfare arguments or regard welfare as a matter of ultra obligation. In addition, there is no reason why we should regard the blood donor system as outlined by Titmuss as a desirable paradigm for welfare provision. This does not imply criticism of Titmuss's account of the blood donor system, only that we have no reason to generalize, as he seems to, and regard much of social policy as a matter of ultra obligation, altruism and fraternity. The only reasons for making this generalization are either of the sort that Nozick gives, and which we have found wanting, or by some appeal to the notion of community, a principle that as we have already seen is far too protean to be of use in detailed thinking about the general principles on which welfare should be based. Welfare can be seen coherently in terms of rights, and the dichotomy between seeing it as a matter of either altruism or a market exchange is a false one.

Of course, this does not mean that altruism is unimportant, but it is perhaps too insecure a basis on which to base the life chances of the disadvantaged. Altruism is much more at home in small contexts between members of a family or a neighbourhood, and it is difficult to see how anonymous altruism of the sort at work in the blood donor system could really make much difference to the sense of community. However, state-provided welfare as a matter of right is never likely to be able to tailor exactly resources to detailed need among the deprived just because the amount of detailed information required is not likely to be available, and it is at the interstices of felt need and state provision that the ultra obligations of altruism and gift-giving are always going to have a place in a welfare society.

It is a false dichotomy to counterpose community and altruism on one side and a set of rights and obligations on the other. While that latter view of welfare organization might seem on the face of it to lead to an attenuation of certain kinds of important human impulses - those of spontaneous and non-criteriological gift-giving - the danger is that the very sponteneity of the former may make it an inappropriate basis for organizing a welfare system as a whole, and in addition the notion of community appealed to is perhaps too vague. Communities can exist within a society, but whether there can be a society-wide conception of community in anything like the present industrial set-up is highly dubious. Within these smaller communities in which the full details of individual need are known there will be always a place for generosity and altruism, and the vision of society as one pared down to procedure with no importance attached to motive and character in the distribution and receipt of welfare is a false one.

NEEDS, WELFARE, THE STATE AND COMMUNITY

We have argued that the recognition of need gives rise to
strict obligations on the part of those with resources.
Needs are means to ends: a subject always needs something
for some purpose. If we morally approve of the purpose or
goal for which something is needed and we think that this
purpose should be realized, then ethical consistency requires that we should help to provide the means, that is
the needs, to that end. If there are any ends that all
human beings share, then there will be basic needs
attached to the realization of those ends and obligations
on those who share the ends - in this case all humans - to
meet such needs so far as they are able. The first account
of needs would relate to the obligations to meet needs in
partial communities. In partial communities there are
limited shared ends which all those who have voluntarily
joined the community share, and there will be needs defined in terms of the necessary means to the achievement
of such ends. The provision of what is needed to those
within the community who may not possess these resources
would perhaps more properly be a matter of strict obligation to the members of that community just because the
person now in need was voluntarily admitted as a member;
and Nozick, as we have already pointed out, is willing
to allow such partial communities to generate by voluntary
contract more extensive obligations than would be rightfully imposed by a state. The other conception of need
would correspond to needs within an overall community in
which those needs required for the achievement of human
ends more generally would be specified and there would
then be obligations on all persons with resources in the
community to meet such needs because *ex hypothesi* all
persons are implicated in the pursuit of the ends that
specify the needs. However, most liberals will want to
reject this account because it makes assumptions about
the identity of human goals and purposes that the consistent liberal does not want to make. At the same time,
however, if he wishes to make use of Titmuss's model he
has to accept the universality of needs to which ultra
obligations correspond. In what follows we want to suggest that the consistent liberal has to recognize certain
universal needs, that corresponding to these there are
strict obligations, and that welfare, understood as the
satisfaction of these needs, is to be seen as a right and
not as a communitarian ultra obligation.
    The liberal wishes to emphasize the diversity of human
goals, values and purposes, and of course it has been a
central argument of those who have wanted to resist the

claims of distributive justice that such distributive
arrangements would require the imposition of a particular
set of ends. Society should be organized on a different
basis, to ensure that each individual using the knowledge
that he has is able to pursue his own good in his own
way. This will require a framework of law to ensure such
mutual freedom. Such a legal framework would be justified
by the view that without it individuals will encroach on
one another's freedom and will not be able to pursue their
ends efficiently. However, it is arguable that if we
recognize a plurality of ends we still need more than
just procedural rules to facilitate the pursuit of these
ends. Such ends, whatever they may be - and of course
the liberal does not want to provide a definitive list -
are still likely to yield a minimal set of the same basic
needs. Any end, in so far as it is an object of value, can
be pursued only by human beings, and as an object of value
can be pursued only by human beings who are capable of
deliberation and choice; and in so far as these are necessary conditions for the pursuit of such ends they will
yield a set of basic needs: the need for physical survival
and autonomy. Any set of ends on this view is going to
imply the same set of basic needs, and if the state is
able to impose a framework of law as a necessary condition
for the effective pursuit by an individual of his own
good in his own way, there is no reason of principle why
the state should not provide resources to meet these
basic needs because these equally are necessary means to
the pursuit of a variety of ends. Indeed, perhaps some
liberals recognize this, at least implicitly - for example,
Hayek's defence of the state's responsibility to provide
a minimum subsistence level in 'The Constitution of
Liberty' (1960), although, of course, no such obligation
is recognized by Nozick (1974). If the state does have
an obligation to meet basic welfare needs, that is those
needs that are necessary conditions for the pursuit of
any end, then at least this dimension of welfare cannot
rest upon communitarian ultra obligations of altruism but
is a strict obligation to which there is a corresponding
right. Such needs, defined as necessary conditions for the
pursuit of any end, have to be met as a strict duty as a
matter of ethical consistency; if we will a society in
which individuals will be able to pursue the most diverse
range of ends possible, then we have a duty to provide
resources necessary for the achievement of ends of that
sort.

There is therefore likely to be a central role left
for the state in the sphere of welfare provision, and we
cannot in consistency allow basic needs to be satisfied

by philanthropy and benevolence alone, even assuming that
altruism is not limited in the ways suggested by some
liberals. While there may be a political equivalent of
love, to echo Unger, and while it is perhaps important for
liberals to pay much more attention to community than they
have tended to in the past and as a way of placing more
responsibility on to voluntary communities as opposed to
the state, there are still going to be grounds compatible
with radical liberalism for having a more than minimal
state, and one that is going to be involved in redistribution to meet need.

Bibliography

ACTON, H.B. (1971), 'The Morals of Markets', Longman, London.

ALTHUSSER, L. (1970), 'Reading Capital', New Left Books, London.

ANDERSON, P. and BLACKBURN, R. (1965), 'Towards Socialism', Fontana, Glasgow.

ANSCOMBE, G.E.M. (1957), 'Intention', Blackwell, Oxford.

ANSCOMBE, G.E.M. (1958), Modern Moral Philosophy, in 'Philosophy', vol. XXXIII.

ARROW, K. (1972), Gifts and Exchanges, in 'Philosophy and Public Affairs', vol. 1.

ARROW, K. (1963), Uncertainty and the Welfare Economics of Medical Care, in 'American Economic Review', vol. 53.

BACHRACH, P. (1967), 'The Theory of Democratic Elitism', Little, Brown, Boston.

BACHRACH, P. and BARATZ, M. (1970), 'Power and Poverty', Oxford University Press, New York.

BACON, R. and ELTIS, W. (1976), 'Britain's Economic Problem', Macmillan, London.

BARRY, B. (1965), 'Political Argument', Routledge & Kegan Paul, London.

BARRY, B. (1973), 'The Liberal Theory of Justice', Clarendon Press, Oxford.

BAY, C. (1968), Needs, Wants and Political Legitimacy, 'Canadian Journal of Political Science', vol. 1.

BELL, C. and NEWBY, H. (1972), 'Community Studies', Allen & Unwin, London.

BELL, D. (1960), 'The End of Ideology', The Free Press, Chicago, Ill.

BELL, D. (1974), 'The Coming of Post-Industrial Society', Heinemann, London.

BENN, S.I. and PETERS, R.S. (1959), 'Social Principles and the Democratic State', Allen & Unwin, London.

BERDYAEV, I. (1960), 'The Destiny of Man', Harper & Row,

New York.
BERGER, P. and LUCKMANN, T. (1971), 'The Social Construction of Reality', Penguin, Harmondsworth.
BERLIN, I. (1969), 'Four Essays on Liberty', Clarendon Press, Oxford.
BERNSTEIN, B. (1971), 'Class Codes and Control', vol. 1, Routledge & Kegan Paul, London.
BIRRELL, D. and MURIE, A. (1974), Ideology and Conflict in Social Policy, 'Journal of Social Policy', vol. 3.
BOULDING, K. (1967), The Boundaries of Social Policy, in 'Social Work', vol. 12.
BRADSHAW, J. (1972), The Concept of Social Need, 'New Society'.
BRAYBROOKE, D. (1968a), Let Needs Diminish that Preferences May Flourish, 'American Philosophical Quarterly Monographs', University of Pittsburgh Press.
BRAYBROOKE, D. (1968b), 'Three Tests For Democracy', Humanities Press, New York.
BRENNAN, P. and BROWN, R. (1970), Social Relations and Social Perspectives Among Shipyard Workers, 'Sociology', vol. 4.
BURKE, E. (1910), 'Reflections on the French Revolution', Dent, London.
CAMPBELL, T.D. (1974), Humanity before Justice, in 'British Journal of Political Science', vol. 4.
CANNON, I. (1967), Ideology and Occupational Community, 'Sociology', vol. 1.
CARRIER, J. and KENDAL, I. (1973), Social Policy and Social Change, in 'Journal of Social Policy', vol. 6.
CARRIER, J. and KENDAL, I. (1977), Social Administration as Social Science, in H. Heisler (ed.) (1977).
CLARK, D.B. (1973), The Concept of Community: A Reexamination, in 'Sociological Review', vol. 21.
COATES, K. and SILBURN, R. (1974), 'Poverty, The Forgotten Englishman', Penguin, Harmondsworth.
COHEN, S. (ed.) (1971), 'Images of Deviance', Penguin, Harmondsworth.
COLLETTI, L. (1973), 'Marxism and Hegel', New Left Books, London.
COMMUNITY DEVELOPMENT PROJECT INTERPROJECT EDITORIAL TEAM (1977a), The Limits of the Law, Community Development Project, London.
COMMUNITY DEVELOPMENT PROJECT (1977b), Gilding the Ghetto, Community Development Project, London.
CONNOLLY, W.E. (1974), 'The Terms of Political Discourse', D.C. Heath, Lexington.
COVAL, S. and MacINTOSH, J.J. (1969), 'The Business of Reason', Routledge & Kegan Paul, London.
COVENTRY COMMUNITY DEVELOPMENT PROJECT (1973), Coventry

Community Development Project Final Report, Coventry.
CRANSTON, M. (1973), 'What Are Human Rights?', Bodley
Head, London.
CRICK, B. (1972), Review of Rawls's 'A Theory of Justice',
in 'New Statesman', May.
CROSLAND, C.A.R. (1964), 'The Future of Socialism',
Jonathan Cape, London.
CROSLAND, C.A.R. (1974), 'Socialism Now', Jonathan Cape,
London.
CULYER, A. (1973), Quids without Quos – a Praxeological
Approach, in 'The Economics of Charity', Institute of
Economic Affairs, London.
CULYER, A. (1974a), 'Need and the National Health Service',
Martin Robertson, London.
CULYER, A. (1974b), 'Economic Policies and Social Goals',
Martin Robertson, London.
DANIELS, N. (1975), 'Reading Rawls', Blackwell, Oxford.
DAHRENDORF, R. (1968), 'Society and Democracy', Weiden-
feld & Nicolson, London.
DEARLOVE, J. (1973), 'The Politics of Policy in Local
Government', Cambridge University Press.
DEARLOVE, J. (1974), The Control of Change, in Mayo *et al.*
(1974).
DOBB, M. (1970), 'Welfare Economics and the Economics of
Socialism', Cambridge University Press.
DONNISON, D. (1961), The Teaching of Social Administra-
tion, in 'British Journal of Sociology', vol. 13.
DUDLEY, E. (1948), 'The Tree of Commonwealth', ed. D.M.
Brodie, Cambridge University Press.
DURKHEIM, E. (1933), 'The Division of Labour in Society',
trans. G. Simpson, The Free Press, Chicago, Ill.
DURKHEIM, E. (1957), 'Professional Ethics and Civic
Morals', trans. C. Brookfield, Routledge & Kegan Paul,
London.
DURKHEIM, E. (1959), 'Socialism', trans. C. Sattler,
Routledge & Kegan Paul, London.
EMMET, D. and MacINTYRE, A. (eds) (1970), 'Sociological
Theory and Philosophical Analysis, Macmillan, London.
EWING, A.C. (1962), 'Ethics', Collier-Macmillan, London.
EYSENCK, H. (1954), 'The Psychology of Politics',
Routledge & Kegan Paul, London.
FEINBERG, J. (1970), The Importance and Value of Human
Rights, in 'Journal of Value Enquiry', vol. 4.
FLATHMAN, R. (1976), 'The Practice of Rights', Cambridge
University Press.
FORDER, A. (1974), 'Concepts in Social Administration',
Routledge & Kegan Paul, London.
FRIEDMAN, M. (1962), 'Capitalism and Freedom', University
of Chicago Press.

FROMM, E. (1973), 'The Anatomy of Human Destructiveness', Basic Books, New york.

FULOP, C. (1967), 'Consumers in the Market', Research Monograph no. 13, Institute of Economic Affairs, London.

GALBRAITH, J. (1962), 'The Affluent Society', Penguin, Harmondsworth.

GALLIE, W.B. (1955-6), Essentially Contested Concepts, 'Proceedings of the Aristotelian Society.

GEORGE, V. and WILDING, P. (1972), Social Class, Social Values and Social Policy, 'Social and Economic Administration', vol. 6, no. 3.

GEORGE, V. and WILDING, P. (1976), 'Ideology and Social Welfare', Routledge & Kegan Paul, London.

GERTH, H. and MILLS, C. (1948), 'From Max Weber', Routledge & Kegan Paul, London.

GIDDENS, A. (1976), 'New Rules of Sociological Method', Hutchinson, London.

GOFFMAN, E. (1968), 'Stigma', Penguin, Harmondsworth.

GOLDMAN, A. (1976), The Entitlement Theory of Justice, 'Journal of Philosophy', vol. 73.

GOODE, W. (1957), Community within the Community, 'American Sociological Review'.

GOODIN, R.E. (1977), Possessive Individualism Again, in 'Political Studies', vol. 25.

GOUGH, I. (1975), State Expenditure in Advanced Capitalism, 'New Left Review', no. 92.

GOULDNER, A. (1972), 'The Coming Crisis of Western Sociology', Heinemann, London.

GREER, S. and MINAR, D. (eds) (1969), 'The Concept of Community', Aldine Press, Chicago.

GRICE, R. (1967), 'The Grounds of Moral Judgement', Cambridge University Press.

HABERMAS, J. (1975), 'Knowledge and Human Interests', Heinemann, London.

HALL, P., LAND, H., PARKER, R. and WEBB, A. (1975), 'Change, Choice and Conflict in Social Policy', Heinemann, London.

HALSEY, A.H. (1974), Government Against Poverty, in 'Poverty, Inequality and Class Structure', ed. D. Wedderburn, Cambridge University Press.

HAMILTON, I. (1965), Affluence and the Worker, in 'American Journal of Sociology'.

HAMPSHIRE, S. (1959), 'Thought and Action', Chatto & Windus, London.

HAMPSHIRE, S. (1972), Review of J. Rawls's 'A Theory of Justice', in 'New York Review of Books', 24 February.

HARE, R. (1963), 'Freedom and Reason', Clarendon Press, Oxford.

HARVEY, D. (1973), 'Social Justice andthe City', Edward

251 Bibliography

Arnold, London.
HAYEK, F. (1944), 'The Road to Serfdom', Routledge & Kegan
Paul, London.
HAYEK, F. (1949), 'Individualism and the Economic Order',
Routledge & Kegan Paul, London.
HAYEK, F. (1952), 'The Couter-Revolution of Science',
Allen & Unwin, London.
HAYEK, F. (1960), 'The Constitution of Liberty', Routledge
& Kegan Paul, London.
HAYEK, F. (1968), 'The Confusion of Language in Political
Thought', Occasional Paper no. 20, Institute of Economic
Affairs, London.
HAYEK, F. (1973), 'Law, Legislation and Liberty. vol. I:
Rules and Order', Routledge & Kegan Paul, London.
HAYEK, F. (1976), 'Law, Legislation and Liberty. vol. II:
The Mirage of Social Justice', Routledge & Kegan Paul,
London.
HEGEL, G.W.F. (1910), 'Phenomenology of Mind', trans.
J. Baillie, Allen & Unwin, London.
HEGEL, G.W.F. (1952), 'Philosophy of Right', trans. T.M.
Knox, Clarendon Press, Oxford.
HEISLER, H. (ed.) (1977), 'Foundations of Social Admini-
stration', Macmillan, London.
HILL, M.J. and ISSACHAROFF, R. (1971), 'Community Action
and Race Relations', Oxford University Press, London.
HILLERY, G.A. (1955), Definitions of Community: Areas of
Agreement, in 'Rural Sociology', vol. 20.
HILLERY, G.A. (1968), 'Communal Organisations', Chicago
University Press.
HOBBES, T. (1955), 'Leviathan', ed. M. Oakeshott, Black-
well, Oxford.
HOBSBAWM, E. (1975), The Idea of Fraternity, 'New Society',
November.
HOOKER, R. (1836), 'Of the Laws of Ecclesiastical Polity',
ed. J. Keble, Rivington, London
HUME, D. (1902), 'Enquiry Concerning Principles and
Morals', ed. L.A. Selby Bigge, Clarendon Press, Oxford.
HUTCHINSON, T. (1970), 'Half a Century of Hobarts',
Institute of Economic Affairs, London.
JARVIE, I.C. (1972), 'Concepts and Society', Routledge &
Kegan Paul, London.
JORDAN, W. (1973), 'Paupers', Routledge & Kegan Paul,
London.
JOSEPH, K. (1975), 'Freedom and Order', Conservative
Political Centre, London.
KAMENKA, E. (1967), Marxism and the Crisis in Social
Ethics, in 'Socialist Humanism', ed. E. Fromm, Allen
Lane, London.
KANT, I. (1974), 'Groundwork to the Metaphysics of Morals',

trans. H.J. Paton, Hutchinson, London.

KERR, C. (ed.) (1918), 'Marx's Contribution to the Critique of Political Economy', Chicago Press.

KINCAID, J. (1973), 'Poverty and Equality in Britain', Penguin, Harmondsworth.

KNIGHT, F. (1933), 'Risk Uncertainty and Profit', Houghton Mifflin, Boston.

KROPOTKIN, P. (1926), 'The Conquest of Bread', New York.

KROPOTKIN, P. (1970), Law and Authority, in 'Kropotkin's Revolutionary Pamphlets', ed. R.G. Baldwin, Harper & Row, New York.

LASLETT, P. (1965), 'The World We Have Lost', Methuen, London.

LASLETT, P. and RUNCIMAN, W.G. (1962), 'Philosophy Politics and Society', Series 11, Blackwell, Oxford.

LUCAS, J.R. (1966), 'The Principles of Politics', Clarendon Press, Oxford.

LUKES, S. (1973), 'Individualism', Blackwell, Oxford.

LUKES, S. (1974), 'E. Durkheim: His Life and Work', Allen Lane, London.

LUKES, S. (1975), 'Power: a Radical View', Macmillan, London.

LUKES, S. (1977) 'Essays in Social Theory', Macmillan, London.

LYONS, D. (1969), The Odd Debt of Gratitude, in 'Analysis', vol. 29.

MABBOT, J.D. (1967), Punishment, in 'Justice and Social Policy', ed. F. Olafson, Prentice-Hall, Englewood Cliffs, N.J.

MACINTYRE, A. (1964), Against Utilitarianism, in 'Aims in Education', ed. T. B. Hollins, Manchester University Press.

MACINTYRE, A. (1966), 'A Short History of Ethics', Routledge & Kegan Paul, London.

MACINTYRE, A. (1967), 'Secularisation and Moral Change', Oxford University Press.

MACINTYRE, A. (1971), 'Against the Self Images of the Age', Duckworth, London.

MACINTYRE, A. (1973), On the Essential Contestability of Some Social Concepts, in 'Ethics'.

MACKENZIE, J.M. (1967), 'Politics and Social Science', Penguin, Harmondsworth.

MCKENZIE, R. and SILVER, A. (1968), 'Angels in Marble', Macmillan, London.

MACPHERSON, C.B. (1962), 'The Political Theory of Possessive Individualism', Clarendon Press, Oxford.

MACPHERSON, C.B. (1973), 'Democratic Theory: Essays in Retrieval', Clarendon Press, Oxford.

MARCUSE, H. (1964), 'One Dimensional Man', Routledge & Kegan Paul, London.

MARX, K. (1942), 'The German Ideology', Lawrence & Wishart, London.
MARX, K. (1959a), 'Capital', Lawrence & Wishart, London.
MARX, K. (1959b), 'Economic and Philosophical Manuscripts', Foreign Languages Publishing House, Moscow.
MARX, K. (1963), 'Karl Marx Early Writings', ed. T.B. Bottomore, Penguin, Harmondsworth.
MARX, K. (1973), 'Grundrisse', ed. McLelland, Macmillan, London.
MARX, K. (1975), 'On the Jewish Question', in 'Early Writings', trans. R. Livingstone and G. Benton, Penguin, Harmondsworth.
MARX, K. and ENGELS, F. (1974), 'Selected Works', vol. I, Foreign Languages Publishing House, Moscow.
MASLOW, A. (1968), 'Towards a Psychology of Being', Van Nostrand, New York.
MASLOW, A. (1971), 'The Farther Reaches of Human Nature', Viking Press, New York.
MAYO, M. et al. (1974), 'Community Work One', Routledge & Kegan Paul, London.
MILLIBAND, R. (1969), 'The State in Capitalist Society', Weidenfeld and Nicolson, London.
MILL, J.S. (1962), 'Utilitarianism', ed. M. Warnock, Fontana, London.
MILLER, D. (1976), 'Social Justice', Clarendon Press, Oxford.
MILLER, W.B.(1958), Lower Class Structure as Generating Milieu of Gang Delinquency, 'Journal of Social Issues.
MINOGUE, K. (1973), 'The Liberal Mind', Methuen, London.
MITCHELL, B. (1971), Law and the Protection of Institutions, in 'The Proper Study of Mankind', Royal Institute of Philosophy Lectures, vol. IV, Macmillan, London.
MORRIS, H. (1968), Persons and Punishment, 'The Monist'.
MORRIS, R. and REIN, M. (1962), Goals, Structures and Strategies for Community Change, in 'Social Work Practice', Columbia University Press, New York.
MOUNCE, H. and PHILIPS, D.Z. (1965), On Morality's Having a Point, 'Philosophy'.
MYRDAL, G. (1960), 'Beyond the Welfare State', Duckworth, London.
NARVESON, J. (1967), 'Morality and Utility', Johns Hopkins University Press, Baltimore.
NISBET, R.A. (1967), 'The Sociological Tradition', Heinemann, London.
NISBET, R.A. (1970a), Moral Values and Community, in 'Tradition and Revolt', Oxford University Press, New York.
NISBET, R.A. (1970b), 'The Quest for Community', Oxford University Press, New York.
NORMAN, R. (1971), 'Reasons for Action', Blackwell, Oxford.

NOZICK, R. (1974), 'Anarchy, State and Utopia', Blackwell, Oxford.
OPPENHEIM, F. (1973), Facts and Values in Politics, 'Political Theory, vol. 1.
PAHL, R. (1970), 'Patterns of Urban Life', Routledge & Kegan Paul, London.
PAHL, R. and WINKLER, J. (1974), The Coming Corporatism, 'New Society'.
PARKER, J. (1975), 'Social Policy and Citizenship', Macmillan, London.
PARKIN, F. (1972), 'Class, Inequality and Political Order', Paladin, London.
PARSONS, T. (1949), 'The Structure of Social Action', Free Press, Chicago.
PETERS, R.S. (1958), 'The Concept of Motivation', Routledge & Kegan Paul, London.
PETERS, R.S. and BENN, S.I. (1959), 'Social Principles and the Democratic State', Allen & Unwin, London.
PINKER, R. (1971), 'Social Theory and Social Policy', Heinemann, London.
PIVEN, F. and CLOWARD, R. (1971), 'Regulating the Poor', Pantheon, New York.
POLANYI, M. (1957), 'The Great Transformation', Beacon Press, Boston.
POLANYI, M. (1951), 'The Logic of Liberty', Routledge & Kegan Paul, London.
POPPER, K.R. (1957), 'The Poverty of Historicism', Routledge & Kegan Paul, London.
POPPER, K.R. (1962), 'The Open Society and Its Enemies', Routledge & Kegan Paul, London.
POWELL, J.E. (1966), 'Politics and Medicine', Pitman, London.
RAPHAEL, D.D. (ed.) (1967), 'Political Theory and the Rights of Man', Macmillan, London.
RAWLS, J. (1972), 'A Theory of Justice', Clarendon Press, Oxford.
RICARDO, D. (1971), 'On the Principles of Political Economy and Taxation', Penguin, Harmondsworth.
ROSE, H. (1973), Who can De-label the Claimant, in 'Social Work Today', vol. 2.
ROSZACK, T. (1971), 'The Making of a Counter Culture', Faber, London.
ROWNTREE, S. (1902), 'Poverty: A Study of Town Life', Macmillan, London.
RULE, J.B. (1971), The Problem with Social Problems, in 'Politics and Society', vol. II, no. 1.
SCHATTSCHNEIDER, E.E. (1960), 'The Semi-Sovereign People', Holt, Rinehart & Winston, New York.
SCHERER, J. (1972), 'Contemporary Community - Illusion or

SCHUMPETER, J. (1934), 'The Theory of Economic Develop-
ment', Harvard University Press, Cambridge, Mass.
SCHUMPETER, J. (1943), 'Capitalism, Socialism and Demo-
cracy', Allen & Unwin, London.
SEARLE, J. (1962), Meaning and Speech Acts, in 'Philo-
sophical Review', vol. 51.
SEEBOHM, F. (1968), 'Report of the Committee on Local
Authority and Allied Personal Services', Cmnd 3703, HMSO,
London.
SELDON, A. (1961), 'Agenda for a Free Society', Hutchinson,
London.
SELDON, A. (1968), 'Choice in Housing', Institute of
Economic Affairs, London.
SENNETT, R. (1976), 'The Fall of Public Man', Cambridge
University Press.
SHONFIELD, A. (ed.) (1971), 'Social Indicators and Public
Policy', SSRC/Tavistock, London.
SIDGWICK, H. (1907), 'The Method of Ethics', Methuen,
London.
SKINNER, Q. (1973), The Empirical Theorists of Democracy
and Their Critics, in 'Political Theory', vol. 3.
SMART, J.C.C. and WILLIAMS, B. (1973), 'Utilitarianism For
and Against', Cambridge University Press.
SMITH, A. (1904), 'The Wealth of Nations', Methuen,
London.
SMITH, D. (1977), 'Human Geography a Welfare Approach',
Edward Arnold, London.
SRAFFA, P. (1971), 'The Production of Commodities by Means
of Commodities', Cambridge University Press.
STACEY, M. (1969), The Myth of Community Studies, in
'British Journal of Sociology', vol. 20.
STEDMAN JONES, G. (1967), The Pathology of English History,
in 'New Left Review', vol. 46.
STEINER, H. (1975), Critical notice of R. Nozick's
'Anarchy, State and Utopia', in 'Mind', vol. 84.
STRAWSON, P.F. (1974), 'Freedom and Resentment', Methuen,
London.
TAWNEY, R.H. (1961), 'The Acquisitive Society', Fontana,
London.
TAYLOR, C.C.W. (1969), Understanding a Want, in 'The
Business of Reason', ed. J.J. MacIntosh and B. Coval,
Routledge & Kegan Paul, London.
TAYLOR, C.C.W. (1976), 'Anarchy and Cooperation', Wiley,
London.
TAYLOR-GOOBY, P. (1977), Welfare Benefits Advocacy in
Batley, 'York University Papers in Community Studies',
no. 11.
TELFER, E. (1976), Justice, Welfare and Health Care, in
'Journal of Medical Ethics', vol. 2, no. 3.

THANE, P. (1974), 'The History of Social Welfare', in 'New Society'.

THOENES, P. (1966), 'The Elite and the Welfare State', Faber, London.

THOMPSON, D. (1958), The Welfare State, in 'The New Reasoner', vol. 1, no. 4.

THOMPSON, F. (1945), 'Lark Rise to Candleford', Oxford University Press, London.

TIMMS, N. and MEYER, R. (1970), 'The Client Speaks', Routledge & Kegan Paul, London.

TITMUSS, R. (1958), 'Essays on the Welfare State', Allen & Unwin, London.

TITMUSS, R. (1968), 'Commitment to Welfare', Allen & Unwin, London.

TITMUSS, R. (1970), 'The Gift Relationship', Penguin, Harmondsworth.

TITMUSS, R. (1974), 'Social Policy', Allen & Unwin, London.

TOWNSEND, P. (1970), 'The Concept of Poverty', Heinemann, London.

WALTON, A. (1969), Need: A Central Concept, in 'Social Service Review', vol. 10.

WATKINS, J.W.N. (1959a), Two Theses of Methodological Individualism, in 'British Journal of the Philosophy of Science'.

WATKINS, J.W.N. (1959b), Historical Explanation in the Social Sciences, in 'Theories of History', ed. P. Gardiner, The Free Press, Chicago.

WATSON, D. (1977), Welfare Rights and Human Rights, in 'Journal of Social Policy'.

WESTERGAARD, J. (1965), The Withering Away of Class, in 'Towards Socialism', ed. P. Anderson and R. Blackburn, Fontana, Glasgow.

WILENSKY, H. and LEBEAUX, C. (1965), 'Industrial Society and Social Change', The Free Press, New York.

WILLIAMS, A. (1974), Need as a Demand Concept, in 'Economic Policies and Social Goals', ed. A. Culyer, Martin Robertson, London.

WILLIAMS, B. (1962), The Idea of Equality, in Laslett and Runciman (1962).

WILLIAMS, R. (1976), 'Keywords', Fontana, Glasgow.

WINCH, P. (1958), 'The Idea of a Social Science', Routledge & Kegan Paul, London.

WOLFF, R.P. (1968), 'The Poverty of Liberalism', Beacon Press, Boston.

WOLFF, R.P. (1970), 'In Defence of Anarchism', Harper & Row, New York.

WOLFF, R.P. (1973), 'The Autonomy of Reason', Harper Torchbooks, New York.

WOLIN, S. (1960), 'Politics and Vision', Allen & Unwin, London.

WOLLHEIM, R. (1976), Need, Desire and Moral Turpitude,
'Royal Institute of Philosophy Lectures 1975',
Macmillan, London.
WOOTTON, B. (1959), 'Social Science and Social Pathology',
Allen & Unwin, London.
WORLD HEALTH ORGANIZATION (1962), 'Deprivation of Maternal
Care: A Reassessment', W.H.O., New York.
YOUNGHUSBAND, E. (ed.) (1968), 'Community Work and Social
Change', Longman, London.

Name index

Althusser, L., 3, 128
Anscombe, G.E.M., 26, 27, 34
Arrow, K., 223, 237–8
Atkinson, 139

Bachrach, P., 108–13
Bacon, R., 2
Baratz, M., 108–13
Barry, B., 28, 95, 126, 127, 130, 196
Bay, C., 55
Bell, C., 206
Bell, D., 2, 101–2, 147
Benn, S.I., 29
Bentham, J., 226
Berdyaev, I., 42, 158, 163, 166
Berger, P., 17, 133, 194
Berlin, I., 12–13
Bernstein, B., 184
Boulding, K., 24
Bowlby, 136
Bradshaw, J., 20, 31
Braybrooke, D., 30
Brentano, 35
Burke, E., 222

Campbell, T.D., 63–6
Carrier, J., 4, 123, 173
Castells, 3
Clark, D.B., 211–12, 215
Cloward, R., 134
Coates, K., 103, 107

Coletti, L., 215
Connolly, W.E., 69, 209
Cranston, M., 55, 73–82
Crick, B., 124, 133
Crosland, C.A.R., 4, 6, 16, 63, 124, 141

Dahrendorf, R., 227
Daniels, N., 5, 124–5, 130
Dearlove, J., 106, 134
Dobb, M., 157
Donnison, D., 1, 3
Downie, 183
Durkheim, E., 142, 183
Dworkin, R., 97

Eltis, 2
Ewing, A.C., 178
Eysenck, H., 191–4

Feinberg, J., 94
Flathman, R., 56
Foot, M., 34
Forder, A., 20, 103
Freud, S., 31, 154–5
Friedman, M., 16, 175–6
Fromm, E., 159–61

Galbraith, J.K., 197
Gallie, W.B., 6, 11, 13, 14, 15, 18, 208–10
George, V., 4, 21, 123, 139, 140–1, 200
Giddens, A., 144–5

258

Subject index

alienation, 163-5
altruism, 56-8, 229, 235-43
anarchism, 40
autonomy, 46-51

benevolence, 53-6
British Hegelians, 218

capitalism, 140-1, 162-8,
   216-20
class consciousness, 120
coercion, 169-72
community, 32, 56-8, 104,
   203-22, 223-46
Community Development Project, 134, 219
consensus, 104-7, 205,
   220-1
conservatism, 225
corporatism, 148-50
cost-benefit analysis,
   39-40

democracy, 102, 137-9, 205
desert, 65-6

education, 51
entitlement, 240
essentially contested concepts, 6-10, 46, 208-15
explanation, 183-6

Fabianism, 4, 16, 141
false consciousness, 31,

   113-21, 132, 152-72
feudalism, 216
freedom, 175-81, 195-6
functionalism, 140-1, 143-4

Gemeinschaft, 220-1

hegemony, 113-15

individualism, 83, 86
interests, 98-100, 129, 155
intuitionism, 125

justice, 54-6, 58-60

labour, 83-6, 240-1
law, 47-50, 245
legitimacy, 54-5, 73-4,
   203-22
liberalism, 223-7, 229-10,
   246
liberty, 12-13, 61-2

market, 14, 22, 61-2, 173-
   201, 223-46
Marxism, 16, 135-7, 215-20,
   225
materialism, 199
mental health, 50
methodological individualism,
   186-91
moral pluralism, 102-3

naturalistic fallacy, 182

Routledge Social Science Series

Routledge & Kegan Paul   London, Henley and Boston

39 Store Street,
London WC1E 7DD
Broadway House,
Newtown Road,
Henley-on-Thames,
Oxon RG9 1EN
9 Park Street,
Boston, Mass. 02108

Contents

*Authors wishing to submit manuscripts for any series
in this catalogue should send them to the Social Science Editor,
Routledge & Kegan Paul Ltd, 39 Store Street,
London WC1E 7DD.*
● *Books so marked are available in paperback.*
○ *Books so marked are available in paperback only.*
*All books are in metric Demy 8vo format (216 × 138mm approx.)
unless otherwise stated.*

International Library of Sociology
General Editor   John Rex

GENERAL SOCIOLOGY

Barnsley, J. H. The Social Reality of Ethics. *464 pp.*
Brown, Robert. Explanation in Social Science. *208 pp.*
● Rules and Laws in Sociology. *192 pp.*
Bruford, W. H. Chekhov and His Russia. *A Sociological Study. 244 pp.*
Burton, F. and **Carlen, P.** Official Discourse. *On Discourse Analysis, Government Publications, Ideology. About 140 pp.*
Cain, Maureen E. Society and the Policeman's Role. *326 pp.*
● **Fletcher, Colin.** Beneath the Surface. *An Account of Three Styles of Sociological Research. 221 pp.*
Gibson, Quentin. The Logic of Social Enquiry. *240 pp.*
Glassner, B. Essential Interactionism. *208 pp.*
Glucksmann, M. Structuralist Analysis in Contemporary Social Thought. *212 pp.*
Gurvitch, Georges. Sociology of Law. *Foreword by Roscoe Pound. 264 pp.*
Hinkle, R. Founding Theory of American Sociology 1881–1913. *About 350 pp.*
Homans, George C. Sentiments and Activities. *336 pp.*
Johnson, Harry M. Sociology: *A Systematic Introduction. Foreword by Robert K. Merton. 710 pp.*
● **Keat, Russell** and **Urry, John.** Social Theory as Science. *278 pp.*
Mannheim, Karl. Essays on Sociology and Social Psychology. *Edited by Paul Keckskemeti. With Editorial Note by Adolph Lowe. 344 pp.*
Martindale, Don. The Nature and Types of Sociological Theory. *292 pp.*
● **Maus, Heinz.** A Short History of Sociology. *234 pp.*
Myrdal, Gunnar. Value in Social Theory: *A Collection of Essays on Methodology. Edited by Paul Streeten. 332 pp.*
Ogburn, William F. and **Nimkoff, Meyer F.** A Handbook of Sociology. *Preface by Karl Mannheim. 656 pp. 46 figures. 35 tables.*
Parsons, Talcott and **Smelser, Neil J.** Economy and Society: *A Study in the Integration of Economic and Social Theory. 362 pp.*
Payne, G., Dingwall, R., Payne, J. and **Carter, M.** Sociology and Social Research. *About 250 pp.*
Podgórecki, A. Practical Social Sciences. *About 200 pp.*
Podgórecki, A. and **Łos, M.** Multidimensional Sociology. *268 pp.*
Raffel, S. Matters of Fact. *A Sociological Inquiry. 152 pp.*
● **Rex, John.** Key Problems of Sociological Theory. *220 pp.*
Sociology and the Demystification of the Modern World. *282 pp.*
● **Rex, John.** (Ed.) Approaches to Sociology. *Contributions by Peter Abell, Frank Bechhofer, Basil Bernstein, Ronald Fletcher, David Frisby, Miriam Glucksmann, Peter Lassman, Herminio Martins, John Rex, Roland Robertson, John Westergaard and Jock Young. 302 pp.*
Rigby, A. Alternative Realities. *352 pp.*
Roche, M. Phenomenology, Language and the Social Sciences. *374 pp.*
Sahay, A. Sociological Analysis. *220 pp.*
Strasser, Hermann. The Normative Structure of Sociology. *Conservative and Emancipatory Themes in Social Thought. About 340 pp.*
Strong, P. Ceremonial Order of the Clinic. *267 pp.*
Urry, John. Reference Groups and the Theory of Revolution. *244 pp.*
Weinberg, E. Development of Sociology in the Soviet Union. *173 pp.*

FOREIGN CLASSICS OF SOCIOLOGY

● **Gerth, H. H.** and **Mills, C. Wright.** From Max Weber: *Essays in Sociology. 502 pp.*

● **Tönnies, Ferdinand.** Community and Association *(Gemeinschaft und Gesell-schaft).\Translated and Supplemented by Charles P. Loomis. Foreword by Pitirim A. Sorokin. 334 pp.*

SOCIAL STRUCTURE

Andreski, Stanislav. Military Organization and Society. *Foreword by Professor A. R. Radcliffe-Brown. 226 pp. 1 folder.*

Broom, L., Lancaster Jones, F., McDonnell, P. and **Williams, T.** The Inheritance of Inequality. *About 180 pp.*

Carlton, Eric. Ideology and Social Order. *Foreword by Professor Philip Abrahams. About 320 pp.*

Clegg, S. and **Dunkerley, D.** Organization, Class and Control. *614 pp.*

Coontz, Sydney H. Population Theories and the Economic Interpretation. *202 pp.*

Coser, Lewis. The Functions of Social Conflict. *204 pp.*

Crook, I. and **D.** The First Years of the Yangyi Commune. *304 pp., illustrated.*

Dickie-Clark, H. F. Marginal Situation: *A Sociological Study of a Coloured Group. 240 pp. 11 tables.*

Giner, S. and **Archer, M. S.** (Eds) Contemporary Europe: *Social Structures and Cultural Patterns, 336 pp.*

● **Glaser, Barney** and **Strauss, Anselm L.** Status Passage: *A Formal Theory. 212 pp.*

Glass, D. V. (Ed.) Social Mobility in Britain. *Contributions by J. Berent, T. Bottomore, R. C. Chambers, J. Floud, D. V. Glass, J. R. Hall, H. T. Himmelweit, R. K. Kelsall, F. M. Martin, C. A. Moser, R. Mukherjee and W. Ziegel. 420 pp.*

Kelsall, R. K. Higher Civil Servants in Britain: *From 1870 to the Present Day. 268 pp. 31 tables.*

● **Lawton, Denis.** Social Class, Language and Education. *192 pp.*

McLeish, John. The Theory of Social Change: *Four Views Considered. 128 pp.*

● **Marsh, David C.** The Changing Social Structure of England and Wales, 1871–1961. *Revised edition. 288 pp.*

Menzies, Ken. Talcott Parsons and the Social Image of Man. *About 208 pp.*

● **Mouzelis, Nicos.** Organization and Bureaucracy. *An Analysis of Modern Theories. 240 pp.*

● **Ossowski, Stanislaw.** Class Structure in the Social Consciousness. *210 pp.*

● **Podgórecki, Adam.** Law and Society. *302 pp.*

Renner, Karl. Institutions of Private Law and Their Social Functions. *Edited, with an Introduction and Notes, by O. Kahn-Freud. Translated by Agnes Schwarzschild. 316 pp.*

Rex, J. and **Tomlinson, S.** Colonial Immigrants in a British City. *A Class Analysis. 368 pp.*

Smooha, S. Israel: Pluralism and Conflict. *472 pp.*

Wesolowski, W. Class, Strata and Power. *Trans. and with Introduction by G. Kolankiewicz. 160 pp.*

Zureik, E. Palestinians in Israel. *A Study in Internal Colonialism. 264 pp.*

SOCIOLOGY AND POLITICS

Acton, T. A. Gypsy Politics and Social Change. *316 pp.*

Burton, F. Politics of Legitimacy. *Struggles in a Belfast Community. 250 pp.*

Crook, I. and **D.** Revolution in a Chinese Village. *Ten Mile Inn. 216 pp., illustrated.*

Etzioni-Halevy, E. Political Manipulation and Administrative Power. *A Comparative Study. About 200 pp.*

Fielding, N. The National Front. *About 250 pp.*

● **Hechter, Michael.** Internal Colonialism. *The Celtic Fringe in British National Development, 1536–1966. 380 pp.*

Kornhauser, William. The Politics of Mass Society. *272 pp. 20 tables.*

4

Korpi, W. The Working Class in Welfare Capitalism. *Work, Unions and Politics in Sweden. 472 pp.*

Kroes, R. Soldiers and Students. *A Study of Right- and Left-wing Students. 174 pp.*

Martin, Roderick. Sociology of Power. *About 272 pp.*

Merquior, J. G. Rousseau and Weber. *A Study in the Theory of Legitimacy. About 288 pp.*

Myrdal, Gunnar. The Political Element in the Development of Economic Theory. *Translated from the German by Paul Streeten. 282 pp.*

Varma, B. N. The Sociology and Politics of Development. *A Theoretical Study. 236 pp.*

Wong, S.-L. Sociology and Socialism in Contemporary China. *160 pp.*

Wootton, Graham. Workers, Unions and the State. *188 pp.*

CRIMINOLOGY

Ancel, Marc. Social Defence: *A Modern Approach to Criminal Problems. Foreword by Leon Radzinowicz. 240 pp.*

Athens, L. Violent Criminal Acts and Actors. *104 pp.*

Cain, Maureen E. Society and the Policeman's Role. *326 pp.*

Cloward, Richard A. and **Ohlin, Lloyd E.** Delinquency and Opportunity: *A Theory of Delinquent Gangs. 248 pp.*

Downes, David M. The Delinquent Solution. *A Study in Subcultural Theory. 296 pp.*

Friedlander, Kate. The Psycho-Analytical Approach to Juvenile Delinquency: *Theory, Case Studies, Treatment. 320 pp.*

Gleuck, Sheldon and **Eleanor.** Family Environment and Delinquency. *With the statistical assistance of Rose W. Kneznek. 340 pp.*

Lopez-Rey, Manuel. Crime. *An Analytical Appraisal. 288 pp.*

Mannheim, Hermann. Comparative Criminology: *A Text Book. Two volumes. 442 pp. and 380 pp.*

Morris, Terence. The Criminal Area: *A Study in Social Ecology. Foreword by Hermann Mannheim. 232 pp. 25 tables. 4 maps.*

Rock, Paul. Making People Pay. *338 pp.*

● **Taylor, Ian, Walton, Paul** and **Young, Jock.** The New Criminology. *For a Social Theory of Deviance. 325 pp.*

● **Taylor, Ian, Walton, Paul** and **Young, Jock.** (Eds) Critical Criminology. *268 pp.*

SOCIAL PSYCHOLOGY

Bagley, Christopher. The Social Psychology of the Epileptic Child. *320 pp.*

Brittan, Arthur. Meanings and Situations. *224 pp.*

Carroll, J. Break-Out from the Crystal Palace. *200 pp.*

● **Fleming, C. M.** Adolescence: Its Social Psychology. *With an Introduction to recent findings from the fields of Anthropology, Physiology, Medicine, Psychometrics and Sociometry. 288 pp.*

● The Social Psychology of Education: *An Introduction and Guide to Its Study. 136 pp.*

Linton, Ralph. The Cultural Background of Personality. *132 pp.*

● **Mayo, Elton.** The Social Problems of an Industrial Civilization. *With an Appendix on the Political Problem. 180 pp.*

Ottaway, A. K. C. Learning Through Group Experience. *176 pp.*

Plummer, Ken. Sexual Stigma. *An Interactionist Account. 254 pp.*

● **Rose, Arnold M.** (Ed.) Human Behaviour and Social Processes: *an Interactionist Approach. Contributions by Arnold M. Rose, Ralph H. Turner, Anselm Strauss, Everett C. Hughes, E. Franklin Frazier, Howard S. Becker et al. 696 pp.*

Smelser, Neil J. Theory of Collective Behaviour. *448 pp.*

Stephenson, Geoffrey M. The Development of Conscience. *128 pp.*

Young, Kimball. Handbook of Social Psychology. *658 pp. 16 figures. 10 tables.*

SOCIOLOGY OF THE FAMILY

Bell, Colin R. Middle Class Families: *Social and Geographical Mobility. 224 pp.*
Burton, Lindy. Vulnerable Children. *272 pp.*
Gavron, Hannah. The Captive Wife: *Conflicts of Household Mothers. 190 pp.*
George, Victor and **Wilding, Paul.** Motherless Families. *248 pp.*
Klein, Josephine. Samples from English Cultures.
    1. Three Preliminary Studies and Aspects of Adult Life in England. *447 pp.*
    2. Child-Rearing Practices and Index. *247 pp.*
Klein, Viola. The Feminine Character. *History of an Ideology. 244 pp.*
McWhinnie, Alexina M. Adopted Children. *How They Grow Up. 304 pp.*
● **Morgan, D. H. J.** Social Theory and the Family. *About 320 pp.*
● **Myrdal, Alva** and **Klein, Viola.** Women's Two Roles: *Home and Work. 238 pp.*
    27 tables.
Parsons, Talcott and **Bales, Robert F.** Family: Socialization and Interaction Process.
    In collaboration with James Olds, Morris Zelditch and Philip E. Slater. 456 pp.
    50 figures and tables.

SOCIAL SERVICES

Bastide, Roger. The Sociology of Mental Disorder. *Translated from the French by*
    Jean McNeil. 260 pp.
Carlebach, Julius. Caring For Children in Trouble. *266 pp.*
George, Victor. Foster Care. *Theory and Practice. 234 pp.*
    Social Security: *Beveridge and After. 258 pp.*
George, V. and **Wilding, P.** Motherless Families. *248 pp.*
● **Goetschius, George W.** Working with Community Groups. *256 pp.*
Goetschius, George W. and **Tash, Joan.** Working with Unattached Youth. *416 pp.*
Heywood, Jean S. Children in Care. *The Development of the Service for the Deprived*
    Child. Third revised edition. 284 pp.
King, Roy D., Ranes, Norma V. and **Tizard, Jack.** Patterns of Residential Care.
    356 pp.
Leigh, John. Young People and Leisure. *256 pp.*
● **Mays, John.** (Ed.) Penelope Hall's Social Services of England and Wales.
    368 pp.
Morris, Mary. Voluntary Work and the Welfare State. *300 pp.*
Nokes, P. L. The Professional Task in Welfare Practice. *152 pp.*
Timms, Noel. Psychiatric Social Work in Great Britain (1939–1962). *280 pp.*
●   Social Casework: *Principles and Practice. 256 pp.*

SOCIOLOGY OF EDUCATION

Banks, Olive. Parity and Prestige in English Secondary Education: a Study in
    Educational Sociology. *272 pp.*
● **Blyth, W. A. L.** English Primary Education. *A Sociological Description.*
    2. Background. *168 pp.*
Collier, K. G. The Social Purposes of Education: *Personal and Social Values in*
    Education. 268 pp.
Evans, K. M. Sociometry and Education. *158 pp.*
● **Ford, Julienne.** Social Class and the Comprehensive School. *192 pp.*
Foster, P. J. Education and Social Change in Ghana. *336 pp. 3 maps.*
Fraser, W. R. Education and Society in Modern France. *150 pp.*
Grace, Gerald R. Role Conflict and the Teacher. *150 pp.*
Hans, Nicholas. New Trends in Education in the Eighteenth Century. *278 pp.*
    19 tables.
●   Comparative Education: *A Study of Educational Factors and Traditions. 360 pp.*
● **Hargreaves, David.** Interpersonal Relations and Education. *432 pp.*
●   Social Relations in a Secondary School. *240 pp.*
    School Organization and Pupil Involvement. *A Study of Secondary Schools.*

6

- **Mannheim, Karl** and **Stewart, W. A. C.** An Introduction to the Sociology of Education. *206 pp.*
- **Musgrove, F.** Youth and the Social Order. *176 pp.*
- **Ottaway, A. K. C.** Education and Society: An Introduction to the Sociology of Education. *With an Introduction by W. O. Lester Smith. 212 pp.*
  Peers, Robert. Adult Education: *A Comparative Study. Revised edition. 398 pp.*
  Stratta, Erica. The Education of Borstal Boys. *A Study of their Educational Experiences prior to, and during, Borstal Training. 256 pp.*
- **Taylor, P. H., Reid, W. A.** and **Holley, B. J.** The English Sixth Form. *A Case Study in Curriculum Research. 198 pp.*

SOCIOLOGY OF CULTURE

Eppel, E. M. and **M.** Adolescents and Morality: *A Study of some Moral Values and Dilemmas of Working Adolescents in the Context of a changing Climate of Opinion. Foreword by W. J. H. Sprott. 268 pp. 39 tables.*
- **Fromm, Erich.** The Fear of Freedom. *286 pp.*
- The Sane Society. *400 pp.*
  Johnson, L. The Cultural Critics. *From Matthew Arnold to Raymond Williams. 233 pp.*
  Mannheim, Karl. Essays on the Sociology of Culture. *Edited by Ernst Mannheim in co-operation with Paul Kecskemeti. Editorial Note by Adolph Lowe. 280 pp.*
  Merquior, J. G. The Veil and the Mask. *Essays on Culture and Ideology. Foreword by Ernest Gellner. 140 pp.*
  Zijderfeld, A. C. On Clichés. *The Supersedure of Meaning by Function in Modernity. 150 pp.*

SOCIOLOGY OF RELIGION

Argyle, Michael and **Beit-Hallahmi, Benjamin.** The Social Psychology of Religion. *256 pp.*
Glasner, Peter E. The Sociology of Secularisation. *A Critique of a Concept. 146 pp.*
Hall, J. R. The Ways Out. *Utopian Communal Groups in an Age of Babylon. 280 pp.*
Ranson, S., Hinings, B. and **Bryman, A.** Clergy, Ministers and Priests. *216 pp.*
Stark, Werner. The Sociology of Religion. *A Study of Christendom.*
  Volume II. *Sectarian Religion. 368 pp.*
  Volume III. *The Universal Church. 464 pp.*
  Volume IV. *Types of Religious Man. 352 pp.*
  Volume V. *Types of Religious Culture. 464 pp.*
Turner, B. S. Weber and Islam. *216 pp.*
Watt, W. Montgomery. Islam and the Integration of Society. *320 pp.*

SOCIOLOGY OF ART AND LITERATURE

Jarvie, Ian C. Towards a Sociology of the Cinema. *A Comparative Essay on the Structure and Functioning of a Major Entertainment Industry. 405 pp.*
Rust, Frances S. Dance in Society. *An Analysis of the Relationships between the Social Dance and Society in England from the Middle Ages to the Present Day. 256 pp. 8 pp. of plates.*
Schücking, L. L. The Sociology of Literary Taste. *112 pp.*
Wolff, Janet. Hermeneutic Philosophy and the Sociology of Art. *150 pp.*

SOCIOLOGY OF KNOWLEDGE

Diesing, P. Patterns of Discovery in the Social Sciences. *262 pp.*

● **Douglas, J. D.** (Ed.) Understanding Everyday Life. *370 pp.*
● **Hamilton, P.** Knowledge and Social Structure. *174 pp.*
 Jarvie, I. C. Concepts and Society. *232 pp.*
 Mannheim, Karl. Essays on the Sociology of Knowledge. *Edited by Paul Kecskemeti. Editorial Note by Adolph Lowe. 353 pp.*
 Remmling, Gunter W. The Sociology of Karl Mannheim. *With a Bibliographical Guide to the Sociology of Knowledge, Ideological Analysis, and Social Planning. 255 pp.*
 Remmling, Gunter W. (Ed.) Towards the Sociology of Knowledge. *Origin and Development of a Sociological Thought Style. 463 pp.*
 Scheler, M. Problems of a Sociology of Knowledge. *Trans. by M. S. Frings. Edited and with an Introduction by K. Stikkers. 232 pp.*

URBAN SOCIOLOGY

Aldridge, M. The British New Towns. *A Programme Without a Policy. 232 pp.*
Ashworth, William. The Genesis of Modern British Town Planning: *A Study in . Economic and Social History of the Nineteenth and Twentieth Centuries. 288 pp.*
Brittan, A. The Privatised World. *196 pp.*
Cullingworth, J. B. Housing Needs and Planning Policy: *A Restatement of the Problems of Housing Need and 'Overspill' in England and Wales. 232 pp. 44 tables. 8 maps.*
Dickinson, Robert E. City and Region: *A Geographical Interpretation. 608 pp. 125 figures.*
 The West European City: *A Geographical Interpretation. 600 pp. 129 maps. 29 plates.*
Humphreys, Alexander J. New Dubliners: *Urbanization and the Irish Family. Foreword by George C. Homans. 304 pp.*
Jackson, Brian. Working Class Community: *Some General Notions raised by a Series of Studies in Northern England. 192 pp.*
● **Mann, P. H.** An Approach to Urban Sociology. *240 pp.*
 Mellor, J. R. Urban Sociology in an Urbanized Society. *326 pp.*
 Morris, R. N. and **Mogey, J.** The Sociology of Housing. *Studies at Berinsfield. 232 pp. 4 pp. plates.*
 Mullan, R. Stevenage Ltd. *About 250 pp.*
 Rex, J. and **Tomlinson, S.** Colonial Immigrants in a British City. *A Class Analysis. 368 pp.*
 Rosser, C. and **Harris, C.** The Family and Social Change. *A Study of Family and Kinship in a South Wales Town. 352 pp. 8 maps.*
● **Stacey, Margaret, Batsone, Eric, Bell, Colin** and **Thurcott, Anne.** Power, Persistence and Change. *A Second Study of Banbury. 196 pp.*

RURAL SOCIOLOGY

Mayer, Adrian C. Peasants in the Pacific. *A Study of Fiji Indian Rural Society. 248 pp. 20 plates.*
Williams, W. M. The Sociology of an English Village: *Gosforth. 272 pp. 12 figures. 13 tables.*

SOCIOLOGY OF INDUSTRY AND DISTRIBUTION

Dunkerley, David. The Foreman. *Aspects of Task and Structure. 192 pp.*
Eldridge, J. E. T. Industrial Disputes. *Essays in the Sociology of Industrial Relations. 288 pp.*
Hollowell, Peter G. The Lorry Driver. *272 pp.*
● **Oxaal, I., Barnett, T.** and **Booth, D.** (Eds) Beyond the Sociology of Development.

Economy and Society in Latin America and Africa. 295 pp.

Smelser, Neil J. Social Change in the Industrial Revolution: *An Application of Theory to the Lancashire Cotton Industry, 1770–1840. 468 pp. 12 figures. 14 tables.*

Watson, T. J. The Personnel Managers. *A Study in the Sociology of Work and Employment, 262 pp.*

ANTHROPOLOGY

Brandel-Syrier, Mia. Reeftown Elite. *A Study of Social Mobility in a Modern African Community on the Reef. 376 pp.*

Dickie-Clark, H. F. The Marginal Situation. *A Sociological Study of a Coloured Group. 236 pp.*

Dube, S. C. Indian Village. *Foreword by Morris Edward Opler. 276 pp. 4 plates.*
India's Changing Villages: *Human Factors in Community Development. 260 pp. 8 plates. 1 map.*

Fei, H.-T. Peasant Life in China. *A Field Study of Country Life in the Yangtze Valley. With a foreword by Bronislaw Malinowski. 328 pp. 16 pp. plates.*

Firth, Raymond. Malay Fishermen. *Their Peasant Economy. 420 pp. 17 pp. plates.*

Gulliver, P. H. Social Control in an African Society: a Study of the Arusha, Agricultural Masai of Northern Tanganyika. *320 pp. 8 plates. 10 figures.*
Family Herds. *288 pp.*

Jarvie, Ian C. The Revolution in Anthropology. *268 pp.*

Little, Kenneth L. Mende of Sierra Leone. *308 pp. and folder.*
Negroes in Britain. *With a New Introduction and Contemporary Study by Leonard Bloom. 320 pp.*

Tambs-Lyche, H. London Patidars. *About 180 pp.*

Madan, G. R. Western Sociologists on Indian Society. *Marx, Spencer, Weber, Durkheim, Pareto. 384 pp.*

Mayer, A. C. Peasants in the Pacific. *A Study of Fiji Indian Rural Society. 248 pp.*

Meer, Fatima. Race and Suicide in South Africa. *325 pp.*

Smith, Raymond T. The Negro Family in British Guiana: *Family Structure and Social Status in the Villages. With a Foreword by Meyer Fortes. 314 pp. 8 plates. 1 figure. 4 maps.*

SOCIOLOGY AND PHILOSOPHY

Adriaansens, H. Talcott Parsons and the Conceptual Dilemma. *About 224 pp.*

Barnsley, John H. The Social Reality of Ethics. *A Comparative Analysis of Moral Codes. 448 pp.*

Diesing, Paul. Patterns of Discovery in the Social Sciences. *362 pp.*

● **Douglas, Jack D.** (Ed.) Understanding Everyday Life. *Toward the Reconstruction of Sociological Knowledge. Contributions by Alan F. Blum, Aaron W. Cicourel, Norman K. Denzin, Jack D. Douglas, John Heeren, Peter McHugh, Peter K. Manning, Melvin Power, Matthew Speier, Roy Turner, D. Lawrence Wieder, Thomas P. Wilson and Don H. Zimmerman. 370 pp.*

Gorman, Robert A. The Dual Vision. *Alfred Schutz and the Myth of Phenomenological Social Science. 240 pp.*

Jarvie, Ian C. Concepts and Society. *216 pp.*

Kilminster, R. Praxis and Method. *A Sociological Dialogue with Lukács, Gramsci and the Early Frankfurt School. 334 pp.*

● **Pelz, Werner.** The Scope of Understanding in Sociology. *Towards a More Radical Reorientation in the Social Humanistic Sciences. 283 pp.*

Roche, Maurice. Phenomenology, Language and the Social Sciences. *371 pp.*

Sahay, Arun. Sociological Analysis. *212 pp.*

● **Slater, P.** Origin and Significance of the Frankfurt School. *A Marxist Perspective. 185 pp.*

Spurling, L. Phenomenology and the Social World. *The Philosophy of Merleau-Ponty and its Relation to the Social Sciences. 222 pp.*

Wilson, H. T. The American Ideology. *Science, Technology and Organization as Modes of Rationality. 368 pp.*

International Library of Anthropology
General Editor Adam Kuper

● Ahmed, A. S. Millennium and Charisma Among Pathans. *A Critical Essay in Social Anthropology. 192 pp.*
    Pukhtun Economy and Society. *Traditional Structure and Economic Development. About 360 pp.*

Barth, F. Selected Essays. *Volume I. About 250 pp.* Selected Essays. *Volume II. About 250 pp.*

Brown, Paula. The Chimbu. *A Study of Change in the New Guinea Highlands. 151 pp.*

Foner, N. Jamaica Farewell. *200 pp.*

Gudeman, Stephen. Relationships, Residence and the Individual. *A Rural Panamanian Community. 288 pp. 11 plates, 5 figures, 2 maps, 10 tables.*
    The Demise of a Rural Economy. *From Subsistence to Capitalism in a Latin American Village. 160 pp.*

Hamnett, Ian. Chieftainship and Legitimacy. *An Anthropological Study of Executive Law in Lesotho. 163 pp.*

Hanson, F. Allan. Meaning in Culture. *127 pp.*

Hazan, H. The Limbo People. *A Study of the Constitution of the Time Universe Among the Aged. About 192 pp.*

Humphreys, S. C. Anthropology and the Greeks. *288 pp.*

Karp, I. Fields of Change Among the Iteso of Kenya. *140 pp.*

Lloyd, P. C. Power and Independence. *Urban Africans' Perception of Social Inequality. 264 pp.*

Parry, J. P. Caste and Kinship in Kangra. *352 pp. Illustrated.*

Pettigrew, Joyce. Robber Noblemen. *A Study of the Political System of the Sikh Jats. 284 pp.*

Street, Brian V. The Savage in Literature. *Representations of 'Primitive' Society in English Fiction, 1858–1920. 207 pp.*

Van Den Berghe, Pierre L. Power and Privilege at an African University. *278 pp.*

International Library of Phenomenology and Moral Sciences
General Editor John O'Neill

Apel, K.-O. Towards a Transformation of Philosophy. *308 pp.*

Bologh, R. W. Dialectical Phenomenology. *Marx's Method. 287 pp.*

Fekete, J. The Critical Twilight. *Explorations in the Ideology of Anglo-American Literary Theory from Eliot to McLuhan. 300 pp.*

Medina, A. Reflection, Time and the Novel. *Towards a Communicative Theory of Literature. 143 pp.*

International Library of Social Policy
General Editor Kathleen Jones

Bayley, M. Mental Handicap and Community Care. *426 pp.*

Bottoms, A. E. and McClean, J. D. Defendants in the Criminal Process. *284 pp.*

Bradshaw, J. The Family Fund. *An Initiative in Social Policy. About 224 pp.*

Butler, J. R. Family Doctors and Public Policy. *208 pp.*
Davies, Martin. Prisoners of Society. *Attitudes and Aftercare. 204 pp.*
Gittus, Elizabeth. Flats, Families and the Under-Fives. *285 pp.*
Holman, Robert. Trading in Children. *A Study of Private Fostering. 355 pp.*
Jeffs, A. Young People and the Youth Service. *160 pp.*
Jones, Howard and Cornes, Paul. Open Prisons. *288 pp.*
Jones, Kathleen. History of the Mental Health Service. *428 pp.*
Jones, Kathleen with **Brown, John, Cunningham, W. J., Roberts, Julian** and
    Williams, Peter. Opening the Door. *A Study of New Policies for the Mentally
    Handicapped. 278 pp.*
Karn, Valerie. Retiring to the Seaside. *400 pp. 2 maps. Numerous tables.*
King, R. D. and **Elliot, K. W.** Albany: Birth of a Prison—End of an Era. *394 pp.*
Thomas, J. E. The English Prison Officer since 1850: *A Study in Conflict. 258 pp.*
Walton, R. G. Women in Social Work. *303 pp.*
● **Woodward, J.** To Do the Sick No Harm. *A Study of the British Voluntary Hospital
    System to 1875. 234 pp.*

International Library of Welfare and Philosophy
General Editors   Noel Timms and David Watson

● **McDermott, F. E.** (Ed.) Self-Determination in Social Work. *A Collection of Essays
    on Self-determination and Related Concepts by Philosophers and Social Work
    Theorists. Contributors: F. P. Biestek, S. Bernstein, A. Keith-Lucas, D. Sayer,
    H. H. Perelman, C. Whittington, R. F. Stalley, F. E. McDermott, I. Berlin, H. J.
    McCloskey, H. L. A. Hart, J. Wilson, A. I. Melden, S. I. Benn. 254 pp.*
● **Plant, Raymond.** Community and Ideology. *104 pp.*
  Ragg, Nicholas M. People Not Cases. *A Philosophical Approach to Social Work.
    168 pp.*
● **Timms, Noel** and **Watson, David.** (Eds) Talking About Welfare. *Readings in
    Philosophy and Social Policy. Contributors: T. H. Marshall, R. B. Brandt, G. H.
    von Wright, K. Nielsen, M. Cranston, R. M. Titmuss, R. S. Downie, E. Telfer, D.
    Donnison, J. Benson, P. Leonard, A. Keith-Lucas, D. Walsh, I. T. Ramsey.
    320 pp.*
● Philosophy in Social Work. *250 pp.*
● **Weale, A.** Equality and Social Policy. *164 pp.*

Library of Social Work
General Editor   Noel Timms

● **Baldock, Peter.** Community Work and Social Work. *140 pp.*
○ **Beedell, Christopher.** Residential Life with Children. *210 pp. Crown 8vo.*
● **Berry, Juliet.** Daily Experience in Residential Life. *A Study of Children and their
    Care-givers. 202 pp.*
○ Social Work with Children. *190 pp. Crown 8vo.*
● **Brearley, C. Paul.** Residential Work with the Elderly. *116 pp.*
● Social Work, Ageing and Society. *126 pp.*
● **Cheetham, Juliet.** Social Work with Immigrants. *240 pp. Crown 8vo.*
● **Cross, Crispin P.** (Ed.) Interviewing and Communication in Social Work.
    *Contributions by C. P. Cross, D. Laurenson, B. Strutt, S. Raven. 192 pp. Crown
    8vo.*

- **Curnock, Kathleen** and **Hardiker, Pauline.** Towards Practice Theory. *Skills and Methods in Social Assessments. 208 pp.*
- **Davies, Bernard.** The Use of Groups in Social Work Practice. *158 pp.*
- **Davies, Martin.** Support Systems in Social Work. *144 pp.*
  Ellis, June. (Ed.) West African Families in Britain. *A Meeting of Two Cultures. Contributions by Pat Stapleton, Vivien Biggs. 150 pp. 1 Map.*
- **Hart, John.** Social Work and Sexual Conduct. *230 pp.*
- **Hutten, Joan M.** Short-Term Contracts in Social Work. *Contributions by Stella M. Hall, Elsie Osborne, Mannie Sher, Eva Sternberg, Elizabeth Tuters. 134 pp.*
  Jackson, Michael P. and **Valencia, B. Michael.** Financial Aid Through Social Work. *140 pp.*
- **Jones, Howard.** The Residential Community. *A Setting for Social Work. 150 pp.*
- (Ed.) Towards a New Social Work. *Contributions by Howard Jones, D. A. Fowler, J. R. Cypher, R. G. Walton, Geoffrey Mungham, Philip Priestley, Ian Shaw, M. Bartley, R. Deacon, Irwin Epstein, Geoffrey Pearson. 184 pp.*
  Jones, Ray and **Pritchard, Colin.** (Eds) Social Work With Adolescents. *Contributions by Ray Jones, Colin Pritchard, Jack Dunham, Florence Rossetti, Andrew Kerslake, John Burns, William Gregory, Graham Templeman, Kenneth E. Reid, Audrey Taylor. About 170 pp.*
- ○ **Jordon, William.** The Social Worker in Family Situations. *160 pp. Crown 8vo.*
- **Laycock, A. L.** Adolescents and Social Work. *128 pp. Crown 8vo.*
- **Lees, Ray.** Politics and Social Work. *128 pp. Crown 8vo.*
- Research Strategies for Social Welfare. *112 pp. Tables.*
- ○ **McCullough, M. K.** and **Ely, Peter J.** Social Work with Groups. *127 pp. Crown 8vo.*
- **Moffett, Jonathan.** Concepts in Casework Treatment. *128 pp. Crown 8vo.*
  Parsloe, Phyllida. Juvenile Justice in Britain and the United States. *The Balance of Needs and Rights. 336 pp.*
- **Plant, Raymond.** Social and Moral Theory in Casework. *112 pp. Crown 8vo.*
  Priestley, Philip, Fears, Denise and **Fuller, Roger.** Justice for Juveniles. *The 1969 Children and Young Persons Act: A Case for Reform? 128 pp.*
- **Pritchard, Colin** and **Taylor, Richard.** Social Work: Reform or Revolution? *170 pp.*
- ○ **Pugh, Elisabeth.** Social Work in Child Care. *128 pp. Crown 8vo.*
- **Robinson, Margaret.** Schools and Social Work. *282 pp.*
- ○ **Ruddock, Ralph.** Roles and Relationships. *128 pp. Crown 8vo.*
- **Sainsbury, Eric.** Social Diagnosis in Casework. *118 pp. Crown 8vo.*
- Social Work with Families. *Perceptions of Social Casework among Clients of a Family Service. 188 pp.*
  Seed, Philip. The Expansion of Social Work in Britain. *128 pp. Crown 8vo.*
- **Shaw, John.** The Self in Social Work. *124 pp.*
  Smale, Gerald G. Prophecy, Behaviour and Change. *An Examination of Self-fulfilling Prophecies in Helping Relationships. 116 pp. Crown 8vo.*
  Smith, Gilbert. Social Need. *Policy, Practice and Research. 155 pp.*
- Social Work and the Sociology of Organisations. *124 pp. Revised edition.*
- **Sutton, Carole.** Psychology for Social Workers and Counsellors. *An Introduction. 248 pp.*
- **Timms, Noel.** Language of Social Casework. *122 pp. Crown 8vo.*
- Recording in Social Work. *124 pp. Crown 8vo.*
- **Todd, F. Joan.** Social Work with the Mentally Subnormal. *96 pp. Crown 8vo.*
- **Walrond-Skinner, Sue.** Family Therapy. *The Treatment of Natural Systems. 172 pp.*
- **Warham, Joyce.** An Introduction to Administration for Social Workers. *Revised edition. 112 pp.*
- An Open Case. *The Organisational Context of Social Work. 172 pp.*
- ○ **Wittenberg, Isca Salzberger.** Psycho-Analytic Insight and Relationships. *A Kleinian Approach. 196 pp. Crown 8vo.*

Primary Socialization, Language and Education
General Editor   Basil Bernstein

Adlam, Diana S., *with the assistance of Geoffrey Turner and Lesley Lineker.* Code in *Context. 272 pp.*
Bernstein, Basil. Class, Codes and Control. *3 volumes.*
●   1. *Theoretical Studies Towards a Sociology of Language. 254 pp.*
   2. *Applied Studies Towards a Sociology of Language. 377 pp.*
●   3. *Towards a Theory of Educational Transmission. 167 pp.*
Brandis, W. and **Bernstein, B.** Selection and Control. *176 pp.*
Brandis, Walter and **Henderson, Dorothy.** Social Class, Language and Communication. *288 pp.*
Cook-Gumperz, Jenny. Social Control and Socialization. *A Study of Class Differences in the Language of Maternal Control. 290 pp.*
● **Gahagan, D. M.** and **G. A.** Talk Reform. *Exploration in Language for Infant School Children. 160 pp.*
Hawkins, P. R. Social Class, the Nominal Group and Verbal Strategies. *About 220 pp.*
Robinson, W. P. and **Rackstraw, Susan D. A.** A Question of Answers. *2 volumes. 192 pp. and 180 pp.*
Turner, Geoffrey J. and **Mohan, Bernard A.** A Linguistic Description and Computer Programme for Children's Speech. *208 pp.*

Reports of the Institute of Community Studies

Baker, J. The Neighbourhood Advice Centre. A Community Project in Camden. *320 pp.*
● **Cartwright, Ann.** Patients and their Doctors. *A Study of General Practice. 304 pp.*
Dench, Geoff. Maltese in London. *A Case-study in the Erosion of Ethnic Consciousness. 302 pp.*
Jackson, Brian and **Marsden, Dennis.** Education and the Working Class: *Some General Themes Raised by a Study of 88 Working-class Children in a Northern Industrial City. 268 pp. 2 folders.*
Marris, Peter. The Experience of Higher Education. *232 pp. 27 tables.*
●   Loss and Change. *192 pp.*
Marris, Peter and **Rein, Martin.** Dilemmas of Social Reform. *Poverty and Community Action in the United States. 256 pp.*
Marris, Peter and **Somerset, Anthony.** African Businessmen. *A Study of Entrepreneurship and Development in Kenya. 256 pp.*
Mills, Richard. Young Outsiders: *a Study in Alternative Communities. 216 pp.*
Runciman, W. G. Relative Deprivation and Social Justice. *A Study of Attitudes to Social Inequality in Twentieth-Century England. 352 pp.*
Willmott, Peter. Adolescent Boys in East London. *230 pp.*
Willmott, Peter and **Young, Michael.** Family and Class in a London Suburb. *202 pp. 47 tables.*
Young, Michael and **McGeeney, Patrick.** Learning Begins at Home. *A Study of a Junior School and its Parents. 128 pp.*
Young, Michael and **Willmott, Peter.** Family and Kinship in East London. *Foreword by Richard M. Titmuss. 252 pp. 39 tables.*
   The Symmetrical Family. *410 pp.*

Reports of the Institute for Social Studies in Medical Care

Cartwright, Ann, Hockey, Lisbeth and **Anderson, John J.** Life Before Death. *310 pp.*
Dunnell, Karen and **Cartwright, Ann.** Medicine Takers, Prescribers and Hoarders. *190 pp.*
Farrell, C. My Mother Said. . . *A Study of the Way Young People Learned About Sex and Birth Control. 288 pp.*

Medicine, Illness and Society
General Editor W. M. Williams

Hall, David J. Social Relations & Innovation. *Changing the State of Play in Hospitals. 232 pp.*
Hall, David J. and **Stacey, M.** (Eds) Beyond Separation. *234 pp.*
Robinson, David. The Process of Becoming Ill. *142 pp.*
Stacey, Margaret *et al.* Hospitals, Children and Their Families. *The Report of a Pilot Study. 202 pp.*
Stimson, G. V. and **Webb, B.** Going to See the Doctor. *The Consultation Process in General Practice. 155 pp.*

Monographs in Social Theory
General Editor Arthur Brittan

● **Barnes, B.** Scientific Knowledge and Sociological Theory. *192 pp.*
Bauman, Zygmunt. Culture as Praxis. *204 pp.*
● **Dixon, Keith.** Sociological Theory. *Pretence and Possibility. 142 pp.*
The Sociology of Belief. *Fallacy and Foundation. About 160 pp.*
Goff, T. W. Marx and Mead. *Contributions to a Sociology of Knowledge. 176 pp.*
Meltzer, B. N., Petras, J. W. and **Reynolds, L. T.** Symbolic Interactionism. *Genesis, Varieties and Criticisms. 144 pp.*
● **Smith, Anthony D.** The Concept of Social Change. *A Critique of the Functionalist Theory of Social Change. 208 pp.*

Routledge Social Science Journals

The British Journal of Sociology. *Editor – Angus Stewart; Associate Editor – Leslie Sklair. Vol. 1, No. 1 – March 1950 and Quarterly. Roy. 8vo. All back issues available. An international journal publishing original papers in the field of sociology and related areas.*
Community Work. *Edited by David Jones and Marjorie Mayo. 1973. Published annually.*
Economy and Society. *Vol. 1, No. 1. February 1972 and Quarterly. Metric Roy. 8vo. A journal for all social scientists covering sociology, philosophy, anthropology, economics and history. All back numbers available.*

14

Social and Psychological Aspects of Medical Practice
Editor   Trevor Silverstone

Printed and bound in Great Britain by
Redwood Burn Limited, Trowbridge & Esher